Challenging Social Issues for Today's Elementary Teachers

Denise L. McLurkin

The City College of New York—CUNY

The McGraw·Hill Companies

Connect
Learn
Succeed™

CHALLENGING SOCIAL ISSUES FOR TODAY'S ELEMENTARY TEACHERS, FIRST EDITION

Published by McGraw-Hill, a business unit of The McGraw-Hill Companies, Inc., 1221 Avenue of the
Americas, New York, NY 10020. Copyright © 2011 by The McGraw-Hill Companies, Inc. All rights reserved.
No part of this publication may be reproduced or distributed in any form or by any means, or stored in a
database or retrieval system, without the prior written consent of The McGraw-Hill Companies, Inc., including,
but not limited to, in any network or other electronic storage or transmission, or broadcast for distance learning.

Some ancillaries, including electronic and print components, may not be available to customers outside the
United States.

This book is printed on acid-free paper.

1 2 3 4 5 6 7 8 9 0 DOC/DOC 1 0 9 8 7 6 5 4 3 2 1 0

ISBN 978-0-07-809770-6
MHID 0-07-809770-3

Vice President & Editor-in-Chief: *Michael Ryan*
VP EDP/Central Publishing Services: *Kimberly Meriwether David*
Publisher: *David Patterson*
Sponsoring Editor: *Allison McNamara*
Marketing Manager: *James Headley*
Editorial Coordinator: *Sarah Kiefer*
Senior Project Manager: *Jane Mohr*
Design Coordinator: *Margarite Reynolds*
Cover Designer: *Kay Lieberherr*
Photo Research Coordinator: *Brian Pecko*
Production Supervisor: *Nicole Baumgartner*
Compositor: *Laserwords Private Limited*
Typeface: *10/12 Times Roman*
Printer: *R.R. Donnelley*

All credits appearing on page or at the end of the book are considered to be an extension of the copyright page.

Library of Congress Cataloging-in-Publication Data
McLurkin, Denise L.
    Challenging social issues for today's elementary teachers / by Denise L. McLurkin.
        p. cm.
    Includes index.
    ISBN 978-0-07-809770-6 (alk. paper)
    1. Elementary school teaching—United States—Case studies.   2. First year teachers—United States—Case
studies.   3. Social problems—United States—Case studies. I. Title.
    LB1556.5.M35 2010
    372.1102—dc22
                                                                                            2009050614

www.mhhe.com

About *The Practical Guide Series*

New teachers face a seemingly endless set of challenges—classroom management, assessment, motivation, content knowledge, cultural responsiveness, inclusion, technology—just to name a few. Preparing for the profession can at times seem overwhelming. Teacher candidates may begin to see solutions to some of the anticipated challenges as they progress through a program of study but know that there are many that await them in their first classroom. Support by mentors and colleagues is crucial for beginning teachers, and this series is designed to bolster that guidance. *The Practical Guide Series* provides another level of support for these new and future professionals.

The series was conceived in response to concerns about teacher retention, especially among teachers in their first to fourth years in the classroom when mentorship and guidance play a crucial role. These titles offer future and beginning teachers a collection of practical advice that they can refer to in student teaching and in the early teaching years. Instructors of pre-service teachers can use these books to reinforce concepts in their texts with additional applications, use them to foster discussion and help guide pre-service students in their practice teaching.

Besides addressing issues of basic concern to new teachers, we anticipate generating a level of excitement—one that a traditional textbook is hard-pressed to engender—that will further motivate entrants into this most essential profession with a contagious enthusiasm. A positive start to a teaching career is the best path to becoming a master teacher!

Alfred S. Posamentier, *Series Editor*
Dean, The School of Education
The City College of New York

Acknowledgments

To my God and loving family—Mom, Dad, Sanci, Julius, Damille, Simone, Elan, Celine, Danielle, Jobe, Shaina, Shamarah, Toastie, Nala, and Louis.

To Allison McNamara and Jill Eccher for supporting this project and keeping me on my toes with frequent emails.

To Dr. Alfred Posamentier, my first dean at the City College of New York. Thank you for your constant words of support and encouragement. I appreciate that you've provided me with this opportunity.

To the wonderful teachers who, even though they were on summer break, were willing to give of their time to share such great advice and suggestions with future teachers: Sanci McLurkin-Patterson, Glenn Allen King, Erin Barnett, Holly DiManno, Karen Hawthore (my favorite expert veteran teacher in the whole wide world ☺), Gina Hernandez, and Blossom Marshall. I couldn't have done this work without you. Please keep inspiring, caring, teaching and supporting our sweeties. They are our future.

To the editors at my editing party: Min. Bill McLurkin, Verina McLurkin, Sanci McLurkin-Patterson, Simone Patterson, Elan Patterson, Autumn Ashley, Jackie Burks, Taryn Burks, Al Frazier, Sade Harris, Rainbo Holland, Pam Holtorf, Janelle Junior, and Derek Burks for watching the puppies.

And, thank you to the full service project manager, Michelle Gardner of Laserwords, Maine, for her great work on seeing this book through production.

To my elementary grade students and their families who have shaped my research and continue to push me to improve teachers' practices all over.

To the future and practicing teachers I have had the pleasure of working with at the University of Michigan, Ann Arbor, Madonna University, and the City College of New York—CUNY Our sweeties need you badly. Please make sure that you give them the nurturing, supportive, compassionate and empathic learning environment that they so deserve. Help them grow, care and thrive.

With all of my heart, I thank you!

Contents

Preface

Challenging Social Issues for Today's Elementary Teachers

I remember my first day of teaching like it was yesterday. I was so happy to have a job that I knew I would love—teaching kindergarten! I had a rambunctious class of 35 kindergarteners from diverse backgrounds. My class looked like a meeting at the United Nations. I had students who were African Americans, White/European Americans, Latinos, Asian Americans, Pacific Islanders, Middle Easterners and Persians, to name a few, and several students who were classified as biracial. I had children who were practicing Christians, Jews, Hindis, and Muslims, and those who according to their parents did not practice any religion. Linguistically, the majority of the class spoke English, but also there were others who spoke primarily Spanish, Hmong, Punjabi, Vietnamese, and Hungarian. Additionally, some of my students' parents and other family members spoke little English or no English at all, thus making conversing with parents extremely difficult.

As far as my students' families, several children came from wealthy socioeconomic backgrounds and some from extremely impoverished socioeconomic backgrounds. I had parents who were teachers, doctors, construction workers, grocery store clerks and secretaries, and some parents who were unemployed or underemployed. Some of my students lived with their married biological mother and biological father, some lived with their unmarried biological mother and biological father, some lived with their biological mother and did not know who their biological father was and vice versa. One lived with two adoptive fathers, many with grandparents, and some with foster parents or aunties and uncles.

Some of my students lived in extremely violent neighborhoods, where they would have to stay in their homes or apartments before and after school because of fear of being killed or randomly shot and because they did not have clean or safe areas such as parks where they could play. Many of these children did not travel outside of their neighborhoods because their families were struggling financially to simply "make it" every single month. At the same time, I had other students who lived in neighborhoods where violent crime was rare and the children could play outside in their backyards on their swing sets or at the local park that was clean and free of drug paraphernalia. Many of these children went on vacations with their family members all over the state of California and even around the United States.

Then, in this same class, I had students who lived in wealthy families, yet rarely saw their parents due to their work commitments. Some of these children came to school and were picked up by nannies, did not consistently turn in their homework, and informed me that they had never been to their local library. For others, although they did not have a lot of financial resources, these children saw their parent, guardian, or grandparent before, during, and after school, were taken to the library on a regular basis, had their school supplies, and completed their homework in a timely fashion. So, thankfully, making sweeping generalizations about "rich people" and "poor people" was impossible in my situation.

As far as previous schooling experience, I had some students who had preschool experience and some who had not ever been in a classroom. I had students who knew how to write their names, knew their phone numbers, knew their parent(s) first and last names, could count from 1–20, could identify all of the letters in the alphabet and numbers 0–20, and knew colors and shapes based on our informal baseline assessment. These children also knew how to stand in lines, share, sit at a desk/table, sit on the rug in the criss-cross applesauce format, knew what "'keeping your hands, feet and objects to yourselves" meant, knew how to use scissors and use them safely, and knew how to actively and appropriately participate during interactive read aloud time. Then I had other students who could do most of the tasks listed above, some who could do some of the tasks listed above, and some who could not do any of these tasks.

What was truly scary to me was that I had young students with family members who were incarcerated, or gang members, or on drugs, or who were alcoholics, or who were physically and sexually abusing them. I also had students who had experienced the death of a loved one, whose parents were going through divorce, and those who had just been removed from their parents' home and placed in foster care. I had overweight students, underweight students, students with asthma, and students who just weren't getting it academically. Admittedly, it was this central issue—working with the whole child and all of the experiences they brought to the classroom, while at the same time ensuring that they learn—that was most daunting of all.

Needless to say, teaching is extremely difficult work. The teaching profession loses an estimated 40 to 50 percent of teachers after just five years of service (Ingersoll & Smith, 2003). While there are many reasons given for these staggering numbers, the heartbreaking truth is that many new teachers leave because they feel overwhelmed and dissatisfied with all that teaching encompasses, feel that they are not financially compensated for all they do, and feel that they are not well-supported (Ingersoll, 2001; Ingersoll & Smith, 2003; Stockard & Lehman, 2004). I had a diverse class in the truest sense of diversity, had to deal with parents, colleagues, administrators, and bureaucrats, all who had different expectations, opinions, values, and standards for what was to occur in my class. I was fortunate to have a father and sister who were seasoned teachers and a mother who had been in the educational field for years, as well as colleagues whom I could trust. Thus, when some of the issues I discussed earlier impacted my teaching, I had several mentors whom I could rely on for support and sound educational advice. However, even with this level of support, I still felt overwhelmed. It was then that I began to question why I hadn't been adequately prepared to deal with these other critical issues prior to ever stepping foot into my classroom. This seemed unfair to me and my students.

Challenging Social Issues for Today's Elementary Teachers is written to prepare pre-service and beginning teachers for the realities of teaching children in the twenty-first century. By relying on my own teaching experiences, as well as the experiences of pre-service teachers, veteran teachers, parents, physicians, and school administrators, three complex vignettes are provided for each of the 24 most challenging social issues that many teachers experience in relation to educating our youth. In each of the vignettes, readers will get a better sense of the complexities of each social issue, as well as see various classroom management styles.

Because these vignettes are based on the lives of children, their families, faculty and staff members, in order to protect the identities I have given each person in each vignette a pseudonym and have taken creative liberty by adding fictional, yet relevant details to make it more difficult for a person to recognize himself or herself or their situation(s) in any of the vignettes. Additionally, I have purposely attempted to keep the teachers in each of the vignettes as cultural, religiously, linguistically, racially, ethnically, sexually, and socioeconomically neutral as possible. That way, readers can better envision themselves as the teacher in each vignette, and contemplate what they would do if they were the *actual* teacher in each of the situations presented.

At the end of each vignette, I have included five discussion questions. These questions have been created to get readers thinking critically about the information presented in the vignettes. They may be used as a springboard to discuss readers' personal views, opinions, and biases regarding each issue, possible legal and ethical responsibilities, and ramifications that teachers face regarding each issue, and how multifaceted each scenario/child/family/school is. Furthermore, because we are mandatory reporters, the vignettes may be used to initiate an exploration of local, state and federal laws, guidelines, resources, and agencies that deal specifically with each of the topics presented, so that teachers are updated on their legal and ethical responsibilities as educators.

Following each vignette and discussion questions, I have conducted several focus groups with veteran teachers who have offered sound advice and suggestions on each topic and situation presented in the book. These sections are called *Advice from Veteran Teachers on. . . .*These teachers; who have a total of over 100 years of elementary teaching experience, offer candid and sincere suggestions on how they would handle the situation, what their colleagues have done in similar situations, as well as provide academic and instructional ideas. Although advice and suggestions are given, these are not exhaustive lists. These are simply launching pads to get pre-service and beginning teaches some ideas to get discussions started.

I recognize that what I am asking pre-service and beginning teachers to do may be difficult as some of the issues in the vignettes and the questions may make readers feel embarrassed, confused, and angry, or cause them to question where they stand on a certain topic. However, we always have to remember that everything we do as educators is about our students. So, while working through the issues presented in *Challenging Social Issues for Today's Elementary Teachers* through discussions, journaling, role playing and even artistic expression, pre-service and beginning teachers can think about what their next steps may be, the support systems available to them and their students, and considering all of these options, make well-informed decisions not only for their students, their students' families, colleagues, but also for themselves, prior to or early in their teaching careers. If a child comes to a teacher and is hurt, depressed, anxious, hungry, or dirty, I want new teachers to feel empowered, courageous and supported enough to make calls, send emails, ask questions, write letters, look on the Internet and initiate conversations with administrators in order to get their students the help they need so that their students have the safest, most nurturing learning environment possible.

References

Ingersoll, R. (2001). Teacher turnover and teacher shortages: An organizational analysis. *American Educational Research Journal, 38*(3), 499–534.

Ingersoll, R., & Smith, T. (2003). The wrong solution to the teacher shortage. *Educational Leadership, 60*(8), 30–33.

Stockard, J., & Lehman, M. (2004). Influences on the satisfaction and retention of lst-year teachers: The importance of effective school management. *Educational Administration Quarterly, 40*(5), 742–771.

Children with Special Needs

Absolutely Not!

I flop on my sofa, sip my hot tea, close my eyes, and take a deep breath. Wrapped in the warm quilt that my mom crocheted for me when I graduated from college, I'm wearing my pajamas and warm, fuzzy socks. I feel so relaxed right now. If only the ambiance were like this in my classroom. Teaching is a lot harder than I thought it would be. Don't get me wrong, I enjoy teaching third grade, but with the lesson planning, meetings, grading papers, and everything else, I am exhausted. I know that it's the beginning of the school year, and everyone on my team, all of whom have been teaching for more than ten years each, has assured me that it will get better. But tonight, I'm tired and it's tough.

On my coffee table are the piles of spelling and math tests and the six journals I brought home to grade this evening. I take another sip of my tea and let the hot liquid soothe my throat. Then I reach over and grab the spelling tests. I look up at the clock and it reads 8:30. "Shoot!" I think to myself. "I probably won't get to bed until 11:00 again." Taking a deep breath, I take my green pen and begin grading the tests. When I get to Richard's paper, I am shocked to discover that he has misspelled every word. Also, his penmanship is illegible. I feel the underside of his paper and wonder how long it took him to retrace every word he's written. Thinking out loud, I say, "Why is he writing so hard?" I look at some of his letters and they are backwards. Once again, thinking out loud, I say, "This just isn't normal." I put the rest of the spelling tests aside and reach for the math tests. I leaf through the pile in search of Richard's test. It looks just like the spelling test.

Now I get up in search of my wheelie cart. I think Richard's journal was one that I grabbed to respond to this evening. I find his orange spiral-bound notebook and head back to the sofa. Sitting on my feet, I open his journal and am shocked by what I see. Most of his entries are just scribbles and he is also retracing his words again. I don't think I've ever seen such heavy print in all my life. On the entries he actually did write, most of the words are misspelled and it looks as if he is drawing the letters—not writing them. I then make a mental note to talk with Caroline, the Special Ed teacher, tomorrow.

The next day, I drag myself into the office to get my supplies together and put away my lunch. I then go over to the vending machine to choose the soda with the highest caffeine content. After I make my selection, I go to my mailbox and head out the side door to my class. As I am walking down the corridor, I look up and see Caroline walking toward me. "Oh my goodness," I say, "You are just the person I want to see." Caroline, who is the happiest person on earth, smiles and says, "Wow, I don't think

I've ever had someone say that to me so early in the morning." I giggle and say, "Well, people should say that to you." We both laugh and then Caroline asks, "How can I help you?" We begin walking to my room and I say, "Do you have time to talk with me about a student of mine?" Caroline nods her head in agreement and says, "You're in luck. The parent I was meeting with had to cancel, so I do have time." When we get to my room, I unlock the door and welcome Caroline in.

When we get settled at the front table, I take out Richard's math and spelling tests and journal. As Caroline goes over his work samples, she lowers her brow and covers her mouth with her hand. She is quiet for some time. Finally, she says, "Is this Richard Brown?" I do not hide my surprise. "How do you know?" I ask Caroline. Shaking her head, she says, "We have been concerned about Richard since kindergarten. We have tried everything to get him tested because he clearly is having problems, but his parents are extremely resistant." I look over at Caroline and actually feel relief. I then confide, "I was so surprised last night when I started grading his work. Especially his journal." Reaching for his journal I say, "I had no idea that he was not completing his journal assignments and that he was this far behind." I reach for his spelling test and say, "I mean, he didn't get any of the words correct."

Caroline shakes her head knowingly. "I know, Rebecca. It can be so heartbreaking." As I nod my head in agreement, I say, "He is one of the sweetest and hardworking kids I have in my class." Lowering my head, I continue, "I just don't know what to do to help him." Caroline looks at me and says, "Have you had a chance to meet with his parents and let them know that you have some concerns about his progress?" Shaking my head, I embarrassingly say, "No." Caroline then says, "Okay, I want you to set that meeting up with them as soon as possible. If you want," she continues, "I will sit in on the meeting with you." She continues, "But for now, I want you to fill out the referral form this afternoon. Make sure you are keeping as many of his work samples as possible." I nod my head to let her know I will. Caroline says, "Pretty soon, we will have an SST (which stands for Student Study Team), where we will meet with other teachers who will give you suggestions on how to help him right now. His parents will be invited to that meeting. Following that, we will have another meeting to see how the suggestions given during the SST are going. If he is still having trouble, we will then begin the process for testing."

I ask, "But what if his parents refuse the testing?" Caroline once again shakes her head. "And therein lies the problem. Like I said before, we have been trying to get him assessed since kindergarten, but his parents have refused." She continues, "But we have to file all of the paperwork and do our part in order to be in compliance." I look up at Caroline and ask, "Do I have to wait until then to get some advice on how to help him?" Shaking her head, Caroline says, "Oh no, honey. I want you to come to my room during lunch and after school. I will give you some resources that you can do with him right now." I look at her as she says, "Once again, that may be all that we can do for Richard." Just then, the bell rings letting us know that school is about to begin.

Caroline stands up to go to her class. But before she leaves, my hand skims over his test, and I ask, "Oh, Caroline, why is he retracing his letters like this?" Caroline looks up at me and then down at his spelling test and says, "He's perseverating." Looking confused, I don't say anything. Smiling, Caroline says, "I have had a lot of students who do that. I see this mainly with students who have OCD tendencies and are trying to relieve some sort of anxiety they are feeling." I must look totally overwhelmed because Caroline says, "Don't worry, Rebecca. I'm here for you. We will get through this together."

Discussion Questions

1. What would you say to Richard's parents during your first meeting?
2. What do you anticipate Richard's parents saying or doing during that first meeting?
3. Why do you think that Richard's parents appear to be resistant to have him assessed?
4. What can your school district do if a child needs to be assessed, but the parents refuse the assessment?
5. In addition to working closely with Caroline, what other resources are available to you in your district and school for children who are functioning below grade level?

In His Own World

I wipe my brow off with a damp paper towel. I am sweating like it is 115 degrees outside. I know it's hot, but I think I may be nervous as well as excited. In two days it will be my first day of teaching kindergarten. I look around my room with pride. Madison and I have really done a great job with our classroom. As I look around the room admiring our hard work, the door opens and Madison comes in. "Ready to go to lunch?" she asks. I look at her and smile. I take a quick whiff of my underarms and say, "Maybe we should order in." Smiling, she says, "They will understand that we are getting our classroom together. We have on Monroe Elementary School T-shirts, for heavens sake." She walks up closer to me and says, "Plus, I don't smell you." We both smile and laugh. Madison then says, "Let me run to the restroom and we'll head on out."

Madison has been teaching kindergarten for five years. I did several of my observation hours in her class, and when this position became available, I kept my fingers crossed the whole time. I will never forget the night when I got the call saying I had gotten the job.

When we get to the restaurant, I request that we sit outside, "just in case my deodorant did leave me." Shaking her head, Madison follows me and our hostess to the patio. After we place our orders, Madison asks, "So, how are you doing, Connie? Are you ready for Thursday?" I take a sip of my water; shake my head and say, "I sure hope so." Unable to contain my excitement, I blurt out, "I just want to do a great job. I want to meet my kids so bad."

Madison giggles, "Now remember what I said. If you get a chance, call several of your students every night just to introduce yourself to their parents. They really appreciate that." I nod my head and let her know, "I have already taken your advice. I'm almost through my whole class list already."

Madison says, "Well, good for you." After a sip of her iced tea she says, "And remember; throughout the year, to call parents whose children are doing a good job, too." Thinking about it some more, she continues, "We don't only have to call to let them know that their children are doing something inappropriate." I make a mental note of her suggestion as I unwrap my place setting.

While we enjoy our salads, Madison continues our conversation. "You know, I think the hardest thing about teaching kindergarten is that you really don't know what you're getting until the students are in your class for some time and you really get to know them and their families." Madison explains, "When I taught third grade, I had the information from their cumulative file." Thinking about it some more, she adds, "Shoot, I also had their report cards, all kinds of testing information, and plus, I could go to their former teachers to find out more information about them or their family." Spearing another bite of lettuce she says, "But with kindergarten, you don't usually have background information, unless they have older siblings or have been going to Sunshine preschool for early intervention services because they were experiencing problems early on."

Now having a clearer picture of what she's talking about, I say, "So do you miss teaching third grade?" Shaking her head, she quickly replies, "Oh no. I'm having a ball." I smile at Madison; our lunch has made me feel a little less nervous.

When we get back to school, I go into the office where Elan Cortez, my principal, says, "Well, there you are. I've been looking for you." Thinking I'm in trouble, I ask Elan "Is everything okay?" She places her hand on my shoulder and says, "Oh yes, don't worry. Nathan and I would just like to talk with you for a bit about a student who will be in your class this year." Nathan is our primary grade full-day Special Education teacher. Elan looks at her watch and says, "If you're free right now, it's a good time." She asks Nichelle, her secretary, to call Nathan and let him know that we will be meeting in her office.

After small talk about my much anticipated first day of school, there is a knock on the door. Elan says, "Please come in," and Nathan enters her office, sits down next to me and says, "Hi there. How are you doing?"

I look at him and smile. "I'm fine. Just waiting for the first day of school." Nathan leans back and says, "Elan, do you remember our first day of school?" Smiling, Elan says, "Oh my." She looks at me and explains, "Nathan and I both started teaching the same year." She asks him, "Has it really been twenty-seven years?" Nathan shakes his head in disbelief. "I know. Time just seems to fly by."

After some more small talk, Elan glances at her watch again and says, "The reason we called you into my office is because we want to talk with you about a student you will be getting on Thursday. His name is Jack McKinley and he has been diagnosed with autism." I look at Elan in disbelief. Slowly, I say, "Really? Okay."

Elan nods and says, "Jack has received speech and language services ever since he was two and has been going to Sunshine since he was three." Nathan jumps in, saying, "He also received services to help him develop his social skills."

I nod my head nervously, trying to take in all of the information being presented to me. Nathan continues, "According to his teacher, Jean, at Sunshine, his speech and social skills have improved a lot; although he does still exhibit a lot of repetitive behaviors, is behind his peers with his verbal skills, and is still having some trouble maintaining eye contact." Elan jumps in, "His parents say that he still gets frustrated in a large crowd or when he finds it difficult to communicate or doesn't get his way." Tapping her lip with her finger she says, "They also let us know that sometimes, he does seem like he is in his own world." Nathan then quickly adds, "But they also did say that was improving." Elan nods her head in agreement.

I look over at Nathan and then Elan and ask, "Have either of you observed him yet?" Both Nathan and Elan shake their heads and reply, "No." Nathan reaches across and says, "I know this is a bit overwhelming, but he does have a personal instructional aide who will be there to shadow him throughout the day." Still trying to comprehend everything, I ask, "I'm just curious, why isn't Jack being placed with Madison? She's been teaching for nine years." Elan says, "Jack needed the afternoon class because he will be receiving speech and language services and occupational therapy in the morning." I say, "Well, I guess I can't wait to meet my little Jack on Thursday."

Discussion Questions

1. How would you prepare for your first encounter with Jack?
2. What cognitive and social areas are usually impacted by autism?
3. What early intervention services are available in your district for children who have autism?
4. What support services are available in your community for parents who have a child or children with autism?
5. Having another adult in one's class can be difficult at times. How would you prepare for working collaboratively with Jack's personal instructional aide?

Then I Don't Need to Do It, Right?

It is right after lunch and my fourth graders are finishing up silent reading time. Arielle waves her hand to get my attention. I nod my head and she knows that she can put her book back in her desk and head to the resource room for reading instruction. Arielle goes to the resource room Monday through Thursday for forty-five minutes each day. She flashes her bright, toothy smile and waves goodbye to me. I wave at her and look back at my class. Gently ringing the bell on my desk, I say, "It's time for social studies, so please get ready. You have. . ." I look up at the clock, "two minutes. You may begin." With that, my students know to finish their paragraph, put their bookmarks in place, take out their social studies book, folder, pencil and paper, and wait patiently for me to begin our lesson on California missions. I then look up at the clock and announce, "You have thirty seconds." I see several kids, obviously reading an arresting part in their book, almost jump out of their seats because they know they need to get it together before their time runs out. "Fifteen seconds," I say as I look around the room. Just as I'm about to announce five seconds, I see that all of my students are ready for the social studies lesson.

"Wonderful job, class."

I ask, "How many of you were at a really good part in your book or magazine?" About half of the class raises their hands. Germaine says, "Oh, Mrs. Simien, I just didn't want to stop." Germaine has finally found books he enjoys. Go figure—he loves westerns. "Well," I continue, "I am so happy to see so many of you enjoying your books. Now let's get ready for social studies."

After about thirty-five minutes, I begin to recap our lesson on the California missions. Before I begin the overview, I look at the SMART Board I've been taking notes on and say, "It is your responsibility to make sure that you have all of your notes written in your notebooks. So make sure you get everything down."

Glancing back at the SMART Board I add, "You will need to remember that all twenty-one of the missions are coastal. What does that mean? That they are *coastal?*" I call on Sammy.

"It means that they were built close to the coast. Or the beach."

I nod my head and say, "Exactly." Looking back at the SMART Board I say, "You will also need to remember that the missions were funded by the Catholic Church in Spain with the goal of ". . . bringing Christianity to the natives." I look up again and ask, "Now what does that mean? Bringing Christianity to the natives?"

Melissa raises her hand. "It means that they thought that the Indians, I mean Native Americans, were not like them. Like they didn't wear clothes like they wore, had long hair, and just weren't civilized like them."

I do not hide how impressed I am with her answer. "Wow, Melissa. Yes," I say, "They did not believe that they were as civilized as they were."

Jason waves his hand frantically and adds, "Plus, they thought that they were natives and beneath them because they were not Christian and worshipped things such as weather and animals."

"You all have learned so much." Looking back up at the SMART Board, I continue, "Now as the story goes, the local Native Americans initially volunteered to be a part of the missions. But they soon found out they would be the ones who would build the missions, which was backbreaking work." They also soon found out that their whole lives had to change. In actuality, most accounts talk about Native Americans having to learn a new language, move from a hunting and gathering society to farmers and carpenters. I ask, "What does this situation remind you of?"

Javonte, an extremely inquisitive young man, quickly raises his hand and I call on him. "How is this situation different than slavery?" Javonte asks. "Slave masters worked slaves against their will for no pay, took away their home languages, and worked them to the bone doing work that they did not do in Africa." Nodding my head, I say, "Good point and good connection."

Melissa, also very inquisitive asks, "Did the slave catchers and owners get slaves for the purposes of turning them into Christians?" My eyes open wide as I say, "That's a great question, and the answer is no." Thinking about it some more, I add, "I know that once the slaves were in America, they did try to change them to Christians to make them more subservient and obedient. However, the primary purpose of the slaves coming to America was free labor."

Just then, our class door opens up and Arielle comes into the class. Flashing her customary smile, she heads to her seat. She looks around, then reaches into her desk and grabs the same materials that her peers have on their desk. I look back at the SMART Board and say, "Before it's time to clean up, who was the most famous priest in the missions?" In unison, my students say, "Father Serra Junipero." Arielle is moving her lips, but it is apparent she does not know what is going on.

Looking up at the clock, I announce "We had a great social studies lessons on the California missions, the Native Americans who built them and worked there, how their situation was similar to the American slave trade, and their most famous priest, Father Serra Junipero." It is now time for us to select our missions for our major project. So please get the room clean and organized. You have forty-five seconds."

The kids are putting their things away and talking quietly amongst themselves. I place a fishbowl on the table that contains folded index cards with the name of a mission on it. Just then Celia, sitting in the front row, waves her hand, pointing to her watch to let me know that their time is up. I smile and say, "Thank you, Celia, for keeping me on my toes." I begin to explain how the projects will be chosen. "In my fishbowl, I have the names of each of the twenty-one missions on an index card. Because we have twenty-eight kids in the class, some of you will be doing a mission that another student in the class will be doing." I raise the bowl over my head and shake it. I walk out to the first row and lower the fish bowl in front of Billy. "Select one index card . . . whatever name is on that index card is the one you will do your project on." Thinking quickly, I grab my clipboard so that I can immediately write down the name of the mission selected next to that child's name.

As I go through the class, I definitely hear some "ahhs" and some "ughs." When I get to Arielle, she excitedly selects an index card, opens it up and says, "I got San Diego." Javonte looks up at me and then at Arielle and asks, "Mrs. Simien, I don't mean to be rude, but how is Arielle going to be able to do her project when she is always out of the class during social studies?" Arielle, looking a bit confused, too, says, "Oh, you're right. I don't need to do it, right?"

Discussion Questions

1. What is your immediate response for Arielle?
2. What can you do during the school day to get Arielle the information from the lesson she is missing when she leaves the room for resource support?
3. What can you do with your resource personnel to make this situation better for all?
4. What are the pros and cons of Arielle completing this project if it is to be completed at school?
5. What are the pros and cons of Arielle completing this project if it is to be completed at home?

Advice from Veteran Teachers on . . . Children with Special Needs

*   Most parents have dreams, hopes, and aspirations for their children. Given that, we know that it is extremely difficult for parents to acknowledge and accept that their children have academic, social, and behavioral exceptional needs. Denial is a reality and a way for many to deal with uncomfortable situations. Additionally, we cannot assume that a parent knows what "normal" behavior or current academic proficiency looks like.
*   We highly suggest that you develop an understanding relationship with your students' parents so that they trust you, know that you have their child's best interest at heart, and then hopefully, will follow through with recommendations that come from the school.
*   Regardless of the need, you should investigate if your school has a Student Study Team (SST). With this team, a group of teachers suggests interventions and if the interventions do not work, then they'll recommend a full assessment. In some schools, the school psychologist and speech therapist sit on this team as well. We strongly encourage you to work closely with the SST or the like in order to get the ball rolling as soon as possible. The earlier we can give the child the additional support services, we will hopefully see a better outcome.
*   In order to prepare for the SST, make sure that you keep work samples, document everything (e.g., phone calls home, progress reports, letters and emails from and to the parents, etc.), and anecdotal notes you keep on the child's specific behaviors and interactions with peers and adults. If necessary, you may have to jot down a child's behavior in minute-by-minute increments.
*   Additionally, for the SST or even a parent-teacher conference, you should have work samples from proficient students (make sure that you remove the student's name from the

work sample). This will provide parents an opportunity to see what proficient grade-level work looks like.

- If you find that a parent/guardian or parents/guardians is/are resistant to even discussing concerns you've observed in your class regarding their child, bring your administrator into the conversation as soon as possible. Hopefully, you will have a strong administrator who will be able to have an open discussion with the parent. Do not continue to handle this situation on your own.

- For some of us, in particular those of us in the upper elementary grades, the child has usually already been assessed and the services are in place. However, we have had cases where this is clearly not the case (the child may have moved or he/she has not been attending school). Thus, continue to be on the lookout for troublesome academic, social, and behavioral issues with your class; these children may need additional services as well.

- At times, Resource Specialist Program (RSP) is so difficult and frustrating. This is when a student receives part-time special education services from a certified special education teacher. This can occur as a pull-out or push-in format. We all agree that having frequent and candid discussions with the RSP teacher is critical to ensuring the best situation possible for all. More important, talk candidly about scheduling. The RSP teacher has a tight schedule and so do you. Compromising is key. Here are a few suggestions that we've found to be very helpful. (1) Push-in programs where the RSP teacher is in your class to assist the child during and after your lesson. (2) The RSP teacher takes your class lesson and assignment to their room and works at a slower pace for the child. (3) Where the RSP takes the child after the regular teacher has done the full lesson. The RSP teacher then helps the child complete the assignment.

Multiculturalism

Dot or Feather?

Wait a minute," Ryland says after I call on him. "We're not gonna get turkey and dressing for our party?" He turns his nose up and pouts. Trying to explain to a room full of kindergarteners that we are going to have the traditional Thanksgiving dinner the Pilgrims and Native Americans observed is pretty difficult. "I believe we are all going to enjoy ourselves." I say to the class, "Remember, this is not about us getting full, but an opportunity for us to learn more about the cultures that were represented and about what the first Thanksgiving was like." Ryland, who still has his arms folded and who still does not look convinced, utters under his breath, "I still want turkey and dressing."

My co-teacher Chelsea jumps in and says, "Most of you will have turkey and dressing on the actual day Thanksgiving is celebrated with your family. But with your class family, we are going to enjoy the foods that were eaten on the first Thanksgiving." She looks on the rug where both classes sit and says, "Does anyone else have a question?" Noelle raises her hand and says, "Are we gonna get to be the Pilgrims or the Indians?" Chelsea says, "My class will be the Pilgrims and Miss Lowell's class will be the Native Americans." Noelle raises her hand again and says, "Miss Lowell, will we be able to wear feathers in our hair and put makeup on?" I answer, "I don't see why not."

Chelsea takes out both examples of the costumes the two kindergarten classes created last year with paper bags. "We are going to need several parents to help us get our costumes created and to help us with our Thanksgiving celebration," I say as I lift up a stack of letters, "So make sure you all take home this letter home to your parents and make sure they read it and let us know if and how they can help us have a great celebration." After that, we answer several other questions before it is time for our students to go home.

Chelsea stands up and says in an even tone, "Okay, sweeties, step one." With that her students stand up—even Ryland. When they are all quiet, standing and looking at her, she says, "Now, step two." With that, her students check the carpet to make sure they did not leave any valuables behind. "Good job, sweeties. Now, step three." Her students tiptoe to the front door and line up quietly. Chelsea waits patiently for their line to straighten up before she says, "Now sweeties, please show your appreciation to Ms. Lowell and her class for their hospitality." As my students move back to their spots on the rug, I hear Chelsea's class say, "Thank you, Room Four." Chelsea squeezes between her students, opens the door, and waves goodbye to me and my students.

As I call my students to get their belongings out of their cubbies, I hand each one a letter and remind them to make sure their parents read the letter and respond if necessary. When my line is straight and the kids are quiet, I say, "Thank you so much for such a great day." Just then, the bell rings signaling the end of school.

As the last of my students are picked up, I head to the office. I see Mr. Birdsong and I can tell that he is steamed. Right next to him is his son, Hunter, who looks like he may have been crying. Looking down at Hunter I ask, "Are you okay, Hunter?" Mr. Birdsong quickly jumps in and says, "Actually, I'm the one who wants to speak with you." He takes a deep breath and continues, "Hunter told me about your plans for your Thanksgiving celebration, and I must admit that I am a bit shocked."

I am having a hard time trying to hide my surprise. "Oh, um, Mr. Birdsong, what in particular shocks you?"

Once again, he takes in a deep breath and says, "Actually, I am not as much shocked as I am disappointed and angry." I say, "I still don't understand what is bothering you, Mr. Birdsong." He looks me squarely in the eyes and says, "I just cannot believe you are letting your class refer to Native Americans as Indians, and are allowing them to portray our people in such stereotypic ways." He adds, "I mean, with feathers and makeup on their face? Are you kidding me?" His eyes are wide as he addresses me.

I now know what he is talking about. "Oh, Mr. Birdsong, I am so sorry. I didn't mean to offend your people. I have nothing but respect for Native Americans." Still fuming, he continues, "We are proud members of the Creek Nation from Muskogee, Oklahoma, and we are much more than the savages I think you are going to allow them to portray during your 'party.'"

Thinking quickly I say, "Mr. Birdsong, once again, I am sorry. I would love it if you would be willing to come to our class and talk about your tribe with our students and help us with our first Thanksgiving celebration." Looking at him with pleading eyes, I ask, "Would you consider helping us, sir?" Mr. Birdsong is now looking at me intently. After what seems like forever, he says, "What day would you like for me to come to your class?" Thinking quickly again, I say, "How about Tuesday? On that day, both kindergarten classes are going to get together for our social studies lesson."

Nodding his head, he says, "Okay." Now breathing easier, he says, "And I apologize for fuming at you the way I did, but I was in shock." I say, "Oh please, don't apologize, and thank you so much for volunteering to come to our class." With that, he and Hunter turn around and leave the school.

As I enter the teachers' lounge, Chelsea is talking with Yvonne, a first-grade teacher. They both look up and Chelsea says, "What happened to you?" As I finish recounting my encounter with Hunter's father, Yvonne looks at both of us and says, "I mean, why was he so upset with being called an Indian?" She then adds, "Oh, I guess it depends on if he is a dot or feather Indian, right?" She then slaps her legs and laughs at her "joke."

Discussion Questions

1. How would you do a first Thanksgiving celebration with your students?
2. If you hear children using politically incorrect names such as Indians in reference to Native Americans, what can you say to correct this situation?
3. Do you think that Miss Lowell handled the situation with Mr. Birdsong well?
4. What are the pros and cons of saying anything to Yvonne about her comment?
5. If you do not feel comfortable talking with Yvonne or other faculty members who make offensive comments, in what other ways can you communicate your displeasure to them?

That Baby Just Needed the Lord

As I enter the office to get my attendance folder, put my lunch away, and check my mailbox, I hear a familiar voice behind me. "Hey there, Miss Crenshaw. How are you doing this fine morning?" Mrs. Wilson asks in her usually cheerful voice. I smile at her and reply, "I'm doing well, Mrs. Wilson. How are you?" She looks up to the ceiling and says, "Well, my arthritis is acting up, I forgot my lunch, and I need gas in my truck." She then shrugs her shoulders and says, "But I know that the good Lord is going to see fit that all of my needs are met, so I'm as happy as can be and ain't stressed in the least."

Still holding the door and making room so she can enter the office, I say, "I just love your spirit, Mrs. Wilson." We both chuckle. "You have a great day, dear," Mrs. Wilson says before heading to the back of the office. "You too, Mrs. Wilson," I say. According to everyone from the cafeteria staff to our principal Mr. Fairbanks, Mrs. Wilson, the school custodian for over thirty-five years, has been this cheerful since day one.

Thinking we had shared a private moment, I hear coming from the left of me, "I love her spirit, too," Rebecca Gonzalez, our attendance clerk, says. I nod my head in agreement. "I just wish I had her outlook on life. Especially when things are going bad. She always seems to have a smile on her face and a good word to say to everyone." Nodding her head, Rebecca continues, "I will never forget a couple of years ago when she was working with Jimmy. He was a fifth grader who had so many problems at home. His mother was in and out of jail. His dad was on drugs, and his elderly great-grandparents were trying to raise him and his two brothers. It was just a rough time." Getting misty-eyed, Rebecca says, "He was the angriest young man I'd ever met. He would fight all the time." She continues, "Now that I think about it, he was always in here during recess because he was fighting or just messing with others."

I am wondering how this story links to our previous conversation about Mrs. Wilson, but I don't have to wait long before Rebecca says, "Mrs. Wilson told us she wanted to have a talk with him and for him to be an apprentice with her." Smiling, she continues, "At first, we weren't sure how it was going to turn out. We didn't know if she was going to just talk to him or spank him." Laughing, Rebecca says, "It was amazing. We're really not sure what she said to him, but he began to think before he acted and stopped fighting so much. As a matter of fact, he actually started smiling and everything." Leaning on the counter, Rebecca says, "He would work with her before school, during lunch, and after school. He took such pride in his work and got so close to her."

Nodding my head, I think about my student Giselle, whom I have been having trouble with since the beginning of the school year. I ask excitedly, "How can I set up something like that with Mrs. Wilson?" Putting my stuff on the counter, I look in my purse for a pen so that I can take notes. Rebecca grabs my hand and says, "Just ask Mrs. Wilson. She loves working with kids." Leaning closer to me she continues, "Who are you thinking about asking her to work with? Giselle?" I am surprised that Rebecca knows exactly who I'm thinking about. She says, "We all know what's going on in your class." She turns around and walks away from me chuckling.

I quickly put my lunch in the refrigerator, grab my attendance folder and mail, and exit the teachers' lounge in search of Mrs. Wilson. It doesn't take me any time to find her standing outside of the library conversing with students. She must've sensed I was behind her, because she reaches her hand out and grabs mine in hers. She looks at the children and says, "Now babies, I've got to go now. Now y'all head on to that playground and get yourselves ready for learning." She looks at me and says, "Now Miss Crenshaw, how can I help you?"

I begin by telling her about the problems that I'm having with Giselle. "Mrs. Wilson," I begin, "she just seems so angry, and I'm not really sure where this anger comes from because she won't open up to me." I turn my head toward the office and say, "Rebecca just told me you worked wonders with a young man named Jimmy, and I was wondering if you wouldn't mind mentoring Giselle just like you did Jimmy." Mrs. Wilson squeezes my hand and says, "Why baby, I would love to work with her. How about I come by your class after school so that we can get the ball rolling?" I am so happy. I can't contain my excitement. "Oh, Mrs. Wilson," I say, "Thank you so much! I just know you are just what she needs." Mrs. Wilson then closes her eyes, shakes her head and says, "Oh no baby. I ain't what she needs. What she need is the Lord. That's what I did with Jimmy. Got him closer to the Lord."

Did she just say she got him closer to the Lord? "Mrs. Wilson, what do you mean?" I ask innocently. With her eyes open again, she continues to shake her head as she says, "I know both his great-grandparents. They go to church with me. But that baby was so angry at the world. As a matter of fact, his grandparents swore he had a bit of the devil in him." Letting go of my hand, she continues, "So, I made it a point to get him closer to the Lord. We prayed, read scripture, and talked about what was going on in his life." Shaking her head with pride, she goes on to say, "And then that baby began to turn around. He began to believe things could get better." Beaming, Mrs. Wilson looks up to the sky, raises her hands in the air and says, "So baby, I can't take any credit for that. It was the Lord."

Just then, the bell rings signaling the beginning of the school day. Mrs. Wilson interrupts my thoughts and says, "So, I'll come on by after school so we can talk more about this baby of yours."

Discussion Questions
1. What is your immediate reaction to what Mrs. Wilson has said?
2. What would you say to Mrs. Wilson during your meeting with her after school?
3. Under what circumstances would you let Mrs. Wilson work with Giselle?
4. Do you feel that it is necessary to report this conversation to your administrator? Explain why or why not.
5. What is your personal opinion regarding religion being practiced and discussed in public schools?

Where's White History Month?

This year for Hispanic Heritage month, I decide I am not going to make my fifth graders do the usual reports on famous and historical figures. This year, they are going to come dressed in costumes and give an "autobiographical" sketch of their lives. In order to make this as fair as possible, I put the names of twenty-eight famous Latinos into a fishbowl and draw slips of paper. Whatever name the student gets, they have to do their project on that individual. So, during the months of August and September, we've had standing dates at the library every Wednesday and most Fridays to use the computers, encyclopedias, and books so my students could adequately research their person's life. I also appreciate that several parents, including Ms. Talbot, a seamstress, have volunteered their time to help us during our library research time.

"Class . . . class," I say. I wait patiently as they reply while putting their hands on their shoulders, "Yes . . . yes." Smiling, I scan my class to make sure I have everyone's attention. "Wonderful job. I really appreciate the way you all quickly stopped what you're doing and looked up at me." I look out again and say, "You may lower your signals." All of my students take their hands off their shoulders and continue to maintain eye contact with me.

"Some of you are having a little trouble finding information about the attire or clothing that Latinos wore during the time that your person lived." I look over at Mr. Jacobs, our librarian, and point out, "Mr. Jacobs is more than willing to help you out before and after school." Several students look relieved. I then ask, "How many of you think you need more help from Mr. Jacobs?" Six students raise their hand. Even before I can grab a pencil, Mr. Jacobs is writing down their names. I smile at how efficient he is and am amazed he knows all of my students' names.

I look up at the clock and realize it's time for us to head back to the class to start our math lesson. In an even tone, I say, "I am going to give you all five minutes to finish what you're writing and get the library clean." Thinking quickly, I say, "For those of you who requested extra time with Mr. Jacobs, please come to his desk so you can sign up for a time." With that, the students begin to move around and get ready to leave the library. I walk over to Mr. Jacobs' desk and say, "Please make sure you all write down the time and date of your meeting. You also need to make sure you have a way to get home after school or to get to school early." All of the students nod their heads in agreement as Mr. Jacobs passes each student a small sheet of paper so they can write their meeting time down.

As my students begin to line up at the door, I say, "Please thank all the parents who were able to donate their time to help us with our projects." In unison with their voices at a level one, their library voice, they all say, "Thank you, parents." Some students giggle every time they say this. Then I add, "And please thank Mr. Jacobs for being so helpful and giving of his time with our projects as well." Once again, at a level one, my students say, "Thank you, Mr. Jacobs." Mr. Jacobs, who I think should get his teaching credential, chimes in, "And thank Mrs. Huff for thinking of such a fun project to do." My students all look at me and say, "Thank you, Mrs. Huff." Chuckling, I say, "Thank you, class. Now let's head on back to class."

Back in the classroom, I am so happy the room is warm and toasty. I usually give my students a minute or two to get themselves together before we move on to our next lesson. I can hear several students bragging about all the information they found today. Francine is sitting in her chair with her arms crossed. Wondering if she's okay, I kneel down beside her desk to talk with her. "Francine," I begin, "Are you okay?" Leigh, who is Francine's best friend and usually jumps in to speak for her, says, "She can't find a lot of information about her person. That's why she's upset." Puzzled, I look back at Francine and ask, "Remind me, Francine. Who do you have again?" Looking up at me with sad eyes, Francine says, "Carmen Miranda." I am rather surprised. "Francine," I say, "Carmen Miranda was a famous dancer and singer. I am sure you can find out information about her." Shaking her head, Francine puts her head on her desk and does not reply.

Leigh then says, "No, Mrs. Huff. She found information on her, but doesn't know what she can wear." Leigh sits down next to Francine and looks at her with concern. Not wanting to baby Francine, I say, "Did you make an appointment with Mr. Jacobs?" Leigh begins to speak for Francine, but I raise my hand and stop her. After a few seconds, Francine looks up like she is surprised that she did not hear Leigh reply. "Um, no." I tilt my head to the side and say, "And why didn't you?" Still wearing her hangdog face, Francine says, "I don't know." Not willing to let her off the hook that easily, I ask, "And did you talk with Ms. Talbot?" Once again, with the sad face, she whispers, "No." I look at Francine, who is now looking squarely at her desk. "Francine," I say to get her to look up at me. "You had several people who could've helped you with your project. As a matter of fact, this is the first I'm hearing about you having any problems with your project on Carmen Miranda." Leigh and Francine both have widened their eyes. "Now," I say, "What can you do to help yourself with your project?"

Francine looks away from me and to Leigh. She then looks back at me, squares her shoulders and says with more confidence than I've ever seen in her, "I don't even know why I have to do this dumb project. We always do stuff on Hispanic people. We even do stuff on Black people and Chinese people. I mean, how fair is that? We never do stuff on white people. I mean, why don't we have White History Month like everybody else?"

Discussion Questions

1. What do you say in response to Francine?
2. What would you say to your class, who probably heard most of this conversation?
3. What would you say to Francine's parents if you had the opportunity to speak with them?
4. If Francine's parents agree with her feeling and do not require her to do this project, how would you handle that situation?
5. How would you handle the situation of one student who is always speaking on behalf of another student?

Advice from Veteran Teachers on . . . Multiculturalism

- We suggest that you talk candidly with your students about what history instruction used to look like and how certain individuals and events were purposely excluded from textbooks, instruction, and assignments dealing with American history. If possible, finding a history or social studies book that highlights this would be great. We would further explain that Black History Month, Women's Month, and the like came about because of those omissions. Thus, we are not purposely excluding white men, but we are purposely including others who have made valuable contributions to our American history.
- We would also make it clear that we are still exploring and learning about the contributions that white men have made in America. As an example, we still teach about our forty-three former presidents and the founding fathers, who were all white men.
- In the case presented, there are Native American parents who could have served as wonderful resources to the teacher. The teacher was correct in asking the parent how to respectfully represent his tribe. Additionally, she could ask him to bring in any

Native American artifacts he may have, tell stories, and/or help the class cook Native American food.

- We have all dealt with inconsiderate, rude, and potentially racist colleagues. We acknowledge that this is a very delicate and troubling situation. Some of us have chosen in the past to talk with these colleagues one-on-one. Some of us have not. This is a personal call. We suggest that you consider what your relationship is with that colleague before you proceed. It may change for the better or the worse following a conversation with them.
- If you feel uncomfortable or the remark is over-the-top offensive, we suggest talking to your administrator about the comment. Hopefully you have a respectful administrator who will keep your anonymity. If not, once again, it's a personal call. You may want to also talk to other colleagues you can trust about the situation.
- In thinking about multiculturalism and diversity, we cannot think of a topic more sensitive than religion. Most of our students have confided in us that they recognize and practice some religious beliefs with their families. Thus, we do not have a problem with our students being religious beings. If a child needs or wants to pray, fast, read their Holy book, or participate or not participate in a holiday because of their religious beliefs, we do not see a problem with that.
- In the case presented, it appears that Mrs. Wilson already had a relationship with Jimmy's great-grandparents and knew that he was Christian. It also appears his family was not opposed to him working with Mrs. Wilson and discussing Christianity with her. In the case of Giselle, we are not sure if she has any knowledge of Giselle's family's religious beliefs. So, unless she knows more about them, we would ask Mrs. Wilson if she would be willing to work with Giselle, but to keep Christianity out of their conversations. Now if, through their conversations, she finds out that Giselle is a Christian and her parents do not oppose this, we would not discourage her from discussing Christianity with her.

Discrimination

Anyone but Her

"Margo, Margo," I say, "Will you please stop messing with the fish tank." Margo is sitting in the front right by my desk where the fish tank is. She is tapping her finger on the tank. I believe she is trying to get one of the fishes' attention because she keeps saying, "Here, fishy, fishy, fishy." "Mr. Pardue," Margo begins, "the fish just won't swim to me if I don't tap on the tank." "Margo," I say for who knows how many times today, "You do not need to concern yourself with the fish because you are supposed to be reading your book right now. So please, sit in your seat, get out your book, and begin reading." I look at the timer and wonder how many more times I will have to redirect Margo. We only have ten minutes left for independent reading time. Margo huffs and gets her book out. However, she stills stares at the fish and leans into the tank. "Margo," I say before she begins tapping on the tank again. "I know, Mr. P.," Margo starts, "Get to reading!"

In the beginning of the school year, I heard from Maxine Holloway, Margo's fourth-grade teacher, that Margo was going to be a handful. According to Maxine, "I have never in all my twenty-seven years of teaching had a student who simply could not pay attention. I mean, it's amazing that she has such a difficult time focusing." After that conversation, I checked Margo's cumulative file and all of her other previous teachers reported similar characteristics—"sweet girl, but has trouble focusing"—"a joy to have in class, but needs to be redirected all day"—"Margo is a bright girl. Wish she could focus more on her class assignments instead of everything else going on in the classroom." Over and over again, teachers, the staff in the front office, the nurse, the cafeteria workers, and the yard duty supervisors all reported that Margo was a nice kid who often got in trouble for her inability to focus well.

What I found when I met Margo and after some time in my class was that she was one of the sweetest students in the class. She was also one of the best writers and artists in my class. Her poems and paintings are phenomenal. I also found out that Margo loves science and especially the experiments we do as a class. She does struggle a bit with math, but I really believe her poor attention span is part of the problem.

In the beginning of the school year, Margo's mother told me that her daughter has been on medication for attention deficit disorder since the second grade. However, her mother reported, because of puberty, she feels that Margo is not responding as well to the medication. "I am trying to get her in to see the doctor as soon as I can, Mr. Pardue," her mother assures me. "But I work during the afternoons and evenings, so I'm having a heck of a time getting her there." Since the beginning of the year, I, too, have noticed that Margo is less and less focused every day. However, until her mother takes her to her doctor, I am not sure how best to handle this situation.

The timer goes off to remind my students as well as me that our independent reading time is over. "Please clean up your areas and get out your journals." I wait patiently as my students follow my directions. "Tap, tap," I hear coming from the fish tank again. "Here fishy, fishy, fishy," I hear Margo saying once again. I take a deep breath in before I proceed. "Margo, is your journal out?" I ask. Margo looks up at me with surprise. "Oh, no, Mr. P." She opens her desk which looks like a cyclone has gone through it and paws through it for her journal. I do not know how she finds anything in that desk. She begins moving loose papers, books, puppets, newspapers, magazines, and notebooks all around. "Margo," I interrupt her, "what color is your journal?" Margo thinks for a second and says, "Oh, it's blue." She finds her blue folder and then closes her desk. "Margo, did you remember a pencil?" I ask. Margo giggles and opens her desk and takes out a pencil so small with several bite marks on it; I am not sure how she will write with it. "Here's my pencil, Mr. P." Margo holds up her small pencil so that I can see it.

"Okay, boys and girls," I tell my students, "Before we leave in twenty-five minutes, I want you to take fifteen minutes and write what you read about in your journal. Remember to include the date, the title of your book, chapter, and page number. Are there any questions?" I ask. "Tap, tap," I hear coming from the fish tank again. "Here fishy, fishy, fishy," I hear Margo saying to the tank. I take another deep breath in before I proceed. "Margo, do you know what you're supposed to do?" I ask. I can tell that she is embarrassed as she looks around the class at her peers. "Um," Margo begins. Trying to give her an out, I say, "Let me get someone to remind you. Samantha, what are you all supposed to do?" Samantha tells the class what I just said. After that, my students get to work.

After twenty-five minutes and redirecting Margo two more times, class is over. I walk my students to the front of the school to catch the bus, meet their parents, or walk home. "Hey Jake," Grace, a fourth-grade teacher says, "You look beat!" "Is it that obvious?" I ask. Grace laughs. "And your day isn't over yet. We still have the staff meeting."

I saunter into the library where the staff meeting is taking place. For forty-five minutes, my principal, Mr. Gerry Cunningham, talks about parent involvement, the book fair, and our test scores. "Now," Gerry continues, "Let me turn things over to Mrs. Holloway, who has some exciting news." Maxine stands up and begins, "Our sister school from London will be sending two teachers and six students to visit our *lovely* school. They will be visiting most of our classrooms and will be having lunch with twenty-one of our best and brightest students. So, we want the upper elementary teams to really think about the students that you are going to invite to lunch because we want to make sure that we make a good impression. I've done the math, so I want each teacher to select three students."

Now this has my attention. Grace asks me who I'm thinking about inviting to lunch. "I don't know, it's so hard," I say. "I think that all of my students should be invited." As I think about this longer, Maxine interrupts my thoughts. "Now Jake," she says, "Please don't invite Margo. Sweet kid, but they may think all of our kids are bad and I just don't have the patience to deal with her all day."

Discussion Questions

1. What are some ways that teachers can configure their classrooms to help children who have attention deficit disorders?
2. What's your opinion regarding medicating children with ADD or ADHD?
3. What ideas can you suggest to parents like Margo's mom to help them get their children to important appointments when their schedules are busy?
4. What do you say to Maxine Holloway?
5. What do you say to your principal regarding this situation?

That's Not Fair!

"Ding, ding, ding . . . " the timer on the front kidney table goes off, signaling the end of math. "Ladies and gentlemen," I begin, "Let's clean up and get ready for physical education." Immediately I hear chair legs scratch the vinyl surface of my classroom floors, as my class of thirty fifth graders begins to mill around and put their math books and remaining homework in their backpacks, clean up the area around their desks, and wait for further directions. After two minutes, I look around the room and begin to praise my students. "Excellent job, ladies and gentlemen. You have all earned six more beans in our pizza party jar. Keep up the great work." As I turn around to put the six beans in the half-full jar, I can hear my students praising themselves and each other.

"Now before we go outside, let's look at our fitness charts." Mrs. Franklin, our principal, announced one month ago that she was holding the first annual marathon in order to promote healthy lifestyles for our students. One component of her plan included exercise, and she decided that all of our students should be able to run one mile in under ten minutes. Although I am not sure where she got the directive from, she is sticking to it. As a matter of fact, she is holding an awards assembly after the marathon in order to recognize the boys and girls who were able to run one mile under ten minutes.

"I know that some of you are running at home," I begin, "So make sure that you jot down your time in your logs." Some of my students nod their heads and begin writing their times in their exercise logs. "Oh, before I forget," I add, "If you are wearing shoes with heels or sandals, please change into your running shoes quickly so that we can go to the track." As my students write in their logs and put on their running shoes, I allow them to talk amongst themselves. "Shoot," Jeremy says, "I could run a mile in eight minutes if I tried hard enough." "Me too," says Timothy, "I hope we get more than a dumb ol' certificate though," he whispers. Some of my girls chime in. "Well, I ran a mile yesterday after school and it took me nine minutes and forty-three seconds," said Jessica. "My dad timed me." "That's nothing," Tanya added. "My aunt timed me two days ago and I ran my mile in nine minutes flat," she says as she hits her hand on her desk for emphasis. "Okay," I say to my students, "Let's line up." After all of the chairs are pushed in, and everyone is in line with water bottles in hand, we go to the track to run our mile.

When we get outside, I set my stopwatch to 00:00. On most days, I run with my students. However, on Wednesdays, I clock them in order to give them an official time that they can record in their exercise logs to note their progress. When all of my students are lined up, I shout, "On your mark, get set, go!" Then they all take off in a cloud of dust.

I have noticed several things about my students during these exercises. First, several of my boys and girls begin sprinting like they are running only a fifty-yard dash. After the first lap, they begin to slow up a little. I have also noticed that a group right in the middle keeps a steady pace throughout the whole mile. All of them finish at ten minutes on most days. Then I have another group who mixes jogging and walking. They work hard and continue to make progress; however, they have yet to get their time under ten minutes. They are close, though, and I let them know it. Then I have the few students who bring up the rear. I can tell that they are trying, but they have to stop every few yards in order to catch their breath. At this rate, I wonder if they'll ever make the ten-minute mark. Shoot, I wonder if they'll make the fifteen-minute mark.

"Come on, ladies and gentlemen," I encourage my students. "You can do it!" I yell as I clap for them for trying their best. Students begin to complete their fourth lap, which is a mile. "Eight minutes, fifteen seconds," I shout as Jeremy crosses the imaginary line. Then I see Maria coming up closely. "Eight minutes, twenty-two seconds," I shout as she finishes. She pumps her arms in the air because this is her best time ever. "Great job, Maria," I shout. Then, students pour in over our imaginary line and I shout out their times. As most of my students are sitting on the grass drinking their water and chit-chatting, we wait for two students who unfortunately have been last every time—Cory and Melissa.

Melissa told me the first day that Mrs. Franklin announced our marathon that she would not participate. "I am not getting all sweaty and out of breath for this." On most days, she tells me that she has cramps, a headache, backache, or just doesn't want to participate. After talking with her mother, I found out that the real reason that she doesn't want to run is because her breasts began to grow in the third grade and she now wears a size 34C bra. Since she can't afford a jogging bra, she is not going to hurt or embarrass herself by running, "no dumb mile for no dumb certificate!" In order to compromise, we decided that she would walk her mile. Most days she will do it. Some days she won't. This is one of the days she doesn't because she joins us on the grass when she finishes her second lap. Her mother says she is comfortable with whatever grade her daughter gets in physical education because she doesn't participate at the level of other students.

But Cory is a different student. He is a bit overweight, has asthma, and tries just as hard, if not harder, than any of my other students. In his journal and exercise log, Cory writes about how he is trying so hard to run a mile in ten minutes because he wants that certificate so bad. However, he is experiencing a lot of difficulty with this assignment. "Come on, Cory," I encourage him. "You can do it!" As he rounds the third lap at seventeen minutes, my other students begin to cheer him on too. As he gets closer, I notice that something is different about Cory this time. His face is red and stained with tears. His breathing is labored and he is holding his chest. "Ms. Robinson," he tries to say, "What's—my—time?" as he falls into my arms. I look at my stopwatch and report to him that he is at seventeen minutes. He then cries and says, "I've been trying to run. I even try at home. I'll never get a certificate, huh?"

Discussion Questions

1. What are some pros and cons of students exercising vigorously during the school day?
2. If students are required to run for physical education, what type of skills should they be taught?

3. What resources might a teacher take outside when doing physical education with his or her students?
4. What other physical problems may make this assignment difficult for some students to fulfill?
5. How might you handle children who are having difficulty completing this task?

That's Too Bad!

As usual when we have an assembly in the cafeteria, there's a buzz in the air. I allow my students to talk quietly to their neighbors, but I have noticed that some teachers do not. For me, it's just easier to let them talk quietly than for me to have to keep shushing them. They are kids, for goodness sake!

I am fortunate to have a hardworking, intelligent, and creative principal this year. An elementary teacher for twenty years, Mr. Peterson knows about classroom practices, resources, and problems. He understands the needs of his teachers and our students. Some of my friends who are also teachers are not as lucky. They are with principals who seem not to care, who are dictators, or who meddle in the classroom too much. I feel very comfortable going to Mr. Peterson with any problem that I may have and if he can't help me, he knows who can.

"Ms. Harris," Monica asks, "What's this assembly about?" "You know, sweetie," I begin, "I'm really not sure." She looks over at me like I'm trying to pull the wool over her eyes, but I am serious. I really don't know what the assembly is about. I get so much stuff in my mailbox that I'm just lucky that I know that there *is* an assembly this afternoon. "I guess it's a surprise," Marcia says to Monica jokingly. "Yes," I say, "That's how we should look at it. As a surprise." Monica chuckles at me and then all our attention is shifted to Mr. Peterson, who is standing in the front of the cafeteria tapping hard on the microphone, shouting, "Testing, testing. Can you all hear me?" All of the boys and girls scream, "Yes!" "Okay," Mr. Peterson continues, not realizing that he is literally screaming in the microphone.

"I am pleased to announce that we have a special guest with us today who is a *real* dance teacher. She is from *Dance America,* the dance studio on 14th and Lincoln, and she has graciously and generously decided to provide free dance lessons to all upper elementary grade students interested." All of the students begin to buzz and talk about this opportunity. I can feel their excitement. "Now, please help me welcome LaVonne Greene." Our students begin to clap to welcome Ms. Greene.

"Hello boys and girls," shouts Ms. Greene into the microphone. "Hello," our students shout back. "Oh, I just love it," Ms. Greene says. "Please feel free to call me LaVonne. I am here to show you the type of dance that you will be taught if you choose to join our team, as well as talk about the specifics such as getting your parents' permission, where to buy your shoes and outfits, competitions, etc." LaVonne coughs slightly, then continues, "Now, before we go further, I want you all to know that dance is for both girls and boys, so I want all of you to consider participating." I look at some of my male students. I'm not sure if they're convinced of this yet. LaVonne continues, "First I have several dancers who will show you an African dance routine, then a hip-hop dance routine, followed by a ballet routine."

For the next twenty minutes, LaVonne's high school and college students wowed our students. To see her students having so much fun and using their bodies in such imaginative ways is unbelievable. My students are very excited as well. "I want to sign up," Benita says to me. "So do I," says Isaac. "I want to join the hip-hop group." I believe that LaVonne has convinced some of my boys to join.

"Well, boys and girls, what do you think?" LaVonne questions our students. Our students begin to clap loudly for what performances and performers they had just witnessed. "Ms. Harris," Monica looks over, "What do we need to do to sign up?" At least ten other boys and girls in my class look over at me with the same question on their minds. "Let's wait and see. She may answer your question," I say.

"Okay, boys and girls," LaVonne starts as the information packets are passed out row by row. "All of the lessons will be given right here in the cafeteria by me and the dancers that you saw today. Also," she says turning to the second page in the packet, "I have to make sure that your parent or guardian gives you permission to participate in our dance lessons because they will be given after school hours and some times, you may need a ride home after school."

"Ms. Harris," Michael begins, "I ride the school bus home. How will I get home then?" Unsure of what to say, I ask him to hold his questions until we get back to the classroom. "Also, please look at the list of supplies." LaVonne instructs the students. "We have been fortunate in that we've received a group discount because we anticipate so many students participating." LaVonne looks over at Mr. Peterson, gives a thumb's up, and continues. "Now, you will need to purchase your shoes, outfits, mats, etc., from Mrs. Fender, who owns the shop next to my studio. The total cost for everything is down at the bottom of your sheet on page four. I quickly turn to page four and am shocked by what I see. "$515!" I whisper. "I thought this was a discounted group rate?" Monica looks over at me with a sad face. "Ms. Harris, I don't think my parents have that much money. What can we do?" Once again, I am unsure of what to say, so I ask her to hold her question until we get back to the classroom.

Surprisingly, LaVonne takes up so much time there isn't any time for questions. When she is done talking about the dance lessons, Mr. Peterson excuses each class to line up for lunch. "Boys and girls," I say before they got up to leave, "Please pass your information packets to me and I will pass them back to you after lunch." My students eagerly comply and go to lunch. Luckily, we brought our bucket with us so the kids who brought their lunch did not have to go all the way back to the classroom to get their lunch. The boys and girls who were buying lunches simply get in line and wait to be served.

As I entered the teachers' lounge, I see LaVonne finishing up a phone call. "Oh great," I say to LaVonne. "I have a question for you." She smiles at me and leans in to hear my question. I begin by saying, "I have some students who are very excited about joining your dance lessons and team. However, $515 is quite a bit for most of my students' families to handle. Do you have any suggestions?" LaVonne thinks about my question for a minute and then replies, "I guess they won't be able to participate then."

Discussion Questions

1. After this conversation with LaVonne, what do you do next?
2. What questions do you anticipate your class having after the assembly?
3. What answers do you give your students?

4. What are some ideas that you have to raise money for students who are unable to financially pay for dance lessons?
5. Why or why do you not encourage your students to participate in LaVonne's dance lessons?

Advice from Veteran Teachers on . . . Discrimination

-   In the case where one child is singled out and not permitted to participate, we would honestly tell the teacher that none of our students can participate. It is not fair and we would take offense that this teacher would assume that she is "bad" because she has ADHD.
-   In special cases; say certain field trips, if the child exhibits behaviors that may make it difficult for you to monitor all of your students closely, we have requested that the child's parent join us, if possible. If the parent is unable to attend the field trip, we have asked for additional parent volunteers so that we can more closely monitor that one student's behavior. The other parent volunteers can help monitor the other students and ensure their safety.
-   In an ideal world we would encourage our administrators not to have school functions where the students have to pay for the school activities. There would be enough money in our school's budget so that all kids could go or participate for free.
-   If there are minimal fees required to participate, we have written letters home to our class parents and asked for the money. Additionally, in the letter, we ask our parents to donate (if they can) money for a child who may not be able to afford the minimal fees.
-   For school extra-curricular activities such as band, dance teams or even field trips, we would encourage the schools to consider fundraising and asking parents or community organizations to make donations for the children who have financial difficulties paying for the activity.
-   We have also had recycling drives where parents and community members bring in newspapers, bottles, and cans to our schools. Every couple of weeks, we take the items to the recycling center and collect the proceeds.
-   For a child who is trying hard but seems unable to meet the criteria set by someone else, we have held our own reward celebration and have printed our own certificates. These children may get a "best effort" or a "most improved" certificate.
-   For children who would not earn or receive an academic or behavioral award (they may exhibit problematic behavior, not show an effort to improve their grades, etc.) at the end of the year, we have held an awards assembly in our classes where certificates such as best dresser, most athletic, or best sense of humor were given out. This way, all of our students receive a certificate at the end of the year.

English Language Learners

Can We Talk?

As I walk out of the office and head to my room to get ready for class, I hear someone calling my name. I turn around and see Mrs. Conrad, our school secretary, standing there. "Yes," I say, stopping. Mrs. Conrad catches her breath and says, "I don't know if you noticed or not, but you have a new student today." I begin to fumble with the mail in my hands and find my attendance folder. I open the folder and see a new name at the bottom of the list—George Parlan.

"Oh," I say, "What can you tell me about George?" Mrs. Conrad looks up at me and says, "Well, his family is from the Philippines. We're not really sure about whether he went to kindergarten in the Philippines, so you'll have to deal with that. We do know that he speaks very little English." She pauses and then says, "As a matter of fact, the lady who came in with his mother says that he knows only the words bathroom, water, and no."

I look at Mrs. Conrad with concern. "Please pardon my ignorance, but do you know what language is spoken in the Philippines?" Mrs. Conrad says, "Tagalog." I am impressed that she knows this information. She then leans closer to me and says, "I looked it up on the Internet." We both smile just as the bell rings.

When I get to my classroom door, there is my principal, Mr. Ishman, standing with a little boy and two women. All of my first graders are standing in line right outside of the class. "Ms. Fernandez," Camilla, one of my students says, "We have a new student." As I get closer to the front of the line where Mr. Ishman is, I look down at the little boy. I kneel down and say, "Are you George?" George looks up at Mr. Ishman and then at me. He smiles shyly and nods his head.

"Ms. Fernandez," Mr. Ishman says, "This is George's mother, Margarita Parlan, and her friend, Isabella." I reach out and shake both of the ladies' hands. Margarita nods her head and then gives me a shy smile like George. I smile back at her. Mr. Ishman then says, "Isabella speaks both Tagalog and English. She is willing to help us out as much as possible, although she works quite a bit." With that, Isabella interjects, "Yes, Margarita and her husband don't speak much English so I'll be the one that you'll have to speak with about stuff going on in school." She hands me an index card with a phone number on it. I slip it into my pocket, and say, "Thank you. Will you two be joining us this morning?" Isabella shakes her head and says, "No, we have to go to work. Our boss was nice enough to let us drop him off, but we really need to go." I look at George, Margarita, and Isabella, and say, "Will you please tell Mrs. Parlan that we'll take great care of George?" Isabella looks at Margarita, says something to her in Tagalog, and then looks back at me. Margarita then says in English, "Thank you," and nods her head.

Isabella leans down and speaks with George, who shakes his head and then leans into his mother and gives her a big hug.

I look over at my students and choose two boys. "Michael and Roger, will you two be George's friends and help him get around school today?" Michael and Roger nod their heads in agreement and walk up to the front of the line. Michael reaches out and grabs George's hand as Roger puts his hand on his back. I open the classroom door and we walk into the room. George looks back at his mother, Isabella, and Mr. Ishman, and waves goodbye.

The morning progresses well. I look up and see Michael and Roger taking George around the classroom. "Fish," Michael says pointing to the fish in the fish tank. "Those are fish." George nods his head and repeats the word, "Fish." George points to the bottom of the fish tank and looks up at Michael and Roger. This time, Roger says, "Those are rocks. Rocks." George looks back at the fish tank and repeats, "Rocks." All three boys smile at each other and continue their tour of the room. I allow the boys to take George on an extended classroom tour and language lesson for about fifteen minutes. George seems to be enjoying himself and learning new words. When the recess bell rings, I excuse the kids and go to the front office.

About five minutes into recess, I hear a commotion in the front office. I see the recess monitor, Michael, Roger, and George, who is crying "Mama!" When I reach the boys I ask, "What's the matter?" Michael, out of breath, says, "George got stung by a bee and it's swelling up." Wheezing, George sticks his arm out and sure enough, it has a bright red bump on it. The attendance secretary, Jackie McDonald, comes into the front office and asks, "What's going on?" Before I can say anything, Roger shouts, "He was stung by a bee!" Mrs. Conrad, who is always thinking, looks into a folder. "There's no indication in his cum file that he's allergic to bees. Maybe we should call his mother."

We all look at each other. "Does anyone here speak Tagalog?" I ask. Mrs. McDonald, Mrs. Conrad, and both of the boys all look up me and shake their heads. I remember the index card in my pocket and immediately dial the number on my cell phone. On the second ring, I hear, "You have reached a number that is disconnected or is no longer in service . . . "

Discussion Questions

1. What is your immediate reaction to this situation?
2. What other information may be in George's cumulative file that may assist you with getting in contact with his parents or Isabella?
3. In your school district, which languages are provided translators?
4. For languages that do not have translators in your district, what are some other resources that you can utilize?
5. What are possible issues for teaching children whose primary language is a non-phonetic language such as Arabic, Hebrew, Chinese, or Japanese, to name a few?

Hi, I'm Jonathan from Hungary

When I walk into the office on Wednesday morning, I see what appears to be a mom, dad, son, and daughter sitting in the four chairs closest to Lillian's, my principal's, office. I give a slight smile, which the parents return with a smile and nod. I then reach into the basket that holds our yellow attendance folders and look for my name. Not finding my folder in the basket, I search again. This time, I put my lunch, backpack, and purse on the counter. I must have a look of panic on my face, because Rasha, our attendance clerk, widens her eyes and begins to move closer to me. She stops at her desk and picks up a yellow folder with my name written on the tab. She says, "I needed your folder because you will be getting a new student today. His name is Jonathan and he is from Hungary."

Behind me, I hear Lillian's door open and I turn around to greet her. "Oh, great!" she says excitedly, pointing to me, "This is Jonathan's teacher, Ms. Williams." The mother, father, and who I am guessing is Jonathan all stand up and bow slightly. The little girl anxiously holds onto her mother's long skirt for dear life. I smile at Jonathan and reach out to shake his hand. "Why hello there, Jonathan. How are you doing?" Jonathan smiles at me nervously, shakes my hand, and then glances up at his father with a worried look. Quickly, Lillian chimes in, "Why don't we all go into my office to talk more about Jonathan?" With that, we all follow Lillian into her office.

As we settle into our seats, Lillian begins. "Gina, this is Dr. and Mrs. Szervan-szky, and you've already met Jonathan, who is in the fifth grade." She smiles and looks at the little girl who is sitting in her mother's lap. "Now this little cutie is Martina and she is in kindergarten." Realizing that she is being talked about, Martina shyly lays her head on her mother's chest and hides her face.

Dr. Szervanszky then begins to speak. "I am a visiting professor in the Geology Department at the university for the winter semester, conducting research and teach-ing several classes." He swallows as he continues, "We are from Hungary and will be returning late summer." He looks at his family and says, "As you can tell, I speak En-glish fairly well, but my wife and children really do not." He looks at his wife and con-tinues. "Now my wife, Graciella, speaks more English than the kids, but she's shy."

I shake my head as I try to process all of this information. Looking over at Lillian I ask, "Whose class will Martina be in?" Lillian finishes swallowing her water and says, "Margaret Dunlap." I nod my head. "Do we have anyone in the district who can help us with Hungarian?" Shrugging my shoulders innocently, I say, "I apologize, but I don't know anything about the Hungarian culture or language." Smiling, I continue, "I mean, I'm assuming that the language is Hungarian, right?" Chuckling, Dr. Szervanszky says, "Yes, it is."

After swallowing another sip of water, Lillian chimes in, "I've checked, and we do not have any Hungarian translators employed with the district." Glancing at Dr. Szervanszky she continues, "But we've talked about the best way for Jonathan to attend school here." She then proceeds to tell me that Jonathan has a national test to take when he gets back to Hungary in the fall. So, according to Lillian, "His parents have requested that he concentrate on learning English, and during instructional times, he will study from the textbooks that he brought here from Hungary."

Admittedly, I am still trying to process all of this information. I think to myself, "Is this legal?" Noticing my baffled expression, Lillian adds, "Don't worry. We've gone through the course of study for fifth grade, and Jonathan is more than prepared to pass our end of the year test. As a matter of fact, Jonathan is doing the math that our seventh graders do." Going through a stack of papers and textbooks on her desk, Lillian con-tinues, "I've been able to go through his textbooks and talk with his parents, so I feel comfortable with this." Thinking about it some more, I say, "Well, if you feel comfort-able then I'm okay, too."

I look up at the clock and realize that we have seven minutes before the morning bell will ring. Dr. Szervanszky says "Now, we've taught Jonathan several important words to help him at least get through his day." He turns to Jonathan and begins speaking Hungarian with him. Jonathan then says slowly, "Hi, I'm Jonathan from Hungary, restroom, Ms. Williams, water, office, police. . ." Smiling, he looks up at his father who is beaming with pride. I look up at Lillian and say, "Well, I think that I'm ready to show Jonathan his new class." I then look back at Dr. and Mrs. Szervanszky and say, "Would you like to follow us to our class?" Dr. Szervanszky speaks with Jonathan in Hungarian again and he and his wife giggle. Dr. Szervanszky states, "Jonathan says that he doesn't need a babysitter, so he doesn't want us to escort him to his class." I nod my head and say to Jonathan, "Okay, let's go to our class." As we get up, Jonathan grabs a red backpack that appears to be full of books. He hugs his mother and father, and then follows me to our class.

When I get to my classroom door, my fifth graders are all lined up and chatting with one another. "Hey," I hear Javier say, "We have a new student." Unlocking the door, I say, "We sure do." I turn around to my class and announce, "Please come in and put your belongings away. I have an introduction to make." After about two minutes, my class is ready. Jonathan is standing right by my side in the front of the classroom. "Now," I begin as I look over at Jonathan, "this is our new student, Jonathan." Several kids say, "Hi Jonathan." He then smiles, waves, and says, "Hi" back to them. I look back at my class and say, "Jonathan speaks just a little English. He is from Hungary, and in his country, they speak Hungarian." "Wow," I hear from my students.

Nahla raises her hand and asks, "Where's Hungary?" I look up at her and say, "Good question." I turn my back to my class and pull down the map above the white board. Jonathan moves closer to the map and points to Hungary. He then looks back at the class and says, "Hungary." Nahla and several other students say excitedly, "Wow." Marcelle adds, "That sure is far." I then scan my class and tell the young men at table six, "Okay, I am trusting you with Jonathan today." I then lead Jonathan over to table six and pull out the empty chair next to Travis. "I want you all to be friends with Jonathan and show him around on the playground today." They all nod and agree to work with Jonathan and be his friend.

The morning progresses well. Jonathan works on his math while we do our Literature Circles. After recess though, several students come running up to me excitedly. "Ms. Williams, Ms. Williams," Kayla yells, "They're teaching Jonathan cuss words." When all of my students are in line to come back to class, I look at Travis who shrugs his shoulders and widens his eyes. I then look at Jonathan as he says slowly, "Hi bitch. I'm Jonathan from Hungary."

Discussion Questions

1. What are the consequences for Travis and his friends' misdeeds?
2. What other problems can you anticipate with having a student who speaks only limited English?
3. What activities can you do to accelerate Jonathan's English language development?
4. What activities can you do to give your students more information about Hungary and the Hungarian culture?
5. How would you communicate with the Szervanszky family on a regular basis?

She Won't Stop Crying!

My class door opens and I hear, "Hi, Mrs. Dunbar." I turn around to find our principal, Lillian, and a man, woman, and little girl, who looks petrified. I tilt my head to the side and say, "Hello to you, too." I then extend my hand and shake the man's hand. He quickly says, "Hi, I'm Dr. Szervanszky and this is my wife, Graciella." I look over at Graciella and say, "It's so nice to meet you." She smiles and looks back at her husband. Dr. Szervanszky smiles and says, "My wife doesn't speak much English and she's rather shy." He then looks lovingly at his wife. I smile and turn my attention to the little girl. I kneel down and say, "And what's your name, honey?" Her eyes get as big as quarters and she looks to her mother. Lillian then quickly jumps in and says, "This is Martina. Her brother Jonathan is in the fifth grade and is in Cheryl's class." Nodding my head, I make a mental note of where her brother is because it looks like she will definitely need him.

Lillian then looks intently at me and says, "Dr. Szervanszky is a visiting professor in the Geology Department at the university. So the family will only be here for this one semester." Nodding his head in agreement, he adds, "We will be going back to Hungary in August." I smile at everyone, as Lillian continues, "Now Martina knows very little English, isn't that correct, Dr. Szervanszky?" He nods his head in agreement and says, "Yes." He then looks down at Martina and says something to her in Hungarian. She widens her eyes again and quickly buries her face in her mother's skirt. Her mother, sensing her daughter's uneasiness, says, "You can say, restroom, office, help. . .," Mrs. Szervanszky looks at her daughter expectantly. Unfortunately, if Martina does know all of these words, she is unwilling to share them with Lillian and me this morning.

Still kneeling, I say, "It's okay, sweetheart." I then stand up and say, "Do we have anyone at the district level. . .", but I am quickly interrupted by Lillian who says, "No. We do not have any Hungarian translators employed with the district." She then looks over at the doctor and says, "But Dr. Szervanszky has graciously extended himself to helping us out as much as possible." He nods his head in agreement and says, "But I will be quite busy, so my wife will be the one who will be here until Martina feels comfortable with school."

I wonder to myself about how much English Mrs. Szervanszky speaks. After a brief moment, she says, "Martina does have some preschool experience, so she knows her letters, numbers, shapes, and colors. But we would like for her to really work on developing her English speaking skills." Inwardly, I say, "Whew! Thank goodness." Mrs. Szervanszky continues, "I am not working right now, so I'll come in whenever you need me." I look down at Martina, who is digging her nails into her mother's thighs and ask in a hopeful voice, "Were you planning on staying today?" Mrs. Szervanszky chuckles slightly and says, "Definitely." Then thinking about it some more, she adds, "But I won't be able to come in tomorrow because I have a doctor's appointment." She then pats her tummy and smiles. Feeling my anxiety level rising, I say in a low voice, "Okay."

Lillian says, "But this is the best situation because she is in kindergarten and this will really give her an opportunity to learn English." She looks at me knowingly and says, "She will get to sing songs, hear great books, write, play with friends, and do art projects." Both Dr. and Mrs. Szervanszky are nodding their heads. Mrs. Szervanszky then speaks to her daughter once again. This time, Martina smiles, but still does not respond. Mrs. Szervanszky tells me, "She just loves music." Lillian then looks up at the clock and says, "Let us give you time to get ready for your class." She then shakes Mrs. Szervanszky's hand and escorts Dr. Szervanszky out of the class. I then say, "Mrs. Szervanszky, if you want, you may walk Martina around the class so that she can get used to her surroundings." Nodding her head, Mrs. Szervanszky leads Martina around the room.

When all of my kindergarteners are in the classroom and are seated on their spots on the rug, I motion for Mrs. Szervanszky and Martina to come to my side. "Hello sweethearts." They all reply, "Hello Mrs. Dunbar." I continue, "Today, we have a new student. Her name is Martina Szervanszky and she is from Hungary." All of my students say, "Hi Martina." Several students wave at her. Martina's eyes widen and then she looks at her mother and smiles. Celine, who is extremely extroverted, raises her hand and says, "Mrs. Dunbar, can she be my friend like I was when Chelsea moved here?" I then look down at Celine and say, "That sounds like a good idea. Maybe you, Chelsea, and Maria can be her friends." Celine then stands up and grabs Martina's hand. Not knowing what to do, Martina doesn't even look up at her mother. She just follows Chelsea back to her seat. Her mother and I look at each other and smile. She then leans down and says, "This went better than I thought." I nod my head in agreement. "Whew!" I think to myself. "Please let this good fortune continue."

The rest of the day was great. Martina, with her mother not too far from her, played with her friends, tried to sing all of the songs, smiled, and even laughed. At the end of the day, Mrs. Szervanszky reminds me, "Tomorrow I have a doctor's appointment, so I won't be able to come in." She looks at Martina and says, "But after having such a great day today, I don't think we're going to have any problems tomorrow."

The next day, Martina and Jonathan arrive at my classroom. "You must be Jonathan," I say. Jonathan says, "Yes, ma'am." Martina looks at her brother and begins to speak to him in Hungarian with pleading eyes. Thank goodness, the bus arrives and Chelsea jumps off. "Hey Martina," Chelsea says as she skips to our door. Martina looks at Chelsea and her brother. Jonathan, sensing her uneasiness, walks with the girls out to the playground.

Unfortunately, Martina comes back into class crying and won't stop. During literacy center time, Chelsea comes up to me and says, "Mrs. Dunbar, I just can't get her to stop crying." I try to soothe Martina, but she is inconsolable. All of the kids have stopped what they are doing to stare at Martina. Chelsea looks over at me and says, "What should we do, Mrs. Dunbar?" Looking back at Martina, she pleads, "What should we do?"

Discussion Questions

1. What would you do to help console Martina?
2. What resources are available to you in a situation such as this?
3. Since Mrs. Dunbar knew the previous day that Mrs. Szervanszky would not be available to come to school the following day, what could she have done to better prepare for this situation?
4. Given that Martina loves music, what can you do musically to help her calm down?
5. What are the pros and cons of Jonathan, her brother, coming into the room and staying with her all day?

Advice from Veteran Teachers on . . . English Language Learners

- Learn as much about the child's first language and culture as possible. Depending on the language, the alphabet may be different or non-existent, the language may or may not be phonetic (as in the cases of Korean and Chinese), and concepts about print may be different (as in the cases of Arabic or Hebrew).
- You may want to label your classroom in all of the languages represented in your class. For instance, English may be labeled in blue, Spanish in red, Arabic in black, etc. That way, even the children who speak English can learn new words in another language.
- Check with your district office to see what types of services are available. You may need extra assistance with reading and writing instruction, writing letters home to the parents, getting permission slips signed, communicating with parents during parent-teacher conferences, etc. We have all had cases where the child is the primary translator in the family. We have also had cases where these same children told us that they were not completely honest with their parents. In particular, with referrals. Getting an objective translator may make the situation less stressful for all involved.
- If they do not have a translator at your school for a certain language, you might want to try restaurants, local colleges and universities, or an ethnic community like Little Italy or Chinatown, or even churches. You may find someone willing and able to donate time with your student.
- If you have a child who continually crys, you may want to ask if one of their parents or guardians can stay in the class until the child is ready to be separated from them. It has been our experience that this usually occurs after they can ask where the restroom is, where they can get a drink of water, and figure out the class routine.
- You may also want to ask several of your students to be the child's friends. These friends will be responsible for walking this child to the restroom, eating with him or her at lunch, and going to the playground with the child. Be purposeful when you select these friends. You do not want the child to be paired with someone who may teach the new student all the latest curse words.
- You may want to allow the children to be involved in a TPR (Total Physical Response). You may ask the children to follow simple directions or even go on a nature walk where the child is told the words for what he or she sees.
- In the best situation, there would be English as Second Language classes for parents at your school site. During these sessions, childcare is provided while the parents learn conversational English. If this option is not available, you might want to suggest that they look into local community centers or organizations such as libraries or local community colleges. They may offer English classes for adults.
- If the previous bullet-point is not an option (i.e., the parent may work, your community may not have such services, etc.), then start with your school. You may have a translator on campus who can help you with this family. Additionally, there may be an older sibling who is able to provide assistance; however, remember that this young adult may also be busy with schoolwork and an afterschool job. So, going through your district may be the best for all.

Non-Standard English Usage

English Only

I admire how good my classroom looks. The kids' portraits hang on one of the bulletin boards. Mr. Manchego, a father of one of my first graders, is an artist and he volunteered his time to help the kids with their portraits. Underneath each portrait the kids wrote down several interesting facts about themselves. I learned what they like to eat, what they do when they are not in school, and what they like to read. I scan the rest of the room. The fish tank is clean, the home center is clean, and finally, we were able to get all the paint off the tables. I also look at our classroom library with pride. This year, I made an effort to diversify the books and magazines in our library. There are books written in different languages, books about different cultures, and books with different family structures. As I continue to scan the room I still see orange crackers on the carpet by the cubbies, but Johnny, the custodian, has assured me he will take care of that.

As I sit down to straighten up my desk, Johnny walks into the class holding a vacuum cleaner. I smile at him. "Thank you so much, Johnny." I say. "I appreciate it." Johnny quickly scans the room and pointing to the cubbies says, "What happened over there?" I shake my head and explain, "Mohammed tried opening a package of those fish crackers. He kept tugging and pulling and finally he got it opened. Unfortunately, the bag popped open and all of those little goldfish landed on the floor." I walk over to the cubbies and continue, "I thought we got most of them up. Do you think the vacuum cleaner can do the rest?" Johnny nods his head and smiles, "Most definitely. This is no regular vacuum. It's a Rug Devil. The best out there." I smile back at him. "Well don't let me disturb you or your Rug Devil." With that, I go back to my desk and continue working.

After Johnny finishes cleaning up the room, he comes over to my desk and says, "Why do you have the class labeled with all of these different cards?" Initially, not sure what cards he's referring to, I look around the room and reply, "Oh, I decided to label the room in the different languages that the kids speak in the class." I walk over to the home center where there are a lot of labels. I point to the index card on the refrigerator and say, "English is written in red, the Spanish word for refrigerator is in blue, the Arabic word for refrigerator is in brown, and the French word for refrigerator is in green." Johnny sucks in his lips and scans the classroom. "That's pretty neat. So, the kids know that anytime they see a brown word, that's the Arabic spelling of the word?" I nod my head. "Exactly. I have so many children and their family members who speak languages other than English; I decided to label the room in all of the languages represented in our class." Johnny, still nodding, adds, "Plus, those who speak only English can learn new words in other languages." Nodding, I say, "Exactly." Following that, Johnny says as he walks out of the door with his vacuum cleaner, "Have a good Open House tonight." As I walk back to my desk I shout, "Thanks again."

It is 6:00 and already a lot of my students and their parents are in the room. I have my little speech prepared where I discuss my expectations for their children this year, my classroom management policy, and the homework policy. Then I encourage parents to please volunteer their time in the class, to donate tissues and paper towels; I then give out information about our upcoming fieldtrips. I recognize Morgan's parents and greet them "Hello, Dr. Speck and Dr. Speck-Martin. How are you two doing this evening?" Valerie Speck-Martin looks at me and says, "We have some concerns about the way your classroom is set up." Admittedly, I am a bit surprised. "Concerns. What sort of concerns?" I ask. Dr. Winston Speck clears his throat and says, "Why do you have all of these index cards with different languages on them all around the room?" He looks around the room and raises his voice. "And the books you have in the library." Then, with disgust in his voice, he says, "This will be too confusing for the kids. We want that stuff out of here now!"

Discussion Questions

1. What is your response to Drs. Speck and Martin-Speck?
2. What are the benefits of children being exposed to and learning different languages in the primary grades?
3. What activities/lessons can you do with your students to teach them new languages?
4. If the Specks decide to push this issue further by having a discussion with your principal, what would be your response to your principal?
5. Would you keep your classroom this way or modify it? Give your rationale.

"I Loveded those Pants..."

I look around the class to check on the progress my second graders are making. The room is almost clean. We just finished science, so we need to straighten up before we move on to arts and crafts. We are going to make Valentine's Day gifts, so the tables need to be as clean as possible. Also, during lunch, I was told by our principal, Mrs. Eleanor Francois, that she is coming around this afternoon with several school board members, including the superintendent. According to her, "They are making their regular rounds to each school, so make sure that you put your best foot forward." She then gave me a sly smile, patted my shoulder, and walked away. "Whew," was all I could muster after that exchange. Just then, Matilda, who has been teaching for twenty-three years, says, "Now you know what she's really saying, right?" Admittedly, I thought I did but now question if I do. Matilda must have recognized my puzzlement because she then explained in a whisper, "Eleanor is into flash and show. As a matter of fact, we secretly call her the Dog and Pony Show principal." Leaning closer, Matilda continues, "So, unfortunately, regardless if the kids aren't learning, things just have to look good." She then looks at me quizzically and asks, "Do you understand?" I nod my head and am thankful that she'll get to see the kids making their Valentine's Day gifts.

Snapping back to reality, I hear the classroom door opening and see several of our class parents coming into the room. They have big yellow stickers on their chests which lets everyone know that they are visitors to the school and have checked into the office. Just then, their children look up and see their parents in the class. Vivienne, Makayla, Shameka, and Benjamin rush to their parents, giving them big hugs around their waists. Mrs. Sweeney looks down at Vivienne and says in her usual booming voice, "Why hello, darlin'." She hugs her tightly and continues, "Now you done cleanin' up your part?" Vivienne looks up at her mother and shakes her head. "Then young lady, you knows what you needs to do." The other parents gently push their children off of their hips, too, and motion for them to go back and help their classmates clean the classroom.

As their children go back to cleaning, I say, "Hello Mrs. Sweeney, Mr. Mendes, Ms. Smith, and Mrs. Marshall. It's so good that you all could come and help us today." Ms. Mendes says, "You know that I just love arts and crafts." Mrs. Marshall looks over at me and says, "Now, although I'm going to know what I'm getting for Valentine's Day, I don't mind helping." Mrs. Sweeney smiles and nods her head in agreement. I laugh too. Mrs. Marshall has five older kids who have all gone to this school. "Mrs. Marshall," I say smiling, "I know that you've gotten all of the Valentine's Day gifts that teachers come up with seeing that you have five other kids." She smiles at me and says, "Yes, and it's getting harder to pretend like it's the first time I've gotten the heart-shaped cards with doilies on them." She thinks about it for a minute and says, "And my husband is having a harder time pretending to be surprised by his Father's Day cards shaped like a necktie." We all laugh. "You see," I say, "That's why I'm doing something a little different this year." All four of them look at each other and then at me. I then explain this year's project. "This year, I decided to do picture frames with the kids. All weekend I was gluing popsicle sticks together to make the frames. The kids are going to paint them, put a flower on them, and put magnets on the back of them so that they can stick to your refrigerators at home." Turning to my desk, I say, "I brought in my digital camera and will take a picture of each of the children while you each help a group of children paint their picture frame." Finally I say, "Then, after I develop the pictures and everything dries we will assemble the pictures and wrap them in tissue paper for Valentine's Day gifts." All of the parents look impressed and excited.

When the timer goes off, I look and see that all of my students are on the rug and that the room is clean. I look back at my students and say, "Magnificent job! Please give yourselves pats on your backs for doing such a fine job, doing it safely and expeditiously." I hear one of the moms behind me saying to the others, "expeditiously." I look back and say proudly, "I like to add those words to our vocabularies because these are the types of words on the SAT and ACT." I then point to our SAT/ACT Word Wall that has several big words on it already. I started this after Christmas break. "We say the words, use the words, write the words, and read the words so we can learn them." All of the parents look at each other and nod their heads. After explaining to my students what they are about to do with the bare picture frames, I then break them up into small groups. When they are each safely working in their group, I plant myself in front of the wall with the rainbow I painted on it and call Lamar over to have his picture taken.

There is a buzz in the air. I can tell that the kids are enjoying themselves and things are moving smoothly. Just then, Mrs. Francois comes into the room with several of our board members. I get up from my chair and greet them. "Hello everyone," I say.

"Welcome to Room 24." Several of the board members begin walking around the room without saying anything to me. The superintendent is standing next to Mrs. Francois. She then asks, "So, what are your students doing today?" I look at her, motion for her to follow me and say, "We are working on Valentine's Day gifts. The kids just love arts and crafts, so I like to give them some time in school to make gifts for their loved ones." She nods her head and continues to look at each table while writing notes on a large yellow tablet.

As we continue to walk around the room, we all end up at Mrs. Sweeney's table. Just then, we all hear Mrs. Sweeney say, "I loveded those pants you gots on," talking to one of the girls at her table. "I seen those in the store and wanted to get my daughter some." I look at the faces of the board members and their eyes are wide. Just then, one of the board members looks at another one and says under her breath, "Oh my goodness. Can you believe this?" Mrs. Francois excuses us and in the corner of the room asks me, "Why would you have that parent come in? Listen to the way she speaks. Don't you think that's a problem for the kids?"

Discussion Questions

1. Do you think that it's a problem for your students to have conversations with people who speak in a dialect of English? Give your rationale.
2. What is your response to Mrs. Francois?
3. What is your reaction to the board members' reaction to Mrs. Sweeney?
4. Do you have a problem with the way Mrs. Sweeney speaks? Give your rationale.
5. What lessons/activities can you do to help your students understand and appreciate dialectal differences, while at the same time teaching them standard English?

"Oh . . . my . . . God"

"Hi, Ms. Fernandez," I hear from behind me. I turn around and see one of my fourth graders, Denise, coming toward me from the cafeteria. "Hello, Denise. How was your breakfast?" Denise looks at me, grabs her stomach and says, "Horrific, disgusting, unbearable . . ." I look at her and say, "My goodness. What did they serve in the cafeteria that was that bad?" Denise scrunches up her nose and says, "I don't like egg sandwich. The eggs weren't even cooked all the way. Sunnyside up at best." I have heard horror stories about those egg sandwiches. "Why didn't you get the cereal?" I ask. "You really can't go wrong with cereal." Denise looks at me and says, "I wanted a hot lunch today and all they had was that disgusting egg sandwich." She then thinks about it for another second and says, "Well, at least the tater tots were pretty good." I smile at her. "Who doesn't love a good tater tot?" Denise nods her head and laughs.

Denise is one of those students who has a wonderful and extensive vocabulary. Her mother attributes this to the fact that her daughter is a voracious reader. Her father attributes it to the fact that she is an only child who is around adults all of the time. Either way, both of them were so uneasy in the beginning of the year that they met with me to discuss their concerns. They felt that Denise was not making friends and was possibly alienating possible friends because, in Denise's words, "They are just plain ignorant." Her father smiled at me when her mother said, "I just don't know where this arrogance comes from. Even at the country club, Denise is still not bonding with the other children like we think she should." Her father quickly chimed in, "Well, that may be the problem. She's always around us or those snooty kids at the country club." He then looked at me and said, "Maybe you can help her be more sociable this year." When I've asked the students about Denise, they've said, "She always has her head in a book and is always correcting the way we talk." So, unfortunately, I still haven't found a way to make her more sociable.

Knowing that I still have some work to do in the classroom before the beginning of class, I look at Denise and say, "Why don't you put your backpack down and go to the playground before the end of morning recess." Denise looks up at me and says, "Do you need any help?" Shaking my head, I say, "Thank you, but I can handle it from here." She smiles, tilts her head and says, "Are you sure?" I nod my head again. She then thinks about it, looks down at the watch on her wrist and says, "Okay. I'll see you in a few minutes." With that, she walks off in the direction of the playground.

Once all of my students are settled in the classroom, I start the writing lesson that will probably take us several weeks. We are going to be working on biographies and each student will interview another student in the class and write their biography based on that information. We will post their typewritten biographies on the bulletin board in the back just in time for Back to School night. It's fortunate that the project coincides with a special evening.

"Okay," I announce to my students. "When I let you know who your partner is going to be for this project, I want you to take several minutes to get to know that person better." I then turn my back to them and write on the board "Informal Interview." I turn around and continue, "We are going to informally interview our classmates." I put the dry-erase marker down and say, "What that means is that we are going to take some time to find out more about that person. Now," I add, "none of our questions are written down because this is informal. We are going to chat with them just like we would one of our family members or friends." I look around my class and ask, "Does anyone have any questions?" Mercedes raises her hand and asks, "So, can we ask them about stuff they like to do and stuff like that?" I nod my head. "That's exactly what you can ask. You may want to know what they are doing this weekend. Who their friends are. Whatever." I look around the room again and say, "It's what you want to know about them right now that will help you better understand who they are as a person." Most of my students are nodding their heads and whispering to one another. I raise my hand and gently tap my bell. When I have everyone's attention, I say, "You will have about five minutes for this part of the lesson." Continuing, I say "Now let me tell you who you are partnered with." And with that, I rattle off the names of the pairs and they begin to informally interview their classmates.

Once everyone is paired, I walk around the room to make sure everyone is on task. They seem to be doing a good job. When I get to Denise's desk, I hear her ask her partner, Suzette, "Now, what will you be doing this weekend?" Suzette looks up at the ceiling and replies, "Ooh, I be goin' to my nana's house. She gon' make me some cake." I look into Denise's face, which has a horrified look on it. "Be goin' to your nana's house. Gon' make you some cake." Denise says mockingly. She then sighs loudly and says, "Oh . . . my . . . God." I look into Suzette's face and she shrugs her shoulders in confusion.

Discussion Questions

1. How do you handle this situation?
2. What are the pros and cons of Denise continuing to work with Suzette on this project?
3. What literature can you introduce to Denise to help her understand and possibly appreciate dialectal differences?
4. What are the pros and cons of sharing what was found out about Denise from her peer's point of view with Denise?
5. What would you say to Denise's parents regarding what took place?

Advice from Veteran Teachers on . . . Non-Standard English Usage

*   All of us wish that not only our students but also we had experienced second-language instruction in elementary school. Research clearly shows that this is the prime time for children to learn another language. For the majority of children, learning a second language probably will not negatively impact their English language proficiency. It has been our experience that those children who do experience difficulties have other academic problems as well. If that is the case, you should begin the referral process as soon as possible.
*   We would tell the concerned parents that we are keeping the room labeled based on the information above. The children will learn new words in other languages, which makes the classroom environment more comfortable and shows respect for our students who speak other languages.
*   Dialect usage and knowing a second language is not a deficit—they are assets. Most of us have found that children who speak in a dialect or in their home language are able to better express their feelings, communicate with their family members, and relate to their community members better when they speak in their dialect or first language. We do not want to encourage any of you to get rid of the children's dialect or first language. But, just like native English speakers, they will need instruction in standard English usage.
*   Kids need to learn how to code-switch—change their speech patterns and behavior depending on the person and situation. You may want to talk about language in terms of formal and casual conversations. We have used the examples of "How would you write a letter to the president?" and "How would you speak with a friend?" These situations require the speaker or writer to recognize that there are different ways to express ourselves.
*   We agree that all of our students need instruction in standard English, not just the dialect speakers or English Language Learners. We have white, middle-class students who are dialect speakers. We do not suggest that you isolate a student as this might embarrass him or her. We suggest that you do mini-lessons and lessons on standard English usage. Be candid and give examples. Some may say hurt-ted, look-ted, like-ted, etc. Then, let them know how to say it in standard English.
*   In order to appreciate dialect usage, you may let them write certain pieces such as poetry in dialect or speak that way at home or on the playground. You may also read books that include dialect usage.
*   As far as Mrs. Sweeney, we would assure our principal and the school board members that all parents in your class are not there to provide instruction, but to support you. In particular, this parent is helping with an art project. Thus, if the children make it an issue, we would deal with it as a whole group. Our conversation would be about not teasing and the need to show respectful behavior. But if the students do not make it an issue, then we would follow

their lead. However, we would still have standard English language instruction, but not because of her or this situation.

- Some children do not realize that they are belittling others. For those children, we would have a frank discussion with them about the behaviors and comments you've observed and heard. For those who do realize that they are belittling others and those you've had a previous conversation with, we would handle it as if it was a violation of one of our classroom rules. Then, depending on how you manage your classroom, consequences are in order.

Perceived Illiteracy

CEO

"What time is the workshop tomorrow?" I ask Al, a fellow first-grade teacher. He replies, "Now you know that I don't know." Turning around, he addresses Mariah, the other first grade teacher, "Mariah, what time is the workshop tomorrow?" Thinking, Mariah says, "It starts at 9:00." Al then spins around, looks at me, and asks, "What time do you think that we need to leave?" I shrug my shoulder, "I really don't know." Mariah, shrugging her shoulders, too, says, "I don't know either." I recently moved, so I'm not as familiar with this area. Just then I remember I have the flyer for the professional development workshop on vocabulary instruction in my mailbox. I look over at Al and Mariah and say, "Hey, don't worry about it. I have the flyer in my mailbox with the address on it and will Google directions from the school and it should tell me what time we need to meet up here." Thinking about it some more I say, "But for right now, let's plan on meeting here at 8:00." Both Mariah and Al nod at me. "Just text us the time." As both leave the teachers' lounge, they shout, "Thanks."

I proceed to my mailbox and retrieve the flyer. We are so lucky our principal, Roger King, found the funds to pay for this workshop. We get a substitute, lunch, and a binder full of suggestions on how to develop our students' vocabularies. I am actually pretty excited. But for right now, I have to get my sub plans ready. Grabbing some paper from the shelf, I sit down at one of the long tables and begin to write down my lesson plans.

As I am deep in thought getting my plans together, Roger comes into the lounge and opens the refrigerator. He then says, "Are you ready for tomorrow?" I look up at him and smile. He knows that this is my first time being away from my students. "Yes," I say. "I just hope that my students are on their best behavior tomorrow. I will be so disappointed if they cut up with my sub." Roger laughs his hearty laugh as he opens his soda. "You know that they are at least going to try. You remember when you were a kid." Nodding my head, I added, "Oh, I also remember when I was subbing as soon as I finished my bachelor's." Thinking about it some more, I say, "Shoot, those subbing days made me reconsider teaching." Once again, laughing, Roger says, "Subbing is so different than teaching though." I nod my head in agreement. "I know," I say. "They know you are with them the whole year, so they don't try as much stuff at they do when they know that you are only going to be with them for several days, max." Taking a long swig of his soda, he says, "Things will be okay. I'll make sure that I get around to your room several times tomorrow." Feeling a bit of relief, I say, "Thanks so much!" He then exits the lounge and I get back to finishing my lesson plans.

After I finish my plans, I remember that I promised Mariah and Al that I would Google the directions to our workshop. I head back to my classroom and boot up my computer. I find out that from the school, it will take about thirty-five minutes to get to the workshop. I then get out my cell phone and text Mariah and Al this information. I still think that we should meet at the school at 8:00 just to give ourselves enough time to get there and to get settled. Both immediately text me back letting me know that they'll meet me in front of the school at 8:00. As I go over the directions, I realize that I am not sure where the majority of these streets are. I think to myself, "I sure hope that Al or Mariah know how to get us there so we don't get lost."

With my plans completed and my printout of the directions, I begin to straighten up the classroom to get ready for the substitute teacher for tomorrow. Just then, my door opens up and Shamarah's father, Mr. Patterson, comes into the room. I extend my hand to shake his. "I hope that I'm not interrupting anything important," he says. I shake my head and reassure him, "Oh no, Mr. Patterson. I'm just getting ready for tomorrow." Smiling, he says, "Oh yes, Shamarah told me that you are going to a conference tomorrow and that you'll be having a sub." I nod my head in agreement. "I sure am. So make sure that you tell Shamarah to be on her best behavior." Mr. Patterson laughs, because he knows that Shamarah can cut up when she wants to. Nodding his head, he says, "I sure will."

I pull out a chair next to the kidney table and offer it to him. As we both sit down, he says, "I wanted to come and talk with you today about a private matter." He puts his hand on his chest and says, "Shamarah told me that you are inviting parents into the class to read books to your students." I nod my head. "Yes. I think that the kids are getting tired of hearing my voice, so I thought that this would be a great way for parents to volunteer." He shakes his head and says, "I agree, but. . . ." Not thinking, I interrupt him and say, "Shamarah tells me that you are an excellent reader. She also tells me that you sound just like all of the characters in the books you read to her." I look over and realize that he is quiet and that his eyes are welling up with tears. I can't hide my surprise. He says, "Miss Spencer, let me be honest with you." He looks down and continues, "I haven't been reading any books to Shamarah. I have just been telling her stories about the pictures in her books."

Admittedly, I am surprised. Mr. Patterson, who is a single father, is the CEO of a lucrative company. He then looks into my face and says, "I know what you may be thinking. How can I run a company and not be able to read and write well?" Not hiding my puzzlement, I nod my head. "Well," he begins, "I inherited the company from my father. I was mentored by him and taught all of the ropes by my uncles." He then continues, "My nephews, who have all gone to Ivy League schools, handle all contracts." Shaking his head, he says, "I am no fool. I have folks I can trust around me who can do all of my reading and writing for me." Thinking about it some more he says with pride, "But don't be fooled. No one can outdo me when it comes to my business. I have made this company into much more than my father ever even imagined." After a pregnant pause, he then leans over and says, "So now you can see my problem." I nod my head silently because I do see the problem that we now both have.

Discussion Questions

1. What services are available in your community for adults who have low literacy skills?
2. How would you handle this situation so that Mr. Patterson can maintain his dignity?

3. What impact do you think a parent's low literacy skills have on a child's literacy skills?
4. What can you suggest parents such as Mr. Patterson do with their children to get them the assistance that their child will need with reading, writing, homework, and other school projects?
5. What does your school do to support family literacy?

I'm Stupid!

"So," I say to my fifth graders, "Toastie the dog had on yellow galoshes. Not only did Toastie have on galoshes, but also a thick blue collar with an ID tag that says "Toastie."' I go into great detail about how Toastie loved going for walks, smelling the flowers, barking at birds or anything else that walked or flew by. "Now, Toastie did not care that other animals would laugh at him for wearing galoshes. He loved the feel of them on his body and loved how they protected him in increment weather." I lean in and continue in a whispering voice, "Toastie looked up at the sky and began to run furiously. He knew it was coming. He could hear the awful noises in the trees. Then he heard a boom." My students' eyes were wide with expectation. "Once Toastie and his master hit the garage, they could hear the tip tap of the drops hit the car in the driveway." I then take a bow and say, "The end." My students begin to clap as I continue to bow.

I look up at the clock and realize that we have about four minutes before recess. I then say, "Let's work quickly on making inferences." I think about the story I just told and ask, "Why do you think Toastie has on galoshes?" Several students have perplexed looks on their faces. Finally, John raises his hand and I call on him. "He didn't want to get his paws wet." I nod my head. "Great, John. Can you please tell the others what galoshes are?" John looks around to his peers and say, "They are shoes that you wear when it rains or it's wet outside. I think they also call them rain boots." Some of my students appear surprised to hear that they are rain boots. Lisa looks up at John and says, "How do you know that?" John then answers, "My grandfather and I were in Louisiana and we were going to go crabbing. He told me to make sure to bring my galoshes to protect my feet." Lisa, then asks, "Why didn't he just call them rain boots?" John shrugs his shoulders and replies, "I don't know. He just always calls them galoshes." After thinking about it some more, John continues. "Plus, I remember seeing several explorers on the National Geographic channel. They were in the rain forest and they had on galoshes. The commentator said that you needed boots such as galoshes because it is usually wet and humid in those parts of the world, and without them, you just can't get around the forest floor."

I look at my class and they are totally enthralled with John. Once again, his experience and vocabulary amaze me. "Brrriiiinnng!" chimes the recess bell. Wow, I can't believe how fast those minutes flew by. "Okay, everyone. Great job!" I say, "You may walk outside to the playground." With that, my twenty-eight fifth graders walk to the playground for fifteen minutes of recess.

John is new to our school. On his first day, he told me that he had been to Europe, Japan, Australia, and most of the states in America with his mom and dad. He also informed me that he just loves watching the History channel, A&E, the Biography channel, the National Geographic channel, all of the Discovery channels, and PBS. He just loves a good documentary and considers himself a biography buff. In my opinion, his vocabulary surpasses most of his peers.

The recess bell interrupts my thoughts. "My goodness," I think to myself, "time sure flies." When my students are back in the class and in their seats, I say, "I need to do several running records for this marking period. So, what I'm going to do is give you time to work on your state projects." I take a look at my clipboard and say, "Peggy, Sylvester, Autumn, and Michael, you may use the computers." I then look up at the rest of my students and continue, "The rest of you may use the books on the cart that I checked out from our library." As students begin to go into their desks to get ready to work on their projects I say, "Any questions?" Everyone looks around at one another and shakes his or her head. "Okay," I say, "You may begin." As I begin walking to my desk in the back of the classroom, I tap John on the shoulder and say, "John, please come to my desk and let's get your running record done."

As I get my testing materials together, I ask John, "So, how are you enjoying our class so far?" John smiles and says, "I like it. I think I'm really going to like doing my project on Vermont. It was beautiful when we went out there. It was fall and all of the leaves on the trees were exquisite." He then nods his head and says, "I even have pictures and everything." I look at John and say, "Great. That will be a great addition to your project."

Since the district wants to see these scores, our principal wants the whole fifth-grade team to begin testing each of our students at a second-grade level. Personally I think this is a waste of time. Especially with students like John, who have an extensive vocabulary. I put the passage in front of John and get my clipboard in position to take the running record. John looks at the passage as if he is waiting for me to give him permission to read. "Oh," I say, "You may begin." John still looks at the passage as if he isn't sure what to do. He puts his finger on the title and begins to read. "The . . . /r/-/r/-/r/ . . . I don't know that word." He squints as if he is having trouble seeing the words and continues, "Um, /t/-/t/-/t/ . . . I don't know that word either." He looks away totally frustrated and says, "I feel so stupid." He then puts his face down and begins to weep.

Discussion Questions

1. What are the pros and cons of continuing with the running record at this time?
2. What would you say to console John?
3. What types of reading materials can you use to improve John's reading skills?
4. What could you have asked John prior to testing him to get a better sense of his reading level?
5. What school personnel should you contact regarding a situation such as this?

Grandpa's Story

"Let me understand," our principal, Karen Simpson, says, giggling. "You have your kindergarteners do book reports?" I laugh. Some folks thought that I was crazy when I announced that I would have my kindergarteners do book reports. Not that they are doing the kind of book reports I had to do when I was growing up. Actually, it's a book report form where whoever read the book to the child asks questions and then writes down the answers the child gave them. I look at Karen and several other teachers in the lounge and say, "I learned about these book report forms in one of my literacy methods classes. We had to think of ways to make read alouds at home more interactive, so I came up with the book report form." I pull three forms from my pile of papers. I hand each of them one and continue, "See, the child will need to describe what the book was about, who the main characters were, where the setting was, the sequence of the story, what they liked about the book, didn't like about the book, and so on." I look up and see all three ladies nodding. "Some of my parents have really appreciated this form."

Kylie, a second-grade teacher chimes in, "I can see how they will learn the vocabulary terms we work so hard to get them to understand when they get to second grade." Christie, the other second-grade teacher says, nodding her head, "I really like this idea." She looks up at me and says, "I thought you had them doing full-blown book reports. I thought you had lost your mind." Karen and Kylie started laughing. "I know," Karen reiterated, "When I asked one of your students in the cafeteria what he did for homework last night and he told me they had to do his book report, I must admit I couldn't hide my shock." She then says, patting my back, "But, he sure did have a lot of pride when he was talking about his book report." When the bell rings signaling the end of first recess and the beginning of P.M. kindergarten, Karen says nodding her head as she walks back to her office, "Keep up the good work, Josephine."

When I get to my line of twenty-four kindergarteners, I see they are lined up in as straight a line as they can get. "Hello there, boys and girls," I say as I walk to the front of the line. "Let's walk carefully into our classroom so that we can begin our day of learning." I place myself right on the side of the front door and greet each of my students by their first name as they pass me. Although we are still in the beginning of the school year, they have caught onto the routine pretty quickly. They know they are to put their homework folders in the crate, hang up their coats and backpacks, and put any lunchboxes or other things in their cubbies. Following that, they are to go to the rug and find a comfortable spot to sit where they can concentrate and be on their best behavior. I will admit the last part about them finding a place on the rug where they can "concentrate and be on their best behavior" is probably the one area we still need to work on with our daily routine, but given that we've only been in school for several weeks, I am proud of what they've accomplished thus far.

I take attendance, the lunch count, do the Pledge of Allegiance, and do the calendar activities. Following these, Mrs. Ramirez, one of our parent volunteers, comes in just as I announce, "While I quickly go through your homework folders, you will go to literacy centers." I hear several students say, "Yes!" when they hear this. "Today," I say, "in our literacy centers, we have our book nook where you can read any of the books in there on our comfortable bean bags." I turn my body and point to the section closest to the door and announce, "We also have the writing center, where you can practice writing your names and letters." I turn again and point to the computers and say, "Three of you may use the computers and work on learning your letters." I look over at Mrs. Ramirez and say, "Mrs. Ramirez will be here today and she is willing to play Alphabet Bingo with six boys and girls." I can see the students are getting antsy now. I hold my hand up and say, "When I finish with your homework folders, I will place myself over there," I say pointing to the rectangular table in the corner and say, "I will be getting out play-doh and the alphabet cookie cutters."

Before I excuse them to pick their literacy center, I say, "Now, can we all go to the Bingo center at once?" "Noooo," my students say in unison. I nod my head and say,

"Exactly." I continue, "So you may not get your first choice, but you will get a chance to be in that center. I am going to set the timer for fifteen minutes, and when the timer goes off, you are going to have to move to another center." I look around and then ask, "Any questions?" When I see that there are no questions, I begin to excuse the students who are quietly sitting on the rug.

As the students move around the room and get into their literacy centers, I go to the folders and find Rashida's on top. Last night for homework, all they had to do was complete the book report form and bring the book in with them today. I have my book report chart and stickers ready so that I can put a sticker on today's date for the students who completed the assignment. As I quickly scan her folder, I find she has completed the form, but there's no book in her folder. Glancing at her book report form, I see that the title of the book is *Grandpa's Story about Kenya*. I look up and find Rashida at the computer center. "Rashida," I call out, "Can you please come here?" Rashida walks over to where I'm seated and says, "Yes, Ms. Regulado." I then ask, "Honey, where's your book?" Rashida looks at her folder and then back at me. "Oh, my grandfather didn't read a book to me. He told me a story about when he was a little boy in Kenya." I look back down and find all of the other questions are answered. "Rashida," I ask, "Who wrote the answers to the questions?" Rashida looks back at her form and says, "Oh, my sister. My grandfather made her."

Discussion Questions

1. What are the pros and cons of Rashida getting a sticker for this assignment?
2. Why is it important that we have a sense of the literacy levels of the family members of our students?
3. What community programs are available for your students' family members who may have limited literacy levels?
4. What is your opinion regarding storytelling as a form of literacy instruction?
5. What other activities can we do as teachers to make sure that books are being read to children at home?

Advice from Veteran Teachers on . . . Perceived Illiteracy

- Unfortunately, all of us have experienced the child who has wonderful oral language skills yet struggles with reading. It can be pretty shocking when you actually assess this student. You need to forgive yourself. This situation is not uncommon to teachers.
- Do not be fooled. We are all familiar with the highly verbal, charming student who is struggling with an academic area. Sometimes these children use their charm to avoid doing work that is difficult for them. You need to have a candid and frank discussion with this child about why it is important for him or her to work on this area.
- Once the student has been assessed, you may want to refer for a SST to get tips on how to best help this student and to get the referral process going, if necessary.
- Once you have his or her reading level, you should talk with a colleague in that grade level to get resources such as books at that level. That way, you can do guided reading/reading workshop and send books home for the student to read.
- Make sure that you keep the parents abreast of this situation. They are the ones who have to monitor their child's at-home reading program. We would also encourage the parents to

let John continue watching the historical and biographical television channels that he loves. This way, he can keep his verbal skills strong.

- In order to protect this child's self-confidence and self-esteem, you may want to put the books at his level in a bag or use book covers so that other kids cannot see which book he is reading. During silent reading time, you may want him to read magazines or anything that interests him.
- We would allow a parent or grandparent to tell their children a story instead of reading a book because they are still getting a story structure, plot, characters, setting, etc. We would also inquire into who else is in that child's life because they may be able to read books to and with the child. This could be an older sibling, aunt, uncle, cousin, etc.
- We would never want to embarrass a parent, grandparent, or guardian. If we find out that a student's family member is unable to read and write, and we have a relationship with that family member, we would suggest an adult literacy program. It has been our experience that most of our parents have been so grateful when this was suggested as they wanted to improve their literacy skills as well.

Gender Identity

When I Was a Girl

"1, 2, 3 . . ." I sing to my first graders while holding up three fingers. Although this is still the beginning of the school year, they already know that this signal means that I want their undivided attention. As my students stop what they are doing and look up at me with their hands placed on their shoulders, I acknowledge their compliance with a nod and a slight smile. When I feel comfortable that all of them are now paying attention, I announce, "It's time for us to clean up our literacy centers. So this is what I want you to do," I say, walking over to the chart listing the names of which children were in which center at what time. "I want you to straighten up the last literacy center you were in. So, Marcus's group will clean up the Coffee Shop center, Wilhelm's group will clean up the US Postal Service Writing center, Maria's group will clean up the *Chicka Chicka Boom Boom* reading center, Pamela's group will clean up the Frank Lloyd Wright School of Architecture center, and Celine's group will clean up the Metropolitan Museum of Art center." I turn around, set the CD player to song #3, and announce, "You have about four and a half minutes to get your center clean. When you are done, please meet me on the rug. You may begin." My first graders begin cleaning up to their favorite song. They know that when the song is over, they are to have finished whatever task was asked of them and be sitting on their spot on the rug. As I walk around, I see my students talking with one another, and yet, still straightening up their centers.

I love the literacy centers for this month. In the coffee shop, they get to read menus, take orders, read books, have conversations, and pretend to cook food. In the Postal Service center, they write letters, bills, postcards, and just whatever. Then they get to mail what they've written. My students now know how to address envelopes. The reading center is just a cool place to read. Especially with the big bean bags that look like moss-covered rocks, the umbrellas, fake coconuts, our big palm tree, and three bookshelves full of interesting books, magazines, comic books, and even newspapers. In the School of Architecture, students get to work on their fine motor skills by using rulers, protractors, and pencils to create blueprints of buildings they would like to build one day. And, in our art center, the walls are covered with paintings by O'Keefe, Van Gogh, Romare Bearden, and Picasso, to name a few artists. The kids can work with watercolors, acrylics, and magazines to create collages. As I sit back, I beam with pride.

"Mr. Chang," I hear one of our parent volunteers say. I look around and see Margeaux Hendricks coming up to me. I look at her and ask, "Yes. How may I help you?" She turns to the other parent volunteers, Al Frank, Jennifer Perkins, and Myra Winslow, and says, "We want to know if you'll need us tomorrow during literacy center time?"

My eyes must have bugged out because she then says, "Oh, we'll be here if you need us. But we thought that you would use the literacy center time for their presentations on their autobiographies." She then asks, "Have things changed?" I let out a breath that I must have been holding for quite a while. I finally say, "You're right. We do have our in-class oral presentations tomorrow. But, Kat is presenting today. As a matter of fact, her parents are coming to videotape it." Margeaux smiles and says, "I know Kat's mother and father and I know they are definitely going to videotape her presentation." Thinking quickly I add, "You are all welcome to stay for Kat's presentation." All of the parents nod indicating that they are staying.

I begin to walk around the class to monitor my students when the classroom door opens and in walk Kat's parents, Emily and Jason Wilson, with a science fair project board. Kat leaves her center and runs top speed into her father, who picks her up and kisses her. "Now Kat," her mother says, "You know you are not to run in this class." Kat looks down at her mother and nods her head as her mother plants a kiss on her forehead. I walk over to the Wilsons and say, "Welcome. We will be beginning soon." Just then, the song ends and my students begin to move quickly to the rug.

When everyone is on their spot on the rug, I take my seat in the front and call Kat up. Her father opens her tri-fold board that has a timeline across the middle and is all decorated and full of pictures. "Wow!" is what I hear from my students. Kat clears her voice and looks out to her peers and says, "I was born on May 16, 2002. I am my mom and dad's first baby. I love spaghetti, popsicles, and playing with my dog, Rocco. I want a brother and a sister. I also want to go skiing, play football, and go swimming." Kat turns her attention to the tri-fold board and begins to point at pictures. "This is when I went to church with my granny. And this is when I went to Disney World with my Aunt Bee Bee. Oh, and this is when I was at my birthday party last year at Peter's Fun Playhouse." She then scans the board closely and finds the last picture on the timeline. She looks up and says excitedly, "Oh, and this was the last time I was a girl." To my utter disbelief, several parents gasp in surprise.

Discussion Questions

1. What would you do if this information is new to her parents, Emily and Jason Wilson?
2. What do you say if one of your students inquires, "What do you mean the last time you were a girl?"
3. How do you handle this situation in the short term and the long term?
4. What social service support systems are in place in your school and community for children like Kat who may be dealing with issues regarding their gender identity?
5. Kat dressing like a boy would not be as noticeable as a boy in your class dressing like a girl. How would you handle a situation like that?

Just Stop That!

On most Fridays, in order to give the children an opportunity to expand their horizons, I allow them to take part in Art. I wish we had art teachers who could teach our students about the specifics regarding the creation of art and art appreciation and the different forms of art. But unfortunately, due to budget cuts, art, PE, computer, and even library time has been cut. It's such a shame that the things the children really love and may consider as possible careers are usually the first things cut.

I am so glad my parents raised me to look at a closed door as a door that can always be opened. Given that perspective, I went to the local college and found under-graduate art students who love working with children and are interested in volunteer-ing in a school. Now, every other Friday they work with two third-grade classes in the cafeteria for an hour.

Our teaching artist is Donovan. I just love how Donovan is with the students. He's a bit effeminate, wears colorful hats, clothes, and scarves, and can dance like Sammy Davis, Jr., Michael Jackson, and Savion Glover all wrapped in one. He is also a magnificent painter. He loves using acrylics and drawing beautiful things he finds around the city that others may only see as trash in a ghetto. His artwork brings to life the environments many of my students live in. What I also love about Donovan is that he is so comfortable with himself. When I first met him, he did not come right out and tell me he was gay, but he told me he and his partner have been in their relationship going on two years. He later told me that after years of denying who he was—a gay man—he decided to accept it and move on. "Now don't get me wrong," Donovan told me, "It wasn't easy. I lost a lot of family members, friends, and folks I thought were friends. They all think I've got AIDS or something. But I'm just a man in America try-ing to get his bachelor's degree, trying to find love, working two jobs to pay for school, and hoping one day to own that new Range Rover." I remember laughing so hard.

When we get to the cafeteria, I am happy because Donovan and our other teach-ing artists, Samantha, Felicity, and Webster, have all the supplies set up and ready to go. When we get the kids settled down, Donovan begins to speak. "Okay, everyone," he begins, "We are going to work with pastels today." Some of our students say, "Oh," and reach out about to touch the supplies on the tables. Even though his back is to the kids, Donovan interjects, "And I sure hope none of you are touching those things on the tables because I don't recall telling you that it was okay to do that yet." I look down at some of my students whose faces are a bit red. "Now," Donovan says standing by the side of an easel with a big sheet of paper in front of it, "This is how you use pastels." For the next ten minutes, he mixes colors, uses a stick made of paper to blend colors and soften edges, and uses bold strokes to create a beautiful ocean scene. "Wow!" we all say in unison. Our students begin to clap. Donovan takes a bow and says, "Now, on the tables you will find some calendars, magazines, and brochures. You may use those and try to copy those images on your sheets of paper. We will be walking around if you need any help. Now remember, this isn't easy, but please don't give up. Just have fun exploring the colors and images that you can create. You may begin."

Melissa and I walk around the cafeteria to watch our students work. "Now only if they worked this hard with math, science, social studies or Language Arts," I think to myself. Just then, in the corner of my eye, I see Donovan talking with Sam, a student in my class. As I look closer, I think Sam is crying and is holding something in his clenched fist. Donovan waves his hand to me and with his lips indicates that he wants me to come over there. When I get over to where they are, we walk into the hallway. Donovan looks at Sam and says, "Tell Ms. Sampson what you told me. Go ahead."

Sam looks up at Donovan and me as I look into his hand. It's a purple crayon he's holding onto for dear life. When Sam does speak, he says, "I love the color purple." Not sure why that's a problem, I say, "Okay, Sam. I love it too." Shaking his head back and forth, Sam continues, "But you don't understand. My dad doesn't like that I like the color purple. He thinks it's a girl color and that's why I want to be a girl." Taking a deep breath, Sam continues, "Ms. Sampson, I really think I am a girl. I feel it in my heart. I love the color purple and combing my hair and doing what most girls like doing." He wipes the tears off his face and says, "My dad saw me switching and walking around my room one night in my sister's purple gown and wearing some of her makeup. He told me to stop because I would end up in hell if I didn't. Now, I can't even use purple crayons at home." Clearing his throat, he finally says, "I just don't think I can. But I'm just so scared that my dad will kill me or I'll even go to hell." Donovan looks at me with tears in his eyes. He then leans into Sam and says, "I know, Sam. I know."

Discussion Questions

1. Who do you need to bring into this discussion with Sam?
2. What are the pros and cons of Sam continuing to work with Donovan?
3. What will you say to Sam's parents when you get the chance?
4. What social support systems are available in your school and community for parents like Sam's, whose children have stated that they are experiencing issues regarding their gender identity?
5. Can you handle this situation in your class or would you need help first?

The Transition

"Mrs. Morton, you aren't going to believe what J.R. did at lunch." I look over my glasses as several of my fifth graders come streaming back into the class after lunch. Javier and Ramona are my class tattletales, so if anything happens on the playground, I am surely going to know about it because they are going to tell it. In all honesty, I don't really think I want to hear what J.R. has done, but I'd better find out before the front office does. I look at the two of them and ask, "What did he do?" in as objective of a voice as I can muster.

"Well," Ramona starts, "He was acting like he was trying out for *America's Next Top Model*." She begins to walk up and down our aisle like she's on a runway, switching her hips in a dramatic way, flipping her hair, fluttering her eyelashes, and smacking her lips. "Oh," Justin, who just enters the classroom, chimes in, "Are you doing J.R. at lunch?" Javier says, "Of course." Most of my students who are in the class are now laughing. In order to get some semblance of order with this conversation, I stop them from continuing. "Okay, you all. I'll have a word with J.R. But I better not hear any of you are teasing or taunting him about this. We are a class who takes care of one another." Ramona jumps in, "But Mrs. Morton, what was scary was that the other fifth graders were talking about how they wanted to beat him up because he's a sissy, a fairy, and a fag." As several students gasp as she says *that* word, she quickly jumps in and says, "I didn't say that, Mrs. Morton. Those mean boys did." I think about my next steps and say, "Do you know who those boys' teacher is?" Ramona shakes her head and says, "I think Mr. Coleman, but I can't be sure." The others in the room are shaking their heads too.

Just then, the bell rings as the final students in my class enter the classroom. As they settle down, take a sip from their water bottles on their desks, they begin to read their independent reading books. They do this for twenty-five minutes every day after lunch. Once everyone is settled, I call J.R. to my desk. Because I know many students are going to try to listen to our conversation, I say, "I need to talk with J.R. privately. So I need you all to do your work quietly. Thanks in advance for being on your best behavior."

I look over at J.R. He is new to our school this year. According to him, he was having problems with bullies at his old school. I remember J.R. telling me, "They would beat me up almost every day. They would pull my hair and try to cut it. Rip my shirts and pants and spit on me." I just couldn't imagine this was happening to a child in a school in America. My goodness. Looking at J.R.'s outfit today, I see he's wearing pink skinny jeans, a white buttoned-up shirt with silver glitter sprinkled on the back that spells DIVA, a pink scarf around his neck, and silver sneakers. His fingernails are painted in a pastel blue and pink color, his eyebrows are arched, his lips are glossy, and his hair is long and curled in a cute hairstyle.

When J.R. sits at the table in the front of the room, I ask him, "What happened at lunch today? Several students said some kids were messing with you." J.R. nods his head and says, "Yeah. Those boys in Mr. Coleman's class are always messing with me. They call me nasty names and everything. I don't even do anything to them. They just keep on bothering me." I look at J.R. and say, "Well, what do you do when they begin to tease or threaten you?" J.R. looks at me and says, "I go to the noon duty supervisor like you told me, but she told me to stop dressing the way I do and I won't get teased." Given this new information, I am really concerned about his safety. Finally I say, "J.R., would you like to eat lunch in the classroom with me until we can figure out the best way to handle this situation? I don't want anything to happen to you." J.R. thinks about it and says, "I don't know, Mrs. Morton. Then they'll think I'm a punk too. So, I don't know." Looking totally defeated, J.R. shakes his head and says, "It just ain't easy being me." He flashes his famous toothy smile and stands up. "May I go back to my desk, Mrs. Morton?" I look up at him and reply, "You sure may." I go to the back of the classroom and take out my cell phone and call J.R.'s mother. I find out that she and her husband have the day off and will come after school to talk with me about this situation.

After school, as I'm thinking about J.R.'s situation, the classroom door opens. "Hello, Mrs. Morton," Dr. Millicent St. Clair says. I put my hand out to shake her hand and her husband's. When everyone is seated, I ask, "Where's J.R.?" Millicent says, "We told him to go on home. We wanted to have this time to talk with you privately." Millicent then says, "As you may already know, I am a psychologist with a private practice and Mike is a psychiatrist who works at the state mental hospital." She looks up at her husband and continues, "So we know what's going on with our son. We have known for years that J.R. is different. He never had the same interests as other boys his age." Looking over at me she says, "He told us that he wanted to be a girl when he was five years old. Of course we were upset." She then looks at her husband who is now nodding his head in agreement. "However," she continues, "we love our son and have decided to accept him for who he is. A transgendered individual." With that, she looks at me and says, "When he is of age we will be there for him as he goes through his official transition with hormone treatments and operations." Michael St. Clair looks at me and says, "I know my wife has placed a lot on you, but do you think you can handle this situation and still teach our son in a loving and an unbiased way?"

Discussion Questions

1. What is your response to Dr. Michael St. Clair?
2. What are some problems, concerns, issues, or questions you have about teaching a fifth grader who is transgendered? (How do you keep J.R. safe?)
3. How can you prepare your students for being in classes with a transgendered student?
4. How would you handle the situation with the noon duty supervisor who suggested that J.R. should change the way he dresses?
5. How do you personally feel about transgendered people?

Advice from Veteran Teachers on . . . Gender Identity

- When we were in school, none of us remember children questioning their gender identity. Thus, this is a new situation for all of us. However, on numerous occasions, we have had children in our classes who have questioned their gender identity. We have found that girls who dress like boys have an easier time than boys who dress like girls and are effeminate.
- It has been our experience that this is very difficult for parents to deal with. Depending on how comfortable you feel with the parents, you may want to ask them how they are feeling regarding this situation. You may want to suggest that the parents seek counseling in order to help them to deal with their own feelings regarding these situations.
- Remember that cultural practices and norms come into play with gender, gender identity, and gender roles. If parents request that their child not use a certain crayon or material such as lace or doilies, or write about certain things, we would let them know that this request is unreasonable as it will be too much for us to monitor those areas that closely. However, if they've had that conversation with their child and the child can remember that their parents do not want them to use or do those things, then we will honor that request.
- We would also talk with our principal and let him or her know what we are planning on doing, ask for any advice they may have, and to see if they would like to join us during our conversation with the parent.
- Initiate counseling services at your school in order to have a professional attend to this child's needs. The counselor is the one who is trained to deal with psychological issues such as the ones presented in the vignettes. Rely on their expertise to help you with dealing with the child who is questioning their gender identity, help you with your class who have probably already began to question this child's situation, and help you deal with the parents.
- Allow a child who is questioning their identity to keep a private journal where you are the only one who converses with the child in the journal. The suicide rate is high among these children, so we want to make sure that the child has someone they can confide in.
- If the other children are teasing this child, you should have a conversation with your whole class about teasing. We suggest that you keep the conversation focused on teasing—not on the child. (See suggestions under bullying for further instructions on how to have a conversation or do role playing with your students.)

Sexual Orientation

It Doesn't Rub Off

"I'm gonna have my party at Yoyo's Fantastic Playhouse," Miriam said with excitement in her voice, as the rest of my second graders say, "Ooohh!" Miriam continues, "I'm having pizza, ice cream, a cake, balloons, and everything." I look around my class and see smiling faces. Although I have never been to Yoyo's Fantastic Playhouse, I have heard good things about it. My nieces and nephews just love the little roller coasters, the games, and the food. When Miriam is finished describing the party, I ask, "Does anyone have a question?" Jose raises his hand and asks, "Is your mom going to give you a lot of tokens so you play a lot of games and win a lot of tickets?" Miriam nods her head and says, "Yes. They told me they are going to give me fifty tokens so that I can try and win the big pink bunny rabbit." Once again, my students say in unison, "Ooohh!"

I look out at the class again and ask, "Does anyone else have a question?" Sarah raises her hand and asks, "Who are you going to invite to your party?" Miriam looks around the room and says, "I get to invite the whole class to my party." I hand her the invitations her mothers gave me this morning to pass out to the class. As she begins to walk around the room and pass out her invitations, Jamal says, "Dang, Miriam. That's expensive. How can y'all afford that?" Jamal's knowledge of the world and curiosity will take him far. Miriam giggles a bit and says, "My mommies said I can invite the whole class because my Mommy Dot works there." Jamal chimes in, "Oh, okay. That makes sense."

As Miriam continues to pass out the invitation, I ask again, "Does anyone else have any questions?" Elizabeth raises her hand and asks, "You have two mommies?" When I look up at Elizabeth, I see a perplexed look on her face like she's trying to make sense of the information she's heard. Miriam, who has just finished passing out the invitations, says, "Yes, I have two mommies. One mommy is Mommy Dot and my other mommy is Mommy Sadie." By the time she finishes this statement she is in the front of the room. Elizabeth, who still has a confused look on her face, says, "But I don't understand how you can have two mommies. That doesn't make sense." Jamal chimes in, "Why don't you understand, Elizabeth?" he asks. "She has two mommies." However, Elizabeth still does not seem to understand. "But how can she have two mommies and not a mommy and a daddy?" Jamal shakes his head and begins to speak. But this time, I interrupt him and say, "Jamal, let me answer this."

I look at Elizabeth and say, "Some families have a mommy and a daddy. Some have two daddies and no mommies. Some have two mommies and no daddies. Some have one mommy and no daddy. Some have one daddy and no mommy. Some kids have families where they are being raised by their grandparents or aunts and uncles. And some kids are in foster families." I look at the rest of the class and then back at Elizabeth. "Does that make sense, Elizabeth?" Elizabeth looks at me and says, "I guess so, Mrs. Davis." I look back at the rest of my class and say, "Does anyone else have any questions for me?" I see my students shaking their heads. "Okay," I say, "Does anyone else have a question for Miriam about her party?" Once again, my students shake their heads. I look at Miriam and say, "Thanks, Miriam, for sharing with us today. And I appreciate my invitation." I then ask her to take her seat.

"Okay class, please get out your math books and a sheet of paper and turn to page 69. Let's get ready for math." My second graders grunt in unison, "Uugghh!"

At the end of the school day, after I check my mail and say hello to friends, I return to my room to get ready for the fieldtrip tomorrow. As I near my classroom, I see Elizabeth and her mother, Blanche Davenport, standing by the door. "Hello," I say to the two of them. Elizabeth runs up to me and gives me a hug. "Hi, Mrs. Davis." I look at her and ask, "Did you leave something in the room?" She shakes her head and says, "No. My mommy wants to speak with you." I look at her mother who asks Elizabeth to go the table so she can talk privately with me.

"Hello, Mrs. Davis," her mother says. "I just wanted to talk with you a bit about this invitation Elizabeth received today." I nod and say, "Oh yes, Miriam's party." She nods, too, and says, "Yes." She clears her throat and says, "I am really not sure about Elizabeth going to Miriam's party. I mean, aren't her parents gay?" I look at her and say, "Yes, they are." She says, "Then you probably can understand my concern. I mean, I don't want Elizabeth to turn out gay like Miriam."

Discussion Questions

1. What do you say to Blanche Davenport after this comment?
2. Is it your responsibility to convince Elizabeth's mother to allow her to go to the party? Give your rationale as to why or why not.
3. If you had a student ask you questions like Elizabeth's, how would you respond?
4. What are the pros and cons of your attending your students' parties?
5. What would you do if Miriam and her parents did not have plans on inviting your entire class?

James Baldwin—My Hero

"Okay, fifth graders. Let's settle down," I say. I raise my hand and hold up all five fingers to indicate that they have five seconds to get quiet. I let them have about three seconds before I put a finger down. I want to make sure they have enough time to get quiet and get things together. When I get to two fingers, all of my students look up and show me they are ready to begin our oral presentations on their biographies of African Americans who have done exceptional things to improve the lives of others. I look over my class and nod my head and say, "Good job! I will put five more cubes in our jar." I can hear them praising themselves as I put five more cubes in our Popcorn Party jar.

When I'm done, I flip through the papers on my clipboard until I find the one with their presentation dates and times on it. I then announce, "Okay, today we will hear from James, Stephanie, and Ryan." I look out at table five to see James stand up and get his tri-fold board from the back wall. "Ladies and gentlemen, please help me welcome James Hendricks." The boys and girls begin clapping as James strolls up to the front of the classroom.

After James puts up his poster with *James Baldwin* written on top on the easel, I see him square his shoulders, look at each table, and clear his throat before he begins to speak. "Um," James says. "Oh, I'm sorry. I'm not supposed to say "Um," he says as he looks at me in sheer terror. I smile at James. "It's all right, James. You may continue." James takes a deep breath and begins to address the class. "I selected James Baldwin for three main reasons. First, James Baldwin was a writer and you all know that I want to be a writer." James looks over at me and winks. I nod my head and wink back at James. "Second," James continues, "his name is James. You can't go wrong with such a great name like that." The class begins to chuckle and so do I. As if jarred back into reality, I hear James say, "James Baldwin was born in Harlem on August 2, 1924. He had nine brothers and sisters, and in fact, he was the oldest kid just like me." Looking back at his index cards, he continues, "He grew up poor, and from the information I found, he lived with his mother, and a strict adoptive father." He looks up and says, "You see, he didn't know his real father and was born to a single mother back when you didn't see that as much." I nod my head in agreement. "But later, she married a man who adopted James and gave him his last name, Baldwin." Looking back down at his notecards, he continues, "Now, he didn't get along with his adoptive dad, but they did have something in common." Shifting his weight to his other hip, James continues "His adoptive father was a preacher, and for three years, James Baldwin preached too." I widen my eyes and say, "Wow, I didn't know that about him." James nods his head and says, "Neither did I. I was pleasantly surprised that we had so much in common."

He looks out at his peers and says, "My dad is a preacher too." He then scans the room and says, "Some of you go to our church." Several students nod their heads in agreement. Laila raises her hand and asks, "Do you think you've been called to preach? My grandmother says it runs in families." James tilts his head to the side and finally responds, "You know, I don't know. I don't know what it feels like to be called." Shifting his weight to his other hip, he continues, "I will probably always evangelize, but to preach? I'm not sure." Several other hands go up and then I interrupt this rich exchange. "Okay, everyone. Let's let James finish his presentation and then we'll have time to ask him questions." James nods his head and continues.

"James Baldwin even went to Greenwich Village in New York City. That's where he met Richard Wright, who is another famous African-American writer." Once again, I am pleasantly surprised, but this time I do not say anything. Last time I did, it led to others asking questions. "While in New York, he was able to get some money and in 1948 he went to Paris." James then looks up and says, "James Baldwin was able to reflect on how bad things were in America while overseas. Racism, poverty, and things like that." Tilting his head once again, he says, "I think I will one day go over there too. It seems exciting and is the place where every writer must go in their lifetime." Then for the next seven minutes, James informs us about the life, trials, and tribulations of James Baldwin.

With about five minutes to go, James turns his back to us and begins to point to his tri-fold board. On it is a list of several of the books written by Baldwin. James clears his throat and continues, "He wrote *Go Tell It on the Mountain* in 1953, *Notes of a Native Son* in 1955, *Giovanni's Room* in 1956, *The Fire Next Time* in 1963, *If Beale*

Street Could Talk in 1974, and *The Evidence of Things Not Seen* in 1985." James puts his head down and says, "Unfortunately, I wasn't able to read any of the books because my mom wasn't too sure if they would be appropriate for me because of my age." He springs up and says, "But as soon as I am of age, I'm reading some of them because they really sound interesting." Looking back at his notecards, James says in a sobering tone, "James Baldwin died on November 30, 1987, of stomach cancer. He is buried in New York State." James then looks up at the clock and says, "In conclusion, James Baldwin was a great man. He was a civil rights activist, a great writer, and had the coolest name on the face of the earth."

Looking at the clock and realizing that we won't have enough time to answer questions, I announce, "James, you've done a great job." My students begin to clap. When they are settled down I continue, "Now we don't have much time, so we'll answer questions when we get back after lunch." Yuri, waving his hand frantically in the air says, "But James said that there were three reasons why he picked James Baldwin and he only told us two." I nod my head in agreement. Thinking this won't take too long, I look over at James and say, "And what is your third reason?" James then stands taller, squares his shoulders, clears his throat and says, "Because he's gay—just like me."

Discussion Questions

1. What do you say to James after this revelation?
2. What do you say to your students following James's presentation?
3. In the future, what can you do as a teacher to be better prepared for surprises such as this?
4. What support services do you seek for James following his declaration?
5. Name other historical figures who are gay, lesbian, bisexual or transgendered. In your opinion, is it important that your students know about their sexuality or gender identity?

What's a Dyke?

"Ms. Jones," I hear several of my fourth-grade students shout to me as I scan the playground during afternoon recess duty, "We won!" Brandon continues to shout as he Alex, William, Steven, Brad, and Makayla run toward me holding a basketball. "Well, good for you all," I say to them. "We beat the fifth graders," Makayla says beaming with pride. I look at them with surprise. "Did you beat Mr. Romano's class?" I ask. Makayla twists her lips and says, "Oh no, we're not ready for them yet," Makayla says with a chuckle. "We beat Mrs. Rohn's class," she says. Steven chimes in, "But don't worry. We'll be ready for them soon. We're getting better and better every day." I give my students a thumb's up and smile at them. The bell rings signaling the end of recess and I follow the six of them to our line by our classroom door.

When we get back into class, the same students are informing everyone about their victory. "I mean, I went up and blocked that shot like I was in the WNBA," Makayla says to Gretchen, showing her exactly how she blocked the shot. Alex chimes in, "Remember when you dribbled the ball between your legs and went up for that layup. They didn't even expect that." Makayla and Alex give each other a high five and move to the other tables to tell other students about their victory. In order to get control of this situation and allow them a chance to cool down, I announce, "Ok, everyone. It's time to relax and cool down." I then say, "You may get drinks and lay your heads on your desks for a few minutes to cool down." Some of my students sip water from the water bottles on their desks, while others line up quietly to get drinks from the faucet in our class. After a minute, I announce, "After our cool down and following our silent reading time, we will take our spelling test. So get your mind ready for it."

While the class is cooling down, and reading, I cut sheets of paper in half. I locate the spelling words for the test and put them to the side. As I reach for my own novel, I can hear several students still discussing the basketball game from recess. I turn around and look at the tables. Of course, it's the table with Brandon, William, Steven, Alex, Brad, and Makayla. I put my finger up to my lips to let them know they need to quiet down. They all go back to reading their books.

Reminiscing, I recall that these six students have been sitting at the same table since the beginning of the school year. As a matter of fact, they have been best friends since kindergarten. I had my students do a "Get to Know You Better" worksheet and short presentation introducing themselves to the class on the first day of school. All six of them begged me to allow them to do their presentation together. During their presentation, which they rapped, we learned they wanted to sit together because they were all on the same sports teams, and they all loved to play soccer, football, baseball, and of course, basketball. I must admit, I was concerned about having only one girl sitting at the table. But I quickly learned that Makayla could handle herself exceptionally well.

Makayla. I smile when I think about how strong and confident she is. In my three years of teaching, I haven't had a female student who has the athletic ability of Makayla. She is the fastest student, is agile, has a great arm, and is as strategic as she is defensive. During parent teacher conference, Makayla's mother told me her daughter has always been a tomboy, and if I could get her to wear a dress for her school pictures, she would be so proud. Well, she refused to wear a dress, but took a cute picture anyway.

After our silent reading time, I look at the classroom chores chart and realize Makayla is the "paper passer outer" for the week. "Makayla," I say, "Will you please pass out the sheets of paper for the spelling test." She begins with the front rows. "Ladies and gentlemen," I continue, "Please get out a pencil and number your papers from 1–20. Make sure that you put your name, the date, and student number on the top." When I scan the room to make sure that my students are following my directions, I see the girls at the front right-hand table whispering to each another. I notice that both Sarah and Margie squeeze their nostrils together as if they smell something that is unpleasant. Just before I was about to say something, Makayla interrupts my thoughts and says, "Here you go, Ms. Jones. I've passed out all the papers." Makayla struts to her seat in the back and begins writing on her sheet of paper.

After their spelling test, my students get ready to go home. "Ladies and gentlemen," I say, "please have a safe and relaxing weekend." Just then, the bell rings and my students line up; I walk them out to the front of the school. When everyone is on their way home, I take a deep breath. "Whew," I think to myself, "I am tired. Maybe a soak in the tub will do me good." Just then I feel someone touching my shoulder. I turn around and see Makayla and the look on her face tells me that something isn't right. She says, "Ms. Jones, I don't know if I should be mad or not, but the girls in class keep calling me a dyke." Makayla puts her backpack on the ground and says, "Ms. Jones, what's a dyke?"

Discussion Questions

1. What do you say to Makayla?
2. How do you define "dyke" for Makayla?
3. What do you say and do to the girls in class who are responsible for making this comment to Makayla?
4. What types of activities/lessons can you do with your students to encourage acceptance of differences?
5. What types of activities can you do with your students' parents in order to help them have conversations with their children about accepting other people's differences?

Advice from Veteran Teachers on . . . Sexual Orientation

*   We are especially concerned that gay and lesbian children and youth have much higher suicide rates than their heterosexual peers. Thus, making sure that all of our students, in particular those who are questioning their sexual orientation, have a comfortable and safe learning environment is crucial. We understand that this may be easier said than done in certain states, cities, communities, and types of schools, and may be much more difficult and seemingly impossible in others. However, we are entrusted to care for and educate ALL of our students and to provide them with the safest and most nurturing learning environment possible.
*   We encourage you to handle any teasing or bullying of gay and lesbian students, female students who appear more masculine, as well as male students who are effeminate, immediately. Some high school and college students have expressed that they were brutalized by their peers as early as elementary school because of the way they dressed, walked, talked or because they preferred their own gender. Some of them considered or attempted suicide, ran away from home, or began to use drugs to deal with this torment. You should, based on the way you manage your class, implement consequences immediately and consistently. Teasing and bullying of any sort should never be tolerated.
*   We have found from our years in the classroom that girls who are more masculine have an easier time adjusting and relating with their peers than boys who are effeminate. Given that, you may want to monitor boys who are effeminate a bit more closely in order to ensure that they are safe on the playground, in the lunchroom, and even in your classroom.
*   There are strict limits to children expressing their sexuality in elementary schools. None of us have taught in elementary schools where the students were allowed to kiss, hold hands or even act like a couple. As a teacher, we must respect this. Be it boy and girl, girl and girl, or boy and boy.
*   Allow a child who is questioning their sexual orientation or who is secure with their homosexuality to keep a private journal where you are the only one who converses with the child in the journal. The suicide rate is high among these children, so we want to make sure that the child has someone whom they can confide in.
*   Families of these children may or may not be understanding about their child coming out. We would start with our school counselor to get tips on how to best handle the situation with the parents, with the rest of our class, and with the gay or lesbian child.

Bullying

I Just Can't Take It Anymore

"Mrs. Stevens," Danny a shy, overweight fourth grader says as I grab my whistle, "can I please keep score for the softball game?" Every time our class has P.E., he volunteers to keep score. "Danny," I say, "it is important that we all exercise. So, you need to play on a team just like everyone else." Danny saunters off, looking at the ground. "Okay, class," I say, "let's line up for P.E."

"Um," Justin says in deep thought, "I pick Violet." I can hear the other team grumbling under their breath. "Excuse me," I say, "you know that I will pack this softball equipment and we will go back to the classroom if I hear anymore of that." Justin and Samantha, the other team captain, try to quiet their teams. "Okay, Samantha," I continue, "who do you pick?" Samantha thinks for a minute and says, "I guess I'll pick Sylvester." I can see that Justin's team is visibly upset, but they know that I truly will end the softball game before it even begins. "Okay, and Danny, you are on Justin's team." Danny does not lift his head up. I can tell that he is embarrassed. This is the part that I hate about P.E.

I get in between both teams, toss the coin in the air, and tell Justin to call it. "Heads!" he shouts. As the coin hits the dirt, we all look and I say, "Justin's team gets to bat first."

When we get back to the room after thirty-five minutes outside, the kids are tired, so I turn out the lights so that they can all cool off. Many of the kids are drinking from water bottles they've brought from home, while others are standing in line getting drinks.

"I can't believe we lost," Patrick says. "I bet if we didn't have *Danny* on our team . . ." I stop him before he continues. "Patrick, flip your card. I will not tolerate you belittling anyone in this class." As Patrick goes to the pocket chart to flip his card, I glance over at Danny, who has his head on his desk. His poor little face is beet red after running around the bases. He was trying so hard to get to home plate, but Marsha is a fantastic centerfielder and throws the ball so fast that he was tagged out at home plate.

"Fourth graders," I say as Simone, the last student in line, gets a drink of water, "I want you to take out your journals and write for fifteen minutes before lunch." The students scoot their chairs back, get out their journals and a pencil, and most begin writing. "Now remember," I begin, "although I am writing too, I can see and hear you as you write. I am looking for tables where everyone is on task, not bothering their neighbors. If there is a problem, that individual will raise his or her hand to ask me their question. For each group who manages to do that, I will add five stones per group to our class jar." The kids begin to get a little excited. There's a popcorn party involved in this community-building activity. "Any questions?" When no one raises their hands, I tell them, "You may get to work."

I, too, have begun to write in a journal when my students are writing. That way, I am modeling good writing habits for them. "Mrs. Stevens," Danny says interrupting my writing, "May I come up?" "Sure thing, Danny," I say to him. Danny ambles up to the kidney table where I am seated. I smile at him and say, "How may I help you, sweetie?" Danny's face is still red. He gives me his half smile and says, "I am still so hot and my throat hurts. Do you think I need to go to the nurse?" "No," I say, "I think you'll be fine. Why don't you get your journal and come up here. I'll turn on my fan because I'm a little hot too." Danny smiles at me and says, "Thanks, Mrs. Stevens," and goes back to his desk to grab his journal and pencil as I turn on the fan. For the next fourteen minutes, we all write in our journals.

As usual, during lunch in the lounge, I sit next to my good friends and colleagues, Yolanda, Kendra, and Dustin. "Why is your face so red?" Yolanda asks. "We were outside playing softball and that heat was a bear," I say. "Whew," Dustin begins, "I sure used to hate P.E." I finish chewing the bite of sandwich and ask, "Why?" Dustin looks up and says, "Cause, I used to be the fat kid who got teased every time we had to play. It's hard being the fat kid," he says as he slices his tomatoes. "You know," I begin, "Danny in my class is overweight. Every time before we go outside for P.E., he begs me to let him keep score." Dustin looks up from his tomatoes and asks, "Do you let him?" I say, "No. We all need to exercise, so I make sure that he participates."

Shaking his head back and forth, Dustin says with a serious look on his face, "But see, what you don't understand and maybe don't see, is that the kids are probably teasing him. I know they sure teased me." Dustin puts his knife down and continues, "I remember I had this fifth-grade teacher, Mr. Schmidt, and he was a star football player in high school and college. When I couldn't run the mile in some unreasonable amount of time, he would make me do it again. I just remember feeling like I was going to die because I couldn't breathe. Now did he *teach* us how to breathe correctly? *Noooo,*" he says. "But he was there to scream at me for not running fast enough." Dustin picks his fork up and moves his salad around his bowl. "Then, when we had to wait to be picked for teams to play on. . ." He put his hand in the air and says, "Oh-my-goodness!! That was the worst!" Still looking down, Dustin says, "I remember trying so hard sometimes, but never making it. It's just hell being the fat kid."

I sat there for a minute thinking about what Dustin was saying. "But don't you think he needs to exercise?" Dustin nods his head. "Yeah," he says, "and I don't have the answer. I just know that it is a hard situation to be in." The next thing I hear is my name, "Mrs. Stevens." Mr. Gaines, our school secretary says, "You have a student in the nurse's office." I wrap up the rest of my lunch and head to the nurse's office. Danny, his face once again beet red, sits there crying.

"Danny, what happened?" I ask. "They got mad at me because we lost again," Danny says between gulping for air. "They said that if I lost the game they were going to beat me up." Surprised, I say, "Danny, why didn't you tell me?" With a puzzled look on his face, Danny says matter of factly, "Cause they'll beat me up." He continues to cry and says, "I love playing softball with my family, but I hate playing with the class. They are always making fun of me, stealing my lunch, tripping me, and hitting me." Danny takes a deep breath and says, "They spit on me, throw food on me, pull my hair, and say they're gonna beat me up." He then leans into me and lays his head on my left arm, still crying.

As I reach around to hold him, I see Dustin standing in the doorway. Just then, in a low tone, but with a firm jaw, I hear Danny say, "I just can't take it anymore. I just can't take it." Then the bell rings signaling the end of lunch.

Discussion Questions

1. After Danny states, "I can't take it anymore," are you concerned? What are you concerned about?
2. What do you do with the students who've threatened Danny?
3. As a teacher, can you think of any better ways to select teammates?
4. What are the pros and cons of Danny not participating in P.E. activities?
5. Do you contact Danny's parents? If so, what do you say to them? If not, why?

My Brother's Keeper

"Hi, Ms. Felix. Is my brother ready?" I look at the door, recognizing the voice. "Why hello there, Josh," I say. I had Josh when he was in kindergarten. Now he is a tall and bright fifth grader. I look back into the classroom and find Johnny playing with the trucks in the dramatic play center. He has on his backpack along with his coat, hat, and mittens. "I guess he's ready to go," I say. Unfortunately, although Johnny has on the appropriate attire to go home for the day, he is not ready to leave. He just loves playing with those trucks. Johnny begins to pout and whine when Josh tells him that it is time to go home. "Johnny," I say, "you can play with the trucks tomorrow. I'll make sure that you get a chance to play with them." Johnny stops pouting and whining long enough to ask, "You promise?" I hold up my two fingers and say with a serious expression, "I promise." With that, Josh and Johnny go home.

The next day, Wednesday, I do not have yard duty. My students know that if they are on their best behavior on Monday and Tuesday, on Wednesday they have the option to go to the playground before class or come into class and play with our educational toys. Breathing heavily and apparently on a mission, Johnny shows up early in class with Josh. "Hi, Ms. Felix," Josh says, "Here's Johnny." Johnny waves quickly to me, then rushes to his cubby to put his backpack away. After he hangs up his coat, hat, and mittens, he makes a beeline to the trucks. "Johnny," Josh says, "you didn't ask Ms. Felix if it was okay for you to play with the truck." Johnny looks up briefly and says, "But you pinky promised? A-member?" He looks at me with those big brown eyes. "Yes," I say, "I remember," emphasizing the "re" in remember.

As Johnny continues to play, I ask Josh how things are going. Josh shrugs his shoulders and says, "Everything is fine, Ms. Felix." I look into his eyes. My gut tells me that things aren't okay. I then look closely at Josh and notice that he has a bruise on his right cheek and a scratch mark on the other one. "Josh," I say, "how did you get that bruise and scratch on your face?" Josh's eyes get big and he says, "Oh, I, um, was playing, um, football, and um, I got tackled." I place my hand on his chin and twist his head from side to side. That way, I can take a closer look at the injuries. Although I still have that gut feeling, his explanation is plausible. So I look Josh in his face and say, "You know if anything isn't fine, you can always talk with me, right?" Josh looks at me and smiles. "Yes, Ms. Felix." He then turns around and says, "I need to get to my class to put my stuff away." Before he turns around to exit the room I reiterate my earlier comment, "You can always come to me, okay." Josh nods and smiles and exits the room.

"Vroooooom." I hear Johnny over in the dramatic play center. Several other students have since come into the classroom. I go over to join Johnny. "You sure love these trucks, Johnny," I say to him. Johnny is smiling and obviously having a great time. "Vroooooooom," he replies holding up a blue truck. I guess that means yes.

Thinking back to my earlier conversation with Josh, I ask Johnny, "So, how's your brother doing, Johnny?" Johnny, barely looking up from the truck says, "I don't know." Then he gives me a big bright smile and returns to playing with the truck. Obviously, talking to a kindergartener is harder than I thought. Especially a kindergartener playing with his favorite truck.

"Johnny," I attempt again. Then I stop. He is so into this truck that it seems fruitless to continue. But, just as I turn to leave, Johnny says, "Ms. Felix, what's bullying?" I am a bit puzzled by his fairly mature question and ask him, "Why do you ask?" Johnny puts his truck down long enough to say, "Josh was telling my mom that Chris and Mark are bullying him. What does that mean?"

"Well," I say, trying to think of words that he can understand, "it means that they are not being nice to him. Do you know if Josh has told his teacher, Mr. Marks?" Johnny then picks up his truck and says, "I don't know that." He goes back to playing with the blue truck as if nothing ever happened.

At my desk I quickly jot down what Johnny just told me. Then, in the dramatic play center, Johnny jumps up and runs to my desk still holding that blue truck. "Oh, Ms. Felix. I have another question." Just as the bell rings, he says, "Um, what's a switchblade? cause my older brother told Josh to put one in his backpack today."

Discussion Questions

1. What is your legal responsibility after hearing that a child has a switchblade at school?
2. How do you contact your principal and Mr. Marks given the fact that the bell just rang?
3. What agencies might need to be involved in this situation?
4. What are the possible outcomes (both good and bad) with this situation?
5. What help is available for children like Josh and Chris and Mark?

Who's the Bully?

Linda, one of my third graders, comes rushing to me after morning recess. She is out of breath and looking over her shoulder as she runs. "Whoa," I say as I put my hands in the air, "slow down, Linda. What's the hurry?" Linda leans over as she tries to catch her breath. "Mrs. Montgomery," Linda pants, "Marquita is doing it again. She just won't leave me alone. Today, she even had her friends in the fifth grade chase me. They chased me all the way here until they saw you." I look over Linda and do not see Marquita or her fifth-grade friends. "That girl hates me," Linda says, "She's always messin' with me." Linda puts her head down and begins to sob.

This situation with Marquita and Linda has been going on for over a month now. Several weeks ago, I talked with Marquita, and according to her, "Mrs. P., that girl gets on my nerves. She is always bothering me. I tell her to leave me alone but she just keeps bothering me." When I talked with Linda about what Marquita said, she said that Marquita was "just lying cause she don't want to get in no trouble." Needless to say, this situation is still unresolved.

After a few seconds of crying with no tears, Linda looks in the direction where Marquita is and puts her hand on her hip and sticks her tongue out. "Linda," I say, "Marquita isn't even looking at you." Then after thinking about it for a few seconds I add, "Is that what you do to her?" Linda's eyes get big as quarters and she says in a soft and innocent voice, "Oh no, Mrs. Montgomery. She just always messes with me." She continues her tearless sobbing.

Shaking my head back to reality, I look down at Linda and decide that enough is enough. If Marquita is bullying Linda, that could lead to serious problems. "Linda, I want you to eat lunch with me this afternoon so that you can avoid this situation. I will have another talk with Marquita and Mr. Carson to get to the bottom of this." Linda begins to beam. "I get to eat lunch in the classroom with you. Okay, Mrs. Montgomery." The bell rings signaling the end of morning recess. "Okay, honey," I say to Linda, "now go and line up."

The rest of the morning goes well. Linda is happier than I have seen her in a long time. During lunch, true to my word, I allow students to join me in the classroom for lunch. Most of my students join me. However, after they eat, most want to go to the playground. Linda is just about to get up to go outside when I say, "Linda, the main reason I asked you to eat lunch with me is because I wanted to give us a chance to go and talk with Marquita's teacher, Mr. Carson, about this problem you are having with her." Linda looks around and pokes her lips out. "But Mrs. Montgomery," she says, "I really want to play tetherball today." She then looks at me with those sad, quarter-sized eyes and says, "Please, Mrs. Montgomery. I promise to be on my best behavior. I'll stay away from Marquita and everything." Shaking my head but needing to go to the restroom, I say, "Okay. But if she continues to bother you, make sure that you go to the noon duty supervisor, Miss Nancy." Linda face brightens up and she says, "Okay, I promise." With that she walks out of the classroom and heads toward the playground.

I look up at the clock and realize that I have about eight minutes before the bell rings signaling the end of lunch recess. As I open the door to the teachers' lounge, I run right into Mark Carson, Marquita's teacher. "Hey there, Mark," I say. "I want to talk with you about one of your students." He tilts his head and says, "Which one?" "Marquita," I say. "Every day after lunch and most recesses, Linda comes into class and says that Marquita keeps messing with her." Mark has a puzzled look on his face, so I ask, "Has Marquita said anything to you?" He smiles and says, "Yes, but the story is a little different. I was told that Linda keeps messing with her and getting on her nerves." Just then the bell rings. Dang! I guess I'll have to wait until the end of the school to go to the restroom. I look at Mark and say, "I have to go back to class. Let's continue this talk later." Mark looks at me and says, "No problem."

Instead of going directly to the classroom, I go to the playground to get my students who should be lined up and ready to go back to class. When I get to our line, I am shocked that I don't see Linda. Just then, I look over next to the girls' restroom and see Linda in Marquita's face. She has her hand on her hip, is rolling her neck, pointing in Marquita's face, and sticking her tongue out. I then see Marquita look Linda squarely in the eyes and say, "Look, little girl. I could really hurt you. Get out of my damn face!"

Discussion Questions

1. What is your first reaction?
2. What do you think is the real story regarding Linda and Marquita?
3. What would you say to Linda?
4. What would you say to Marquita?
5. What would you say to Linda's parents?

Advice from Veteran Teachers on . . . Bullying

- Having learned from Columbine and all the other school shootings, dealing with bullying is so important. Bullying is a form of violence and it can lead to murder. Kids can either kill others or kill themselves. Do role playing in the beginning of the year and include several scenarios on bullying. That way, you can have an open conversation about bullying.
- Make a class rule of no bullying. Be very specific. Name it and let them know what bullying is, what it looks and feels like, and where it can lead to. Then be firm and consistent with consequences for bullies. Also, let the children know that they need to contact you if they or a classmate is being bullied. We have to encourage them not to be silent about this serious issue.
- Ask the parents what advice they have given their child on how to respond to a bully or someone hurting him. To hit back, walk away, etc. Having this information may explain the child's behavior.
- In the case with Danny, we would encourage you to handle this head on. Send him out of the room and talk with your entire class about what you've heard and observed. Ask them, "How do you think Danny feels?" Then tell them what you've observed with their interactions with Danny. Then do role-playing exercises. Children have to be taught how to empathize. Suggestion—encourage them to help Danny become a better player. "Why don't you all help him practice running so he builds up some speed?"
- Do not let the kids pick their teams. Do 1-2, front row/back row, or odds and evens after assigning numbers to your students. Otherwise, the most athletic and popular will always be chosen first. Also, stop keeping score with the games. They're playing for fun and for exercise. One person can't make a team lose. What does it mean to be a team?
- If a child brings a weapon to school but is not in your class, contact their teacher and the principal immediately.
- If a child is being bullied, call the child's parents to get more information. They may know the names of the kids who are bullying their child.
- Contact the parents of the bullies. Let them know what's going on. Encourage them to talk with their child about the situation.
- What would you say to Johnny? Let him know that neither he nor his brother is in trouble right now. Tell him he did the right thing to let the teacher know.
- If you are the teacher of a child who brings a weapon to school, when the child is suspended, do a role-playing exercise with your class. What could've happened if the child had used the weapon? Also, have the principal come in and talk with your class.

- With children who are annoying others, start with the one causing the problem. Be candid, saying "I observed you do this or that." Let them know that they are bothering another child to the point where you can't control the reaction of the other child. Ask "Do you know why that happened? What can you do so that this situation does not happen again?"
- If the annoying child has a younger sibling, link that situation to the problem they are causing. They may not be aware that they are annoying another child but may connect the dots when they link the school problem to their own situation with their younger sibling.

Child Abuse

He's Such a Boy

"Boys!" I blow my whistle and then shout to the group of second graders near the slide, "Please move out of the way so that Justin can go down the slide safely." Shawn, one of my first graders from last year, gives a thumb's up and yells, "No problem, Mrs. Merritt." He then flashes a million-dollar smile and he and his friends move to the side of the slide.

As I monitor the children during yard duty, I make sure that my back is not toward the playground. I remember when I was student teaching and one of my friends, a fellow student teacher named Morgan, missed a child jumping off the top of the slide and breaking his arm and leg because she had her back to the playground while talking to several students. When it came time to file the official report, she couldn't report anything because she hadn't seen anything. Now don't get me wrong. I know teachers don't have eyes in the back of their heads, but Morgan still has issues and guilt because she made that one mistake. So I walk around the playground like a cop.

Once again, I blow my whistle and move quickly to the girls in front of the swings. "Girls," I shout, "You are too close to the swings. Please move back a bit so that you don't get hurt." The two girls move back a few steps and continue to count to twenty-five so they can swing next. As I continue to walk around the playground, I go next to Sandra, a fellow first-grade teacher who has been teaching for over twenty years. She has on her big floppy hat and huge sunglasses. "Hello there, Rebecca," she says to me, still scanning the playground, "I'll send the new science kit to your room after recess." I forgot she had the science kits. "Thanks so much." I say. "Do you want me to send over some of my students to help?" Still scanning the playground, Sandra places her whistle in her mouth and says, "No, that's okay. I'll send four of my students over to your room with the kits." Just then, she blows her whistle and shouts, "Melissa, Randall, Lisa, and Roman. Please stop running or you'll get hurt." The kids do exactly as she asks and Sandra turns to me and says, "Okay then. I'll see you later." She continues walking and scanning the playground like a cop, too.

I notice one of my students, Damien, playing roughly in the sandbox. He throws sand at several kids, then picks up the plastic pail and lifts it over his head aiming toward Rachel. I quickly walk over to him and blow my whistle. "Damien," I say, "You have lost your recess because of your behavior. Please go to the wall and take a time-out." Damien looks at me with big doe eyes and says, "But please, Mrs. Merritt . . ." I put my hand up and say, "No, Damien. No excuse. Please go now." Damien looks at the two students in the sandbox, then at me, and slowly exits the sandbox. He then slowly walks to the wall. Unfortunately, as soon as Damien gets to the wall, the bell rings signaling the end of recess. And just like that, all of the kids on the playground move to their respective lines.

At the end of school, I am in my room cleaning up after what seemed like a long day. As I am about to sit in my chair and put the children's stickers on our homework chart, Damien and his mother, Lydia Smith, come through the door. I look up and smile and say, "Why hello there, Mrs. Smith. How are you doing?" She smiles at me and says, "I'm fine, Mrs. Merritt. I just wanted to check the pocket chart because I want to make sure that Damien is following the rules in school." She looks down at Damien with her eyebrows elevated, which indicates she isn't playing. "Damien," she says to her son, "Please show me your cards." Damien is a bit nervous, but he points to the colored cards on our pocket chart. Mrs. Smith scans the cards and finds his name. Without saying anything, she sucks in her cheeks and then looks down at Damien. Finally, she asks, "Damien, why did you have to flip your card today?" Even more nervous now, Damien looks at his mother and then me. Just as I am about to explain to his mother what happened on the playground, she raises her hand to me and repeats, "Damien, why did you have to flip your card today?" Damien then drops his head and says, "I got in trouble on the playground for being mean in the sandbox." Still looking at her son intently, Mrs. Smith says, "I am disappointed with you, Damien. What do I tell you every day before you go to school?" Damien, still looking at the ground says, "to behave." Mrs. Smith then says, "And what did you do?" Damien, still not looking at either of us says, "Not behave."

Mrs. Smith shakes her head and looks me squarely in the face and says, "Excuse us, Mrs. Merritt. I need to take Damien into the restroom." From the restroom I can hear her spanking him and him crying, "Please, Mommy. I promise I won't do it again!"

Discussion Questions

1. What is the legal definition of child abuse?
2. What are parents' rights regarding disciplining their children with the use of spanking?
3. Is this type of situation defined as child abuse? Give your rationale for why it is or isn't.
4. To whom are you responsible to report this type of incident?
5. What would you say to Mrs. Smith when she exits the restroom with Damien?

Under One Roof

"Ladies and gentlemen," I say to my fourth graders, "I have always loved to write in journals." I look up to the ceiling and say, "Writing in journals has been one way for me to get my feelings out when things got difficult in my life or when I wanted to remember something great that happened in my life." Some of my students nod their heads in agreement, while others roll their eyes up to the ceiling like they are bored. "Now," I continue, looking at my students, "Some of you are barely writing in your journals and others are only doodling in your journals." I walk down the aisle and say, "The journals aren't meant for tic-tac-toe. They aren't meant for you to just scribble." Some of my students giggle. Probably the ones who are doodling or playing tic-tac-toe in their journals. I then continue, "They are meant to give you an outlet to express yourself and improve your writing skills." As I come back to the front of the room, I notice that Theresa has her hand raised. "Yes, Theresa," I say. "Do you have a question?" Theresa scrunches up her nose and says, "But what about when I don't have anything to say? I don't always want to write in my journal because sometimes I just don't have anything to say." Of course, Theresa would be the one to ask the question that plagues all teachers. Before I answer her, I turn the question back on her. "Well, Theresa, what would you suggest a teacher do if his or her students didn't have anything to say in their journals?" Theresa looks up to the ceiling and says, "Um, I don't know. Maybe like give us something to write about. Or let us write stories. Or let us write poems or songs or something like that." I nod my head at her good idea. "Done," I say. "That's a really good idea." Theresa then beams with pride.

I turn to the dry-erase board and write the date on the board. "Okay, ladies and gentlemen," I say, "You may write about something personal in your journal, may write a story, poem, song, or whatever else may be in your heart to write today." On my right side, I can see John's hand waving in the air. "Mrs. Yukon, can we write comics?" My face lights up. "By all means," I say smiling, "You may definitely write comics." Some of the students nod and say, "Yes!" to John's suggestion. "Okay," I continue, "Any other questions?" When no one raises a hand, I say, "Then you may begin. Remember, you have twenty-five minutes to write so please get to work."

As my students begin to work, I am impressed with how engaged they are in this journal time. Usually, it is like pulling teeth to get them to write. Maybe the fact that they have more options with regards to their journal writing time may make a difference in the products I receive. I look up and realize that we actually have seven minutes before it's time to go home. Since I don't want my bus riders to miss the bus, I announce, "Ladies and gentlemen, I am so proud of you. You all worked so hard. Thank you." I then say, "Now give yourselves a pat on your back." The students then pat their own backs and John gets up and takes a bow. "Leave it to John," I think. He's such a ham.

I then say, "It is time to get ready to go home, so please put away your journals, take out your planners, and make sure that you have all of your assignments written there." There is a mass movement as students push their chairs back to get into their desks. I ring the bell on my desk to get their attention and continue, "Also," I say as I look around the room, "Please make sure that you clean up around your area."

When the bell rings and my students are lined up at the door, Hillary walks over to me and hands me her journal. I look at her and say, "Oh no, honey. I'm not taking them home today." She looks up at me and says, "Can you please just read mine tonight? Especially the one I just wrote today." Not thinking much about it, I nod my head and say, "No problem." Hillary smiles at me and then bounces out of the classroom.

When I return to the classroom, I see Hillary's purple journal sitting on the front table. Just as I promised, I open her journal to today's entry and begin reading. Hillary wrote, "I'm tired of my brother hitting me every day. He hits me for going into his room, eating his cookies, and taking too long in the bathroom. Maybe I should do something to him to make him stop. But what? Please help me Mrs. Yukon. ♥ Hillary"

Discussion Questions

1. What is your first reaction to this journal entry?
2. Is this just normal brother and sister relations? Give your rationale for why or why not.

3. Who are you responsible for reporting this to?
4. If you have Hillary's parent-teacher conference the next day, what would you say to her parents regarding this situation?
5. If her parents feel that this is simply normal brother and sister relations, yet Hillary continues to tell you that she is experiencing problems with her brother, what steps would you take next?

Can You Keep a Secret?

Whew! It is the end of a long day. Actually a long week. In reality, a long few months. We just finished our end-of-the-year testing today after studying for the test for the past several months. I just hate that I have to devote so much time to cramming for these tests. Especially since I believe that the tests don't really measure all we do as teachers and all our students learn. Thankfully, it's over now! In order to celebrate, I decide to go to the office with my change and treat myself to a soda and a candy bar from the vending machines. Unfortunately, my principal, Joe Simmons, comes into the teachers' lounge and asks me to meet him in his office. I roll my eyes up to the sky thinking, "I wonder which one of my students has gotten into trouble this time?"

When I enter Joe's office, I once again admire how he's decorated it. He has children's books in three cherry wood bookshelves behind his desk, along with children's art and inspirational sayings hanging on each wall. He also has a very cozy area in the corner of his office with two comfy leather chairs, a beautiful rug on the floor, and a lamp providing soothing light on an end table. His office is painted in a calming buttercup yellow. When I asked him about his office décor at my interview, he stated he did it for the children. "I usually see children and family members who are in distress. When they come into my office, I want them to feel comfortable. Also, I want to show them the importance of reading children's books as well as inspire them with words." I was so impressed with his response, that even though it was my first interview, when I was offered the job, I quickly accepted. I have not been disappointed with that decision.

"Hello, Susan," Joe says in a friendly manner. "Please have a seat." I sit in one of the leather chairs. After small talk about how my year is coming along, Joe asks, "So, what do you know about Will Matthews?" I think about it for a minute, and reply, "He's a great kid. He cares about his peers. Is hard working. And very, very creative." I look over at Joe wondering why he is asking about Will. "Is there a problem with Will, Joe?" I ask. Joe is in deep thought. "Oh no, Susan. Will just came into the office and asked to speak to me. But once he got in here, he froze up. He wouldn't talk about anything, so I'm not sure what to make of the situation." Surprised, I say, "Will? I just can't imagine why he would want to come and talk with you. Was he acting oddly? Did he look scared?"

Joe shakes his head and says, "Oh no. The message he left with Lucille was that he had to meet with me today because he had something important to tell me. But then he gets in here and clams up. So, I just wanted to know if you have heard or seen anything." I shake my head and reply, "No. Have you tried contacting his parents? They are wonderful people. I just can't imagine that they would have done something to him." I shake my head in disbelief. Sensing my uneasiness, Joe says, "Now Susan, we don't have enough information to panic yet. Let me look into this situation a little more and

I'll get back with you as soon as I can." I get up to leave when he continues, "Now, if you hear or see anything, please let me know ASAP." I shake my head and let him know that I sure will.

As I head back to my class, I am obviously bothered by this situation. Will has never expressed there were problems at home. 'Oh my goodness!' I think to myself. "Did I miss a bruise or something on him today?" Just as I was about to head back to the office, I hear someone say, "Ms. Gomez, can I talk with you?" I look up and see Will standing in front of our locked classroom door. "Will," I say relieved. "How can I help you?" Will looks around, leans in, and says, "Can I talk with you in private?" I shake my head and without saying anything, I unlock the door and we walk into the classroom.

We both sit at the first table and Will puts his backpack on the floor. Waiting impatiently, I ask, "Will, what's bothering you?" Will looks at me with pleading eyes and whispers, "Can you keep a secret?" I look at Will with concern. I then say, "Honey, I can't make that promise to you. If someone or you are getting hurt, I have to get help." I shake my head and reach across the table to touch Will's hand. "Do you understand that?" Will, who looks up quickly and then back down, replies, "But I don't want someone to get in trouble." I continue looking at Will and say, "I don't want anyone to get hurt or worse. Honey, you have to tell me what's going on." Will, still looking down, finally replies. "Okay. Um, one of my friends in Mrs. Smitherman's class was in the restroom today and he told me that his grandfather beat him up with his cane." Will finally looks up and says, "Mrs. Gomez, he had bruises and cuts all over his back. He was bleeding. He showed me and everything." Just as soon as he finished, Will jump up and in a panicked voice says, "But please, Mrs. Gomez, he begged me not to tell. So please don't tell."

Discussion Questions

1. What is your immediate reply to Will?
2. How do you bring your principal into this conversation when Will wants you to keep this a secret?
3. What are the legal steps that will be taken in your district with a situation such as this?
4. Will may be very upset this evening. What would you say to his parents to prepare them for possible difficulties?
5. If children are pulled from the homes they are living in, what are the next steps that will be taken if they are then placed in the system (i.e., if they are subsequently labeled as a child in need of service)?

Advice from Veteran Teachers on . . . Child Abuse

- Once again, teachers are mandated to report any known or suspected incidents of child abuse. Teachers cannot cast a blind eye or hide behind ignorance. The law is very clear and precise.
- Teachers can be held personally liable for not reporting cases of child abuse. The school administrator and the Board of Education may also be held responsible if teachers are not properly trained to report child abuse.
- Promises of confidentiality do not exempt a teacher from reporting incidence of suspected child abuse.

- Teachers should report, not investigate, matters of suspected child abuse. Leave the responsibility of investigation to the professionals.
- Incidents of child abuse should be reported whether the suspected abuse is inflicted by an adult or by a sibling.
- While a child abuse investigation is being conducted the teacher should not discuss the matter with the parents at the parent conference. Instead, the parent conference should focus on the academic progress and social development of the child.
- If a child is removed from the home and placed in a safe house, foster home, or with another relative, it is highly likely that he or she may be removed from your school and class. If your students want to know more information about that child's whereabouts, simply let them know that they've moved.
- If the child is still allowed to attend your school and be in your class, then we suggest that you communicate with your school's psychological expert on how to best handle this delicate situation. You'll need to know what signs and signals you should be on the lookout for just in case the child is having a hard time dealing with the changes to his or her home life and to get information on what you can reasonably expect academically and socially from a child who's been through a very difficult situation. Veteran teachers and principals are also excellent resources in cases like this.

Sexual Abuse

Don't Eat the Hotdogs!

"This is so nice," Melanie Miller says. Melanie is our room mother and is such a creative and sweet person. Our parties all year have been great. If her daughter Stephanie says that she wants her friends to have a piñata, Melanie will make a piñata. As I look around the picnic area at our local park, I am amazed at how organized she is. All of the parent volunteers know exactly what they are supposed to do, and the kids are enjoying playing games, singing songs, and finding things on their scavenger hunt. All I had to do was show up and get the kids there safely. I am so spoiled.

Melanie says, "Ms. Chan, I think we'll get the hotdogs, hamburgers, and veggie burgers ready for the kids." I am amazed once again. "You even thought of veggie burgers?" I ask. Melanie smiles at me and says, "Stephanie told me that Jamal and Katie are vegetarians. So she insisted that I have food they could eat too." I nod my head, then go over to my first graders in the play area. They are having such a good time. "Ms. Chan," I hear Corrine say, "Come play with us, please." I walk over to the swings and sit on one. Most of my students laugh as I begin to pump my legs. "Wow," Samantha says, "You sure can go high." I chuckle and continue to swing for several more seconds. When I get off the swing, I hear Marcus on top of the slide shouting, "Ms. Chan, come over here and slide down the slide." Not one to disappoint, I go over to the slide and climb up the ladder. When I get to the top, I see all of my students looking up at me. I then slide down to the laughter of my students. When I get to the bottom of the slide, Maddie's mother, Selina, is there shaking her head. "You know you are tiny to be able to climb up that ladder and slide down that slide like that." Maribel's mother, Judith chimes in, "I could get up there and slide down. But I'm sure I'd have to put Icy Hot all over my body tonight." We all laugh. Just then, more of my students are shouting and asking me to join them on the equipment they're playing on. I wave my hands in the air and say, "Ms. Chan can't. I'm tired!" But I don't go too far away from them. I am still the teacher, regardless of how many parents are there. So I need to monitor to make sure they are all safe.

As I walk around the perimeter of the playground area, Jesus comes up to me and asks, "Ms. Chan. When is it gonna be time to eat? I'm starvin'." I smile at Jesus. "I know. I'm hungry too, Jesus." I look over at the area where the picnic tables are located and say, "It probably won't be long." Omar, who is Jesus' best friend, says while licking his lips, "It smells so good. I want to eat right now." I smile at both boys. "You won't have to wait much longer. Why don't you go and play a little more while they get everything together." Both boys rub their bellies and walk off in the direction of the jungle gym.

Several minutes later, Melanie comes to my side and says, "Everything is ready. You may call the kids over whenever you like." I take out my whistle and blow it hard. All of my students stop what they are doing and put their hands on their shoulders and look my way. I shout, "Thank you, boys and girls. You may take your signals off." I look around as they put their hands by their sides and wait for further instructions. "Okay," I say, "It's lunchtime. Please walk carefully and safely over to the picnic tables and form one line." With that, my students begin to walk, albeit a bit faster than a normal walking pace, to the picnic tables.

Melanie has outdone herself. On each picnic table, she has cute tablecloths, chips, and juice boxes. Martin, Selina, and Judith then bring over the platters of hotdogs, hamburgers, and veggie burgers to the main table. When Jesus and Omar reach for hotdogs, out of nowhere, I hear Tasha gasp and then begin screaming, "Don't put those in your mouth! They can hurt you." I try to get hold of Tasha to calm her down, but she is now crying uncontrollably. "Don't let them eat those, Ms. Chan. They taste nasty and squirt yucky stuff." I look out at my students and they look just as confused as the parent volunteers.

Discussion Questions

1. How do you handle this situation immediately and long term?
2. Who should you notify first? Principal? Parents? Counselor? Social worker?
3. What do you do to console Tasha?
4. In the case above, this actually happened to a preschool teacher with a preschooler. However, there could be other reasons why Tasha may not want her peers to eat the hot dogs. What do you think could be other reasons that Tasha doesn't want her peers to eat the hot dogs?
5. What are some of the signs of children who are being molested that we should look for in our classrooms?

Mommy's Little Boy

My classroom looks pretty good. I came to school four days last week and early this morning to get ready for the first day of school. All of my copies are made, my bulletin boards are prepped, the room is clean, and I have my attendance folder. Now, for a cup of tea to calm my nerves and I'll be set. "Hey," Marilyn, another third-grade teacher comes in. "Are you ready for the first day?" I smile at Marilyn. "As ready as I'm gonna get." As Marilyn looks around my classroom she comments, "It really does look good in here." She glances at the colorful bulletin board in the center of the classroom with just butcher paper on it. "Now," she begins, "What are you going to do with that board?" I say, "That one is for our autobiographies and photos. I brought in my digital camera and will take photos of all of the kids. Then, we'll begin writing autobiographies so that we can get to know one another and so that I can assess their writing skills." Marilyn looks back at my blank, yet colorful bulletin board and says, "I really like that idea you have about the autobiographies and the photos. Do you mind if I steal it?" I smile back at Marilyn, "Just like I learned in student teaching. It's not stealing. It's sharing." Marilyn smiles at me and says, "Thanks for sharing." With that, she leaves my room.

In order to busy myself, I begin to straighten up my already straight desk. My tea is cold, but I don't have time to go to the office to microwave it. Just then, the front door opens up and a man walks in toward me with his arm extended. I get up and meet him in the middle of the room. "Are you Ms. Patel?" he asks. I nod my head. He says, "It's nice to meet you." We shake hands. "I'm Brian White, and you have my son in your class this year." I say, "Oh yes. I saw his name on my list." Mr. White looks at me and says, "I'm sorry for staring, but you look so young. Are you sure you're the teacher and not a student?" I laugh, nod my head, and say, "I'm sure." I point to the wall behind my desk where I've hung my degree and my teaching certificate. Mr. White glances at them with a smile.

"So, Mr. White, how may I help you?" I ask as I begin walking back to my desk. I have a chair next to my desk for conversations just like this with parents or even students. Mr. White takes a seat and says, "I apologize for not coming to see you sooner, but things have been so crazy for me with work and with all that has gone on with Brian this summer. He touches a tissue to his nose and begins to tell his story.

"I found out early this summer that Brian was being molested by his mother. I had no idea." Mr. White continues, "We were never married and broke up soon after Brian was born. We had joint custody of Brian, so his mother would get him during the week and I would get him on the weekends and most holidays." Mr. White sniffs and wipes his nose with the tissue again. Mr. White leans closer to me and says, "Apparently, it first started out with kisses and fondling. But at the end, they were engaging in oral sex." My eyes are as wide as saucers. "I could beat myself up because I did notice his grades had begun to go down, he was acting out, losing weight, and it was like pulling teeth getting him to go his mother's after our weekends. But I never thought anything like this could be going on." Shaking his head, Mr. White continues, "Well, after Brian finally told me what was going on, I notified the police and they arrested his mother." His voice then begins to shake and he says, "She hung herself in jail and Brian is now blaming himself for killing his mom. I tell him that he isn't to blame, but he is having a really hard time with this." "Brrriiiinnnggg!" the bell chiming interrupts our conversation. Mr. White looks at his watch and says, "I'm going to be late for work." He gets up and says quickly, "We will need to work together to help him get through this." Still in shock, I nod my head in agreement.

We both get up and walk to the front door. I open the door to find my students lining up. Mr. White looks over at me and says, "That's Brian right there." I look out and see a skinny boy who looks petrified. Mr. White hugs Brian and leans down and whispers something to him. Brian closes his eyes and then opens them and looks into his Dad's eyes. "I'll be okay, Dad," Brian says to his father. With that, Mr. White leaves me with my students.

Discussion Questions

1. What are some ways that you and Mr. White can work together to help Brian?
2. What sort of activities can you do in class and for homework to help Brian process what has happened to him?
3. What is your legal and ethical responsibility regarding a situation such as this?
4. What are your immediate and long-term concerns with a student such as Brian, who has been molested and is also dealing with the death of a parent who has committed suicide?
5. What support services are available to students such as Brian who have experienced incest and the death of a loved one?

My Girlfriend, Cathy

"Okay, let's get ready for recess." I say to my fifth graders. I hear many of them say, "Yes" under their breaths. Unfortunately, I have yard duty today. I grab my cell phone, whistle, and clipboard and stand in the front of the line. Turning to my students, I say, "BJ, please make sure you close the door behind you." One of the most popular kids in the class, BJ flashes his smile and says, "No problem, Mrs. Anderson. I'll take care of it for you." I laugh and begin to take my students to the playground.

BJ is an extremely charming young man and seems a bit worldlier than his peers. He always sports the latest clothes, shoes, hairstyle, and technological gadgets. The kids in the school congregate around him like flies to honey. I remember when Leslie, his fourth-grade teacher, told me he was going to be in my class. "Now watch out for him," she said. "He thinks he can talk and charm his way out of and into anything. Although he is smart as a whip, he can be lazy at times. So watch out when he flashes that smile of his and compliments you on everything. He wants something." At first I had a hard time believing this, but I , too, have found it to be true. But so far, I haven't had any problems with him.

As I walk around the playground making sure the kids are safe, Nabila, a student in my class who has been skipped two grade levels so is two years younger than her peers, rushes to me. Unfortunately, she is a tattletale. "Mrs. Anderson," Nabila says, "BJ is talking dirty to the kids over there." I'm not really sure how to handle this situation. Do I deal with the fact that she is tattling (something her parents really want me to help them curtail) or with what she is telling me? I decide to deal with the latter. "Nabila," I ask, "What did BJ say?" Nabila says, "He is talking about kissing a girl." I look up and gaze at BJ and the crowd around him. They are listening intently to him and laughing. I say, "Are you sure that you heard him say that he is kissing a girl?" Nabila nods and continues, "Yes. He said that he was kissing his girlfriend and that her name is Cathy. She lives next door to him and she likes to wear tight shirts and low-rider jeans." Just then, the bell rings. I look at Nabila and say, "Thanks, Nabila. I'll make sure that I look into this."

Right before lunch, Mrs. Rogers, our school secretary, calls and says that BJ needs to come to the front office because he has a dentist appointment. I make a mental note to talk with BJ tomorrow about what Nabila told me during recess. BJ packs up his belongings and heads to the office.

At the end of school, I see BJ in the front of the school where the kindergarteners are picked up. "BJ," I say, "I thought that you had a dentist appointment?" BJ flashes that famous smile and says, "Yeah, but we had to come back to school and get my kid brother." I look down and see a little one who looks just like BJ. "Oh," I say, "I almost forgot about Jeremy." Just then, BJ and Jeremy's mother comes by their side with a female companion. "Hi, Mrs. Anderson," Linda Washington, BJ's mother, says. "How is BJ doing in class?" BJ looks like he wants to crawl into a hole. I say, "He's doing fine." I look over at BJ and say, "Did you get your homework before you left?" BJ smiles and says, "Why, of course."

After a few seconds and more small talk, Linda says, "Oh my goodness," gently tapping her forehead. "Please forgive my manners, Mrs. Anderson." She turns to the lady next to her and says, "I would like you to meet our new neighbor, Cathy. Cathy, this is BJ's teacher." Cathy shakes my hand. "It's nice to meet you. I am a phys. ed.

teacher at Logan High School." she says. She continues, "We're off today because it's midterms, so that's why I'm dressed so casually." I nod my head and say, "It's nice to meet you too." To my surprise, Cathy looks like she is well into her twenties, if not thirties.

Discussion Questions

1. What is your immediate reaction to this situation?
2. What school personnel do you need to immediately involve in this situation?
3. With more media attention on this issue, what are the short-term and long-term effects of boys being intimately involved with older women such as teachers?
4. What do you do with a student like Nabila who is gifted, yet very young in relation to her peers?
5. What kind of boundaries do you need to set for students who appear to use charm to get out of doing work?

Advice from Veteran Teachers on . . . Sexual Abuse

- Suspected sexual abuse of a minor is a form of child abuse and must be reported to the appropriate authority.
- Brian showed a lot of courage in reporting his mother for abusing him. He will need a lot of counseling and nurturing for years to come. He may exhibit character traits that are negative toward females, including female teachers. This issue might be discussed at a SST meeting with the school psychologist present.
- It is a huge leap to suggest that Tasha's concerns about the hotdogs are sexually based. Her concerns may be derived from her parents warning about the meat contents of hotdogs. I would suggest that the teacher remove Tasha from the area and try to calm her down so that she can determine the nature of Tasha's concerns. If the conversation reveals a sexually abusive incident, the matter should be reported to the appropriate authority. If it does not reveal anything of a sexual nature, a call to the parent to report the child's response would be appropriate.
- In BJ's case, as soon as we could, we would let our principal know the whole situation—from what Nabila informed us about on the playground to your meeting a woman by the same name (Cathy) who appears to be much older than BJ. We would hope that our principal would investigate this situation, which means that he or she would contact BJ and his mother to get more information. BJ could be making this all up and just telling stories to impress his friends. However, if during that conversation it is revealed that there is a relationship between BJ and Cathy, that does constitute sexual abuse and the appropriate authorities would need to be contacted immediately.

Violence

Child's Play

"Good morning, A.M. Kindergarten," I say to my students sitting on the rug. "Good morning, Mr. Frazier," they say back to me. So many people are shocked that a 6′4″ man is teaching kindergarten, but it's such an important time in children's lives; I feel compelled to teach this grade "Did everyone put their homework in the new homework bin?" I ask. Most of their little hands go up. "For those of you who didn't, please go to your cubbies and place your homework in the homework bin." Several of my students who forgot get up and put their folders in the bin. It takes some time for them to get used to new routines.

"Hi, Mr. Frazier," Bianca says coming into the classroom late. "Here's my tardy slip." "Lately, Bianca has been tardy more often," I think to myself. Just as I am about to close the door, Bianca's mother comes into the room and hands her daughter a sheet of paper. "Here sweetie," she says, "You forgot your homework." Bianca quickly takes her homework, goes to her cubby, and then remembers the new routine. She quietly places her homework in the homework bin and joins the rest of class on the rug. I turn around and say, "Mrs. Johnson, I would like to talk with you about . . ." my voice trails off as I notice she has a black eye and her lips are swollen. She quickly puts on her glasses and says, "I know she's been coming to school late, Mr. Frazier. My husband has a new job so we're trying to work out the kinks." She waves to Bianca and leaves the room.

"Mr. Frazier," Jimmy shouts, "Are we going to do calendar?" I turn back to my students and get out my pointer for calendar. After calendar, we spend the next thirty-five minutes doing patterning with unifix cubes. Jimmy, my official timekeeper, looks up and says, "Mr. Frazier, it's time for recess." I look at Jimmy and then my watch. "All right class," I say, "Recess time. Please put your unifix cubes away in the math bins." I give them several minutes to clean up from their patterning activities. Now that they are all sitting on the rug I say, "If you have on pink or purple today, please tiptoe to the cubbies and put on your snowsuits, mittens, and hats, and go to the door." After waiting a few seconds, I announce, "If you have on red or white, please tiptoe to the cubbies and do the same." I continue this until all the boys and girls are lined up and ready for recess. I grab my whistle and take my class to the playground.

After recess, it is time for centers. "Class," I say to them before we walk into the classroom. "I want you to find a spot on the rug and listen to the story that I have on tape. Pay close attention to what the boy in the story is trying to do. Any questions?" All of the kids shake "no." Once the kids get into the classroom and settle down, I hit the play button on the tape recorder and begin to set up for center time. Ms. Robertson, a parent who's the president of the Parent-Teacher Association, helps me with center time. She loves to work with the kids on their language development in the home center.

"Hello," Ms. Robertson says. "What are we working on today?" I say, "I would love for you to have conversations with them about cooking. I really want them to think about the different types of utensils they'll need to make dinner, the ingredients they'll use in whatever they are trying to make, how to make it, safety issues, and the utensils they'll need to clean up." Nodding her head, Ms. Robertson says, "You know, when my other kids were in kindergarten, they didn't really work on vocabulary and language development like you do in play center. They just played." I look at her and say, "I think they're both important. So, why not do both at the same time?"

Once the tape has ended, I ask the kids questions about the story. Then, I go to the pocket chart and begin to explain the different centers. "Okay, table one will go to the writing center. You get to write letters to someone special. Table two, you will go to the listening center. You have a very funny book over there. Kenneth, you are in charge of the tape recorder and Melissa, you are in charge of passing out all the books. Table three will go with me to the guided reading center. We are going to begin reading a new book today. And table four will go with Ms. Robertson to the play center. You are going to pretend that you are making a dinner for your family. Remember, you have to clean up the kitchen and dining room once you finish dinner. Are there any questions?" They all nod "no." "You may tiptoe to your center," I say, moving to the guided reading table.

The kids are active in their centers. I learn to place myself in a spot where I can always see all my students. After scanning the room, I hit my bell and say, "I just want you all to know I am very proud of you. You are doing such a fantastic job. Keep up the great work." It's amazing how well they respond to praise. After fifty minutes, it is time for the kids to clean up and get ready to go home. I hit my bell to let them know it is time to clean up, and I walk around the room to make sure that everyone is on task and not getting into trouble.

"Mr. Frazier," Ms. Robertson says as we walk to play center, "I think there is something you need to see." She whispers, "Bianca has been playing with these dolls the whole time, but in my opinion some of the stuff she's talking about with the dolls is inappropriate." I thank Ms. Robertson and go to see for myself. "What did I tell you?" I hear Bianca say, holding up a girl and a boy doll. "You were supposed to have dinner ready before I got home. You good for nuffin." Bianca smacks the doll on her plastic face and pulls her hair. She turns the doll over and hits the doll on her back and bottom. "When I say I want dinner on the table, I mean it. Do you understand me?" Bianca turns the doll to face her and says, "Yes, I do. I promise. I won't have dinner late again. Don't hit me. Please." She holds up the other doll and says, "You deserve this, you little witch. You make me sick." She then hits the doll again.

"Bianca," I say, not really knowing what to say, "It's time to clean up." Bianca looks startled and says, "Okay, Mr. Frazier. I sure love play center." She neatly puts away the dolls, helps her classmates finish cleaning up the classroom, and sits on the rug to be excused. Ms. Robertson asks me, "Would you like me to go to the office to talk with Mrs. Shelton about this?" I quickly say, "Oh, no. I'll take care of it." She nods in agreement and goes outside to wait until her son, Micah, is excused.

When the bell rings, I walk the children out. I see Ms. Robertson talking with several parents. "Oh goodness," I think to myself, "I hope she's not talking about the situation in play center." I can't dwell on that right now because I have twenty-four kindergarteners to get on the bus or to join parents or siblings.

Releasing my students can be a madhouse. Luckily, I am tall enough to see over most folks' heads. I can see if my bus riders have gotten on the correct bus, those being picked up by their parents are in the line, and those waiting for older siblings are sitting on the bench. After the madhouse clears up, it's only Bianca and me waiting for her mother to come and pick her up. Just then, I see Bianca's mother trot up with her infant daughter on her hip; she is wearing dark glasses and a wide-brim hat.

Bianca jumps off the bench and runs right into her mother. Mrs. Johnson keeps walking toward me and says, "Oh, Mr. Frazier. I want to bring something for the party tomorrow. What should I bring?" "The list is in the classroom," I say. "If you'll follow me into the room, I'll check." When we get to the class, I notice that she's taken off her glasses to read the list along with me. "Well," I say, "We don't have anyone down for sodas yet. Would that be too much of a bother?" "Oh no. That's fine." she says. Just then, Mr. Johnson comes barging into the classroom. "What is taking so long?" he says with an angry expression on his face. Mrs. Johnson quickly puts back on her glasses and says, "Oh honey, they're having a party tomorrow and I just wanted to know what to bring." Looking around the classroom, he says, "Oh, hi Mr. Frazier. Sorry about that, but I'm going to be late for work if we don't hurry." I look at him and say, "I understand." As they turn to leave, Bianca waves goodbye to me and says, "Goodbye, Mr. Frazier. I can't wait for the party."

The next day, Bianca is absent from school.

Discussion Questions:

1. What do you say to Bianca about what you observed in home center?
2. What are your legal or ethical responsibilities regarding this situation?
3. Should you be concerned about Bianca's absence from school the next day?
4. What are the pros and cons of discussing this situation with your school administrator?
5. What are the pros and cons of discussing this situation further with Ms. Robertson?

In the Neighborhood

Hitting my bell signals my first graders to give me their undivided attention. "Good job, boys and girls. Now, I'm going to remind you because we have some new students," I say looking directly at the two new students. "I am going to put the CD on, and when *Beary-Beary* starts laughing at the end, this room should be clean with you all sitting on your spots on the rug. You may begin." I turn on *Beary-Beary's Good Time,* a three-minute song, and monitor the kids as they clean to get the classroom . With his robust laugh, *Beary-Beary* signals to my students they've had enough time to get the room in order. "Um," I say rubbing my chin, "Good job, boys and girls," as I walk around the classroom inspecting their work. "Give yourself a pat on your left shoulder," and they all give themselves a pat on their left shoulder. "Now, give yourself a kiss on your right hand," and they all give themselves a kiss on their right hand. "Now, give yourself a round of applause." And in our usual first-grade style, they all begin clapping in big circles.

"Now, boys and girls," I begin, "we have a couple of minutes before recess." I look over to the board and see that it is Abigail's day for show and tell. The kids love when Abigail brings things in for show and tell because they are usually "shiny" as she describes them. One time she brought her father's $20,000 Rolex watch, another time she brought her mother's $50,000 diamond brooch, once her grandmother's limited-edition canary yellow Tiffany diamond ring worth $100,000, and finally, she brought her brother's baseball autographed by Babe Ruth. On each of these occasions, her nanny contacted the school to inform us about how valuable the items were and to request I put them in a safe place until she could come to the school to safely bring them back home. After the watch, brooch, and ring, Abigail promised to show someone at home her show and tell surprise before bringing it to school. However, she was able to get her brother's autographed baseball to class without anyone at home knowing about it.

"Abigail," I begin, "It's your turn for show and tell. Did you bring something?" "Yes I did, Mrs. Gomez. Can I go get it?" Abigail asks. I look at her and say, "*Can* you?" I correct her. She laughs and says, "I mean, *may* I go to my cubby and get it?" I tell her that she surely may. Abigail walks over to her cubby and retrieves her pink backpack. In it is a small box and I get concerned. "Oh goodness. What priceless jewel did this little one bring today?" But then, she pulls out what appear to be two pieces of brass-colored crumpled metal. "Abigail," I say, "what are those?" Looking at her hands, she says, "I just found them this morning on my way to school and brought them to show and tell. They're not shiny, but they are pretty for fingernails." She places one of the metal objects on her right index finger and the other on her middle finger. She raises her hand up to admire her new fingernails. Several of my students say, "Oohh, that's pretty." Rachel raises her hand and says, "Can I try on your new fingernails, Abigail?" Before Abigail has a chance to answer, I say, "Abigail, may I please see those?"

Without questioning, Abigail takes them off her fingers and hands them to me. Shocked, I immediately think that I know what they are. Spent shell casings! "Abigail," I say, "Where did you find these?" Playing with a long curl on her forehead, she says, "In a hiding place in the street. Where the water goes?" I could be concerned that a first grader is walking in the street, apparently by herself and looking in the storm drain, but I decide to focus my attention on the shell casings. "Abigail, have you shown these to anyone?" Shaking her head, she says, "No, I just brought my fingernails to show and tell."

Just then, Myra stands up and says, "Those aren't fingernails. Those are bullets." Several of my students' eyes widen, and I'm not sure if it's because of what Myra said or because she said it without raising her hand and being called on. "Those aren't bullets, Myra," says Alicia, "Those are fingernails. Abigail says so." Myra is still not convinced. "Those aren't fingernails, Alicia," Myra continues. "My grandfather has a gun and some rifles 'cause he likes to hunt for deer and squirrels and stuff. And he has those at home. But I can't mess with them until I'm older and with him right by my side cause you can get hurt and die and stuff. Ain't that right, Mrs. Gomez?" I feel like I am totally caught off guard by this whole situation. So, all I can muster is, "Yes, you can get hurt or killed with guns and rifles. We shouldn't play with them." Myra then jumps in, "And unless I'm hunting with my grandfather, right?" Once again, I feel caught off guard. "Yes, Myra," is all I can say.

Abigail interrupts my thoughts. "You know, Mrs. Gomez," she begins, still playing with that curl, "Our next door neighbor shot his wife and killed hisself yesterday.

Maybe they were playing with guns and got hurt and dieded." I am so alarmed by this news that I do not correct her grammar. I had heard about a murder-suicide shooting on the west side of town but did not know that it was Abigail's neighbors. "Abigail, you know about that?" Still twisting with her hair, Abigail says, "Yeah, my daddy told me because I heard the pops when I was outside playing on the trampoline. I had to talk with the polices and everything." Several students look shocked. "You had to talk with the polices?" Margaret asks with wide eyes. Abigail continues, "Yeah, cause they wanted to know if I saw anything. But I didn't. I just heard firecrackers," I look at Abigail with concern. "How are you doing with all of this, Abigail?" I say. She says, "Fine. My daddy says that I don't have to worry cause bad stuff like that only happens in the ghetto."

Once again, I can't believe my ears. I think to myself, "If it only happens in the ghetto, then how did it happen in your neighborhood?" Luckily, I realize that it is time for recess. Thank goodness. I turn to Abigail and say, "I would love to show your fingernails to a few people. Is that okay?" Abigail nods her head up and down and says, "No problem, Mrs. Gomez," sounding like *Beary-Beary*. Most of the kids laugh at this. "But wait, Mrs. Gomez," Felix interrupts, "We didn't get to ask Abigail three questions." I look at Felix and say, "Don't worry about it. We'll do them later." I am not sure if I will keep that promise. Clutching the shell casings, I begin to excuse the kids for recess.

Discussion Questions

1. What are your next steps?
2. What concerns would you have if you were Abigail's teacher?
3. What are the pros and cons of contacting Abigail's parents?
4. In some parts of the country, children are taught how to handle a gun appropriately, learn how to hunt with rifles, and live in homes with guns, rifles, and ammunition. What is your opinion of children hunting with a responsible family member or other adult?
5. What activities/lessons can you do with your students to promote gun safety and being safe in general?

Three Strikes—You're Out!

"5, 4, 3, 2, 1 . . . all eyes on me," I say to my fifth-grade class of sixteen girls and fourteen boys. I look around and realize I have almost everyone's attention and shoot *that* look over to the two who are not focusing on me. I then say, "It's time for P. E." The kids begin to clap and move their chairs back and shove their journals in their desk. "5, 4 . . . " I begin again . . . and then I hear the familiar, "Sshhuusshh! We won't get to go out if you keep talking," Shanice says, with her everpresent authority. Should I remind her *again* that she, too, is making noise when she does that? Oh, forget it—she gets the job done. "Before we go out," I continue, "I want you to dog-ear three of your favorite journal entries for these past two weeks." After a few minutes, I say, "Now, I want the table leaders to collect the journals and place them on my desk." I then call each table to line up for P.E.

My fifth graders have been playing baseball against Sam Hernandez's class all year long. It's a fierce competition because his students are in sixth grade and they consider my students the babies. But with Danny on our team, pitching strike after strike, there's no way we can lose. "I just can't believe how good Danny is," Sam said to me behind the plate. "I know," I answer. "His mom and dad are so proud of him. They've even signed him up for the team at the Y." Sam looks over and says, "How's his brother, Matt, doing? I had him several years ago in the sixth grade. Real good baseball player too." I think for a minute before I reply. Danny has talked about his brother in his journal, and from what I gather, his brother is not doing well in school or at home. "Mrs. P," Danny wrote, "I think that my brother is hanging out with some bad kids. I mean my brother isn't bad. But some of his friends are."

"Rose," Sam says interrupting my thoughts, "Have you heard a word I said?" Shaking my head, I say, "I'm sorry. I guess his brother is doing okay. You know, just regular teenager stuff, I guess."

"Strike three! You're out! Mrs. Patrickson's class wins the game!" hollers our custodian, Mr. Monroe. My students run up to me screaming and jumping up and down. I shake Sam's hand and say, "We'll see you bright and early tomorrow for the real game." Sam gives me a smile, lines his students up, and takes them back to their class. Once we are back in our room, I make sure the kids write their homework assignments in their planners, clean up the space around them, and put their chairs on their desks. "5, 4, 3, 2, 1," I say over the kids' chatter. When I have everyone's attention, I say, "Okay, folks, we have our big game tomorrow. Make sure you get a good night's sleep, eat a good breakfast, and get to school on time." Then, the bell rings ending another busy school day.

I clear my messy desk so that I have space to read the journals. On the top of the pile is Danny's journal. Usually, although he has grammatical errors and misspelled words, his journal entries are riveting. I get out my signature green pen and begin to read. "Date: March 15th: Dear Mrs. P, I am really getting scared about my brother. I don't think he's doing drugs or is gonna shoot nobody. He's tripping at home. Well, he ain't really tripping, but he keeps bringing home these fools my Pops hates. Pops thinks that they in a gang or something like that cuz they wear bandanas and got tattoos and stuff. They don't even go to no school, Pops says. I don't know what to do. They are argueing all the time and stuff and its makeing all of us mad."

His next selection reads, "Date: March 22nd: Dear Mrs. P, my brother was in the room last night and he looked all sad and stuff. When I asked him why he was looking all scared and stuff, he told me to shut up. We was really supposed to be sleeping cuz it was like 2 in the morning I think. Later on he said to me that they want to jump him in the gang. I know that Pops is gonna kill me is all he keep saying. I said why would they want you? You a nerd. He says because he's smart. In the morning, he got me in a corner and told me I better not tell Pops. I promised. But now I'm scared too.'

I sit there afraid to even read the third entry. But I just have to. "Date April 1st: Dear Mrs. P, my brother came home yesterday with a black eye. At first he said he tripped and stuff, but I knew that he was lying. When Pops came home he went off. He wanted to call the cops and stuff. So did Moms. They did call the cops, but nothing really happened with that. They wrote stuff down and stuff."

Closing his journal, I begin thinking, "What should I do?' 'Do I *have* to do any-thing?" I believe that the counselors are gone for the day and Mrs. Roth, our principal, left for a meeting, so I can't talk to them. Then, a voice booms over the PA system and interrupts my thoughts. "Mrs. Patrickson," says Mrs. Logan, our school secretary, "You have a phone call." "Thank you," I say to her. Before leaving the room, I put a Post-it note on Danny's journal reminding me to talk with someone about the situation. "But who?" I say to myself. Then I shrug my shoulders and say, "Oh, I will just handle this tomorrow."

Bright and early the next day, the kids are so excited about the baseball game. "My dad took off work, Mrs. P., so that he could videotape the game," Shanice says proudly. "My grandmother is here too," says Byron. "5, 4, 3, 2, 1 . . . all eyes on me," I say to my fifth graders. "I need to take roll and do the lunch count before we go out." As I go through my roll, it becomes apparent that Danny is absent. "I knew Danny wasn't gonna come," Shanice says. "Ladies and gentlemen," I say, "We aren't going out for another half hour. Now, get out your journals and begin writing." I am so happy that we decided not to start the game right when school starts. That may give Danny enough time to come to school. Unfortunately, forty minutes later, there's still no Danny and the kids are extremely disappointed. "We don't have a pitcher!" "We're gonna lose for sure!" "I hate Danny!" The kids are trying to say these things under their breath so they don't get in trouble, but loud enough for other students to hear. "Ladies and gentlemen," I begin, "We are going to go out there and try our best. Now, get your . . ."

Just then, the kids begin to clap. "Danny's here!" some shout. Admittedly, I am happy, but disappointed with his tardiness. I have a high tardy rate this year and need to crack down on it. Ready to read him the riot act, I say in a stern voice, "Do you have a tardy slip from the office?" Danny looks up blankly and says, "No," in a low voice with his eyes fixed straight ahead. As I get closer to him and look into his eyes, I can tell that something is wrong. Terribly wrong. He is breathing heavily and now opening his mouth like he wants to speak. He then looks at me, and with wide eyes says, "I had to hide in the bushes because I thought I saw them this morning when I was coming to school." Not following him, I kneel down and ask, "Danny, what are you talking about?" He then says, "The gang I was telling you about. They jumped my brother in the alley behind our house." He takes a deep breath and continues, "They hit him with bats and chains and everything!" Still holding on to my shirt, Danny says, "He was all bloody, Mrs. P. All bloody." Now holding on to him I ask, "Danny, is he okay? Where are your parents?" Nodding his head, he says, "They're at the hospital with my brother." Danny then looks around the room at his stunned peers and then back at me. Tears begin to fall down his cheeks as he says, "I don't understand, Mrs. P. I don't understand!"

Discussion Questions

1. What is your immediate course of action with Danny, your students, and notifying the office?
2. What are some actions you could have taken after reading the initial journal entries?
3. Are the contents in student-generated journals confidential and protected under law?

4. Would you need to secure parental permission if the police want to examine the journal?
5. What are the pros and cons of playing the baseball game that day? Another day?

Advice from Veteran Teachers on . . . Violence

*   Teachers should remember that it is their responsibility to report, not investigate, these types of incidents. In fact, the involvement by a teacher could hinder the investigation by the qualified professional.
*   The psyche of an elementary student is very fragile. It is important that students who experience these types of violent acts should be given access to professional help, such as a school psychologist or counselor.
*   Teachers should seek guidance from professionals as to how to best create a safe and nurturing environment for these students so that they can have a successful academic year.
*   In order to protect the privacy of the student, teachers should be very careful not to talk about the specifics of these types of incidents with the other students in the classroom. However, teachers should talk to students about what to do when they see or experience things that make them uncomfortable.
*   It is important that adults take all reports of violence of any kind from students very seriously. While the above incidents do not constitute child abuse, the acts do create a very hostile living environment for the students and should be reported to the appropriate authority for a full investigation.

Religion

I Don't Pledge Allegiance

"It sure was hot out there," I say to my third-grade students as they settle down. Their red faces and sweaty hair tell me I am correct. "Mrs. Connors," Tatiana says, "I wonder if we could cook an egg on the ground." Some students stop what they are doing and look up at Tatiana. "I saw it on a cartoon," she continues. "I bet it will work." I say to my students, "Now that sounds like a science project to me. We may have to really think about that and conduct that science project as a class." Most of my students begin to cheer at this thought. While they are cooling off, it's time for independent reading. I give them twenty minutes every day at the beginning of school to take out their favorite reading material and read before we move to Language Arts. I really think this allows them to collect their thoughts, get ready for school, relax, and do something that most of them enjoy. Also, during this time, it gives me time to take roll, do the lunch count, collect the homework folders, read notes from parents, and all of the other stuff that goes with being a teacher.

During any reading time in our class, I let them read books, brochures, magazines, catalogs, newspapers, lyrics to songs, cookbooks, and anything else they choose to read as long as it is age appropriate. I have gone into quilting stores, gyms, malls, colleges and universities, airplanes, photographers' studios, clothing stores, automotive stores, and any place that has some type of written reading material and have asked the owner if I may take them for my students. I have found that even some of my reluctant readers are now exploring more. I think maybe it's because they have more options.

Several minutes later, the school's PA system blares into the classroom at its regular time. "Hello, Wilmington Wildcats," an unidentified student shouts into the microphone. Most of my students cover their ears. This happens every single day, yet they always act like it's new. The unidentified student continues, "This is Slick Steven from Mr. Malone's Magnificent fifth grade classroom." Slick Steven continues, "We have a few announcements today." We then hear him shuffling papers and asking questions while he attempts to cover the microphone. I chuckle and shake my head. I am now questioning how "slick" Slick Steven is. Just then he comes back on. "Okay, everyone. Don't let that slight faux pas fool you." He says, emphasizing *faux pas*. "For those of you who don't know, a faux pas is a mistake in French." He then chuckles and continues, "You see, Slick Steven is here even to help you with learning a new language." We can all hear him laugh and Mr. Simpson, our principal, say, "Hurry up, Steven." Clearing his throat, Steven says, "In the cafeteria you have a choice of a hot-dog or a ham and cheese pretzel. The salad bar is closed for the day." I hear some of my students grunt at that news. "Also, band practice is today. So please make sure that you go to the gym at 1:20 on the dot. According to Mr. Kietz, if you come sooner or later, you're going back to your room."

Then, as if he is reading over his notes, Slick Steven finally says, "That concludes the announcements for today. Please stand for the Pledge of Allegiance." With that, all of my students stand up and begin to recite the Pledge of Allegiance with Steven. When I look out, I see our new student, Terry, shaking his head back and forth and seated with his arms folded. When the pledge is over, Terry looks around and says out loud, "I don't have to say the pledge because I don't believe in a God. I can't believe you believe in a God you can't even see. You are all so stupid!" My students look up at me in utter disbelief.

Discussion Questions

1. What do you say to Terry regarding this outburst?
2. What are your personal feelings regarding the recitation of the Pledge of Allegiance?
3. How would you handle this situation with Terry or other students like Terry who refuse to say the Pledge of Allegiance?
4. How would you handle the situation about Terry's comment about not believing in a God and feeling that those who do are stupid?
5. How different do you think this situation would be handled in a public school, private school, charter school, or parochial school?

Reasonable Requests?

"This math is driving me nuts," I say to Juan, another first-grade teacher. "With all of the projects, worksheets, and homework, I would think that my students would be doing great," I continue. Unfortunately, right before recess, we had a mid-point quiz. When I saw Mrs. Flynn, one of our parent volunteers, grading the sheets, I was saddened. I mean, we work so hard to see such dismal results. Interrupting my thoughts, Juan steps in and says, "I know. My kids love the games and all. But shoot. The prep alone is killing me." Vanessa, the other first-grade teacher, catches up with us just in time to hear Juan's last comment. "Oh," Vanessa says, "You must be talking about math." She looks at me and asks, "How did your kids do?" I look at her and put my thumb down. "They worked so hard. I know they are going to be heartbroken." Vanessa, who has been teaching first grade for several years, nods in agreement. Just then, the bell rings, signaling the end of recess.

After several minutes, my students are back in their seats sipping water from water bottles on their desks, getting drinks from the faucet in the class, and munching on their midday snack. About an hour and a half before lunch, our principal allows students to eat nutritious snacks in the class. I believe that when Mr. Peters initiated this, he was thinking more in line with fruits and vegetables. But now I feel like I'm on the Junk Food Police Team, trying to rid my classroom of snack cakes, candies, cookies, and the like. Since we've been doing this for most of the year, my students pretty much have the hang of it. Since they are now settled in, I announce quietly, "You need to get out your journals and finish writing your poems."

While the kids are snacking and writing, I notice that Bridgett is in the back writing, but she does not have her usual snack of carrots and celery sticks. "Bridgett,"

I say quietly, "Please come here for a second." Bridgett is one of the sweetest kids in my class. When I first got Bridgett, I was admittedly scared because her parents told me that they were a very religious family. In their family, the children aren't allowed to watch television, listen to music, or celebrate mainstream holidays; they have to get their parents' permission when selecting reading materials, and are on a strict diet. Because of this, Bridgett usually reads a children's Bible in the class during independent reading time.

Once Bridgett gets to my desk, she asks, "Yes, Ms. Donerson." I look at her and ask, "Where's your snack, Bridgett?" With sad eyes, Bridgett says in a low whisper-like voice, "We are fasting this week. So I can't have my snack or lunch." This is actually a surprise to me. Not knowing what to say next, I ask, "Can you drink water?" Bridgett says, "Momma says that I can sip water only when I'm real thirsty. But I have to pray first." I look at Bridgett and continue, "You know what, I'm not going to eat my snack either to help you." Bridgett's little face lights up. Following that, she goes back to her seat.

After a great social studies lesson on community organizations, we get ready for lunch. I am so hungry. Thinking about that, I ask Bridgett, "Honey, would you like to go to someone else's class while the others are eating so that you don't have to see them eat?" She looks up at me and once again in a low whisper-like voice says, "Yes I would, ma'am." So, as I take my other students to the cafeteria, I take Bridgett over to Margo's class. She teaches fifth grade and we usually pair up in cases like this.

Just as I take a big bite of my big sandwich, Mrs. O'Leary, our school secretary, comes from the front of the office. "Roni," she says, "There's a problem in Margo's class that needs your attention." At first, I am a bit puzzled. Then I remember Bridgett. So I rush out of the lounge and head to room 34. When I get there, Margo is leaning over talking to Bridgett who is crying uncontrollably. Margo looks up at me and gives me that, "See, that's why I teach the older kids" look. I get on my knees and hug Bridgett. She begins to calm down and I pull away from her so I can see her face. "Bridgett, honey," I say, "What's the matter?" She looks up at me, rubbing her head and eyes, and says, "I am so hungry. My head hurts." She looks up and says, "I don't want to fast. I want to eat."

Discussion Questions
1. What is your legal responsibility with this situation?
2. What is your ethical responsibility with this situation?
3. What school personnel should you bring into this discussion/situation?
4. In order to better prepare yourself as a teacher, how can you encourage parents to notify you if their children are fasting or need time throughout the day to pray?
5. What would you say to Bridgett's parents when you get the chance?

Stop Staring

LaShayla, who is staring out of the window says, "I think the principal is coming." She turns around and shouts, "Who's in trouble?" I shush everyone to quiet them down. "Just because the principal comes to our class doesn't mean that someone is in trouble," I say to my students. Some of them look at me with sly smiles like they don't believe a word I've just said. Mr. Clark opens the door and says, "Hello, Mrs. Phelps, and all of the first graders." My students know the routine. "Hello, Mr. Clark," they say in unison. Then with bated breath, it is apparent that they are waiting to see who Mr. Clark is going to call into the hallway. Mr. Clark looks at me and says, "May I speak to you in the hallway for a second, Mrs. Phelps." The stunned look on my students' faces was priceless. Some even say, "Oooohhhh!" In order to get things back in order I turn to my class and say, "Now boys and girls. You know I'm not in trouble. So get back to reading and mind your own business." Some of the kids giggle while others still look at me suspiciously.

When we get right outside the door, Mr. Clark says, "Why would they think you've gotten in trouble?" I shake my head. "It's a long story. They think that anytime you or Mrs. Simms comes to a room, someone's in trouble." Mr. Clark shakes his head and begins to chuckle. "The little ones always amaze me." He then clears his throat and continues, "The reason I came down was to tell you I was able to get you a part-time paraprofessional. Her name is Farzana Akbar, and she is finishing up her bachelor's degree in liberal arts. She wants to be a teacher one day." Taking a breath, he continues, "She will be working with you in the mornings until lunch." I am shocked. I have been asking for some assistance in my class ever since my numbers shot up to thirty-four. I think this is out of compliance with the union. Finally things worked out. "When does she come? Is she married? Does she have kids?" I ask. Mr. Clark thinks about it for a second and says, "She'll be here first thing in the morning, not married, no kids." He then smiles at me and says, "So congratulations." With that, he walks off.

When I get back in the room, my students are sitting there with eyes the size of quarters. Obviously, my little speech did little to calm their notions about getting in trouble. I then announce, "Tomorrow, we are getting a teacher's assistant in the class. Her name is Miss Akbar. She wants to be a teacher one day like some of you want to be." Some of the kids cheer. I look around the room and see Josh's hand up. "Mrs. Phelps," he begins, "Why don't we ever get boy assistants?" I think about that for a second and say, "Once again, a great project to undertake. We may have to look closely at that one too." Josh smiles with pride.

When I get home for the evening, I work out, cook a grilled cheese sandwich, shower, grade a few papers, and crash on the couch. When my alarm goes off, I think I will faint. I am so tired! But then I think about Miss Akbar coming and I jump out of my bed excited. I was told she had already taken her literacy methods courses, so she would know about reading workshop, writing workshop, and the like. Those, in addition to math, are the key areas that are so difficult with thirty-four students.

When I get to my classroom, I notice a person in my room clothed in a black robe from head to toe. I look at my desk and see Mr. Clark hanging up the classroom phone. "Hello there, Mrs. Phelps." He looks over at the young lady and says, "Monica, please meet Farzana Akbar, your new assistant." I put my hand out to shake her hand, which is sheathed in a black glove. From the front, I can see her face and slivers of her hair. Other than that, everything else is covered. "Well," I begin, "I can see that you've had a chance to see the comic strips the kids have been working on," I say pointing to the wall that she was admiring when I first came in. "Oh yes," she says with a bright smile. "They are so cute." Mr. Clark, who was observing this whole exchange, touches my back and says, "I'll leave you two alone. I know you have planning to do." With that, he walks out of the room.

Farzana and I look at the clock and realize that we have twenty minutes before the students will be coming into the class. I brief her on our reading and writing workshops and am really impressed with her body of knowledge. While we are talking and laughing about student teaching, the bell rings. My students line up in front of the classroom and just before I open the door, I turn around to Farzana and ask, "How would you like the kids to address you?" Farzana thinks about this for a second and replies, "Miss Akbar is fine." Nodding my head, I open the door, greet them all, and let them come into the room. While I am greeting those students in the back, I notice that the line is stopping from the front. To my horror, most of my students are staring at Miss Akbar with eyes the size of silver dollars. She is attempting to greet them and has her hand out to shake their hands. But no one is shaking her hand. Just then, I hear Jonathan say, "Is she a terrorist?"

Discussion Questions

1. What is your immediate reaction to this situation?
2. How will you introduce Farzana Akbar to your students?
3. What could you have done to better prepare yourself and your students for Miss Akbar's entrance?
4. What are the different forms of attire that women who practice Islam wear?
5. What activities can you do in the short term and long term to help your students understand and appreciate differences?

Advice from Veteran Teachers on . . . Religion

- We have all had the case of the parents who do not want their children to participate in any Halloween celebration, birthday or holiday parties, or to recite the Pledge of Allegiance. We recognize that is their right. We have all accommodated these requests by asking another teacher if that child could stay in their room until our class party is over, or allow them to sit quietly while the rest of the class recites the Pledge of Allegiance. If the other teachers are also having parties, we've asked the school secretary or librarian if that child could help him or her during the time of the party. If you take the time to develop a respectful relationship with the staff members, it has been our experience that they are more than willing to accommodate such requests.
- For the child who is calling other students stupid for reciting the Pledge of Allegiance, this is unacceptable. Once again, we all have zero tolerance for teasing, ridiculing, and bullying as these can lead to other more extreme behavioral problems. Thus, consequences are in order.
- Having Miss Akbar in a class is a great opportunity to talk about her religion and the religious/cultural practices that she adheres to. We would have Miss Akbar come up and introduce herself. We would then ask her questions about her attire and then open it up to questions from our students. Children are inquisitive and will stare. That is normal. Thus, giving the children an opportunity to ask questions and to receive correct information helps dispel myths and misconceptions. After a short while, most children will see Miss Akbar as another member of our class family.
- We all really wish that we could do objective units on religion. With so many wars being fought over religion, we feel that learning more about religions would help our students develop empathy, care, and understanding. More religious education would dispel myths and misconceptions because students are misinformed, not informed at all, or receive their information about various religions through the news alone, which is extremely biased.

We would make sure that we did not proselytize, but would teach religion from historical, political, and cultural perspectives. In the primary grades, we could focus on the holidays, traditions, and customs of various religions.

- We've all wished that we could tell parents who request to know in advance every book and resource that we will be using with our classes to either home school their child or to send them to a private or parochial school. But since we are professionals, we don't. We do tell them that their request is unreasonable because a lot of times, teaching is so in the moment, in particular read alouds, that there would be no way for us to get that information to them every single day. However, we do assure them that if we select a book or resource that we think will be unsettling for that parent's child, we will send the child to another class.

- If a child is fasting and begins to cry or gets weak, you need to contact your school nurse as soon as possible. The nurse should then contact the parents to discuss this situation further. We also suggest that you ask the nurse how you should immediately handle the situation if that child is in your class.

Poverty

No More Books

"Mr. Wallis," Greg says, "Can I take my library book out to recess? I'm at a really good part." I look up and say, "No problem, son. Just make sure that you take good care of it because they are expensive to replace." Greg says as he walks briskly out of my class-room clutching his beloved book, "Thanks, Mr. Wallis."

Most of my fourth-grade students like to read. However, I haven't ever encoun-tered a student like Greg who *loves* to read. He is so enthusiastic about science fiction, nonfiction, mysteries, poetry, humorous stories, serious stories . . . you name and he loves it. I have really been pleased about his decision to begin checking out picture books so that he can read them to his younger brother at home. "Mr. Wallis," he wrote in his journal. "We don't have a lot of money, so we really don't have books at home. So, I want to start checking out the books for little kids that my baby brother would love to hear me read. He loves books with trains, trucks, cars and lions right now. I'll make sure I try and find some of these books when we go to the library on Wednesday." So, although he just loves to check out books for himself, he is willing to sacrifice one of the three books he gets to check out one for his brother.

When the bell rings indicating that recess is over, my students slowly walk back into the room to get ready to go to the library. On the other hand, Greg excitedly bounces back into the room. "I finished the book, Mr. Wallis," Greg announces. "Was it good?" I ask him. "Yes," Greg says. "I just loved the way the author talked about how to create computer games. I want to do that one day when I grow up." I am actu-ally shocked by this. "I thought you wanted to be a writer, Gregory," I ask. "A writer *and* a computer programmer," Greg corrects me. I think about it for a minute and say, "You know what Greg? I bet you'll do it." Greg looks at me sheepishly and says, "Thanks, Mr. Wallis."

"Table one, please line up," I announce to my class. Lately, my students have been running to get in line, bumping into one another, and continually talking while they are lining up. "Now look, class," I begin to address my students, "See how table one is walking to the line. They are not bumping into one another. They are not talk-ing and they did not scratch their chair legs on the floor. Thank you, table one." I wait for a few seconds to let the information sink in for the rest of the students. "Now, table four," I continue, "Please show me how you can walk like fourth graders to line up." When all my students have lined up and are quiet, we begin walking up to the library. Surprisingly, we do not have problems walking to the library, cafeteria, playground, or any other place. Maybe it's not surprising because when they get a compliment from a faculty or staff member, I put four beans in our cookie jar.

When they enter the library, they all sit in chairs and wait for instructions from me or from Mrs. Neal, our librarian. I notice that Mrs. Neal is busy assisting another student, so I tell my students we will need to wait patiently until she is ready for us to proceed. Mrs. Neal looks up at my quiet students, praises them for being considerate, and tells them that all of their books have been checked in, so they may begin searching for their new library books. My boys and girls get up and begin looking through the stacks.

We stay in the library for thirty minutes. "Mr. Wallis," Greg says to me looking down at his books, "I found another book by the same author." "Great, Greg," I say. "What did you get for your little brother, Kevin?" Greg gets excited, "I found him a pop-up book with trains, boats, cars . . . just everything. He'll love this one." I look at Greg and say, "I just bet that he will."

The next day, Jasmine, another student, comes in early in the morning and tells me that she saw Greg with his father in library. She tells me that Greg's face was red and it looked like he had been crying. "Jasmine," I say, "Are they still in the library?" Jasmine, who I can tell has genuine concern, shrugs her shoulders and says, "I'm not sure, Mr. Wallis." I thank Jasmine for letting me know and go in search of Greg and his father. When I get to the library, Ms. Neal tells me that Greg and his father went to the office. When I finally get to the office, I find Greg sitting in a chair and next to him his father.

Mr. Foster stands up, extends his hand to shake mine, and says, "Hello, Mr. Wallis." I reply, "It is good to see you." I look over at Greg and ask, "Is everything okay, son?" Greg shakes his head and looks up at his father. When Greg does not answer my question, his father replies, "Mr. Wallis, unfortunately, my three year old got a hold of the book that Greg checked out from the school library. He ripped out all of the cars and wrote in the book with a crayon. I talked with Mrs. Neal this morning and she told me that it will cost $65.00 to replace and restock the book." Mr. Foster looks down at Greg and says, "I just can't afford to pay for this. Not since their mother's cancer came back and I'm the only one working right now." I can tell that Mr. Foster is really having a hard time with this, as he continues. "I talked with Mrs. Neal and she put me on a payment plan. I will play $5.00 per week until the book is paid off." Mr. Foster then looks back down at Greg and says, "But, I do not want Greg to check out any more books because I just can't afford this ever happening again." With that Greg begins to cry.

Discussion Questions

1. What do you say to Mr. Foster?
2. What do you say to Greg?
3. What activities/lessons can you do with your class in order to get books donated to your class library?
4. What's your opinion regarding the inflated cost of the library book?
5. What would you say to your librarian or principal regarding these charges?

Those Homeless Shelter Kids

"Good morning to you, good morning to you. We're all in our places with bright sunny faces. And this is the day, to start a new day," sing my twenty-six kindergarteners. Every morning at 7:45 on the dot, we sing our kindergarten theme song. I thought they would get tired of the song, but the students seem to love it, as every morning at the same time, they begin to sing it. "Ms. Manning," Joyce, the school secretary's voice booms over the PA system. "You have a new student coming to your class today. His mother is walking him down now." "Wow, everyone," I begin, "We have a new student." Marcus raises his hand and asks, "Do you think he's a boy or a girl?" Thinking, I say, "Let's vote. How many of you think that our new student is a boy?" Twenty-six little hands go in the air. "Now, how many of you think our new student is a girl?" The same twenty-six hands go back up into the air. I guess I'll have to work more on the rules of voting only once next time. Just then, our door opens up, and a little boy walks into our class-room followed by woman. "He's a boy!" Marcus shouts as the other students begin to clap. The boy and his adult appear to be shocked by all of the commotion.

"Hi," I say extending my hand to the little boy, "You must be our new student." He looks up at his adult and doesn't say anything. Finally, the adult says, "This is Mitch and I'm his mother, Geraldine Hilbert. And yes, he is your new student." I bend down so I can have eye contact with Mitch and say, "The reason that they were so happy was because we had just taken a vote to see if you were a boy or a girl. As you can see," I say turning around to my students, "They are very happy to have you in class." Once again, Mitch doesn't say anything and looks up at his mother.

"Okay, let's see if we can find Mitch a few friends to help him find his way around his new school," I say to my students. Marcus quickly raises his hand and volunteers to be Mitch's friend. "Ms. Manning, me and Chris and Benny will help him." I look around and say, "Mitch, would you like sit with Marcus?" This time Mitch doesn't look up at his mother and goes and sits between Marcus and Chris on the rug, with Benny sitting right behind him. "Ms. Manning," Mitch's mother says, "Is there anything else that I need to do?" I turn to my class and say, "Sweethearts, you may talk quietly to your neighbor." I turn back around to face Ms. Hilbert. "No, Ms. Hilbert. You are more than welcome to stay if you want to." Geraldine looks at me and says, "Oh please, call me Geraldine." Geraldine looks over at her son and says, "I think he'll be okay." She looks back at me and continues, "I don't have a phone right now because they cut off my cell phone. But if you have any problems, please call the office at the Sunrise Shelter on 15th." Geraldine then hands me a Post-it note with a phone number on it. "They will come and get me and I will be up here as fast as I can." Mitch comes back up to his mother, hugs her leg, and goes back to sit with Marcus, Chris, and Benny. I think he's going to be okay as well.

Our morning was great. The kids went to their literacy centers without any prob-lems and I was able to get to two of my guided writing groups. During our math time, I call Mitch over to the front table so I can assess where he is academically. At the time he is in block center with his new friends, Marcus, Chris, and Benny. When I call his name, he eagerly comes to the table and takes a seat. "Hello there, sweetie," I say. "I just want to ask you a few questions so that I can learn a few things about you. Is that okay with you?" Mitch gives me a shy grin and shakes his head. I take out my interview questions and literacy assessment sheet. "Mitch, did you go to school before you came here today?" Mitch looks at me and responds, "No. I was in the Begas." In the Begas? I wonder what that means. "What's in the Begas, Mitch?" I ask hoping that he can fill in the blanks. "Um," Mitch replies, "in the Begas." Okay, so that didn't work. "What did you do in the Begas?" I ask. "It was really hot, so we had to stay in our car," Mitch says. "Oh, do you mean Las Vegas?" I ask. Mitch looks at me and says, "Yes, the Begas."

Now that we have that taken care of, I say, "Okay, Mitch, tell me what do you like to do when you're at home?" "Um," Mitch thinks, "We just got a home." I totally forgot that Geraldine said that she could be reached at the Sunrise Shelter. I didn't really give it much thought, but I guess that Geraldine doesn't work at the Sunrise Shelter; they live there. I also wonder if they lived in their car when they were in Las Vegas.

This is proving to be a lot harder than I thought. I decide to just begin with my literacy assessment. To my surprise, Mitch was able to get 100 percent on all of the sections. He could identify all twenty-six of lower- and upper-case letters, could recite the alphabet, could identify and count to 20, knew all of his shapes and colors, and could write his first and last name. I praise Mitch for a job well done. "Wow, Mitch, you have done an excellent job with this. How did you learn all of these things?" Mitch gives me that smile again and says, "My mommy teached me." I ask, "How did she teach you all of these things? How did you learn to count so high?" Mitch goes on, "Um, my mom would make me count the stars and the trees." Tilting my head to the side, I say, "Really?" Mitch nods his head and says, "Yeah, and I would tell her the colors of cars too." After that, Mitch told me that he learned his shapes by looking at windows, tires, and other stuff like that, and that his mother would have him identify the letters on signs and billboards. She totally used the environmental print that my literacy professors were always talking about.

Just then, the timer goes off indicating that it is time for my kindergarteners to go to lunch. Mitch joins the others as they clean the classroom and get ready for lunch. I walk my students over to the cafeteria and head to the teachers' lounge. Several primary grade teachers are already in the lounge when I arrive. "Oh, Danielle," I hear Rosaline call out to me, "I heard that you got a new student from that shelter on 15th."

"Whew," Marron calls out, "I am so glad that I don't have another one of those kids. They don't know anything. They are just poor white trash." My eyes bug out because I can't believe what I'm hearing. "I know," Mark says, "I am glad my numbers were so high because that meant I wouldn't have to get him." Seeing my surprised look, Marron says, "I can call them poor white trash because I have family members who are poor white trash." And with that, she leaves the teachers' lounge.

Discussion Questions

1. What's your opinion regarding Marron's comment that she can call others poor white trash because she has family members who she considers to be poor white trash?
2. What do you say to your colleagues?
3. What do you anticipate may be some challenges and solutions in working with families who are homeless?
4. What are some activities that your students can do to help the homeless in your community and/or our world?
5. How can you incorporate some of the literacy activities Geraldine used with Mitch into your literacy program?

Science Fair Project

"Wow," Jose says, "I can't believe I can win a computer for doing a project for that science fair." As my fifth graders enter our classroom after the assembly, I hear them commenting on what Dr. Johnson, a retired scientist at the college in our town, offered to them to encourage them to participate in this year's science fair.

"Hello everyone," Dr. Johnson began, "I am offering to the winner of the science fair a free laptop computer with all of the bells and whistles. You will be able to do your homework assignments and hopefully search on the Internet to help you with your future scientific endeavors." After, Dr. Johnson said, "free laptop," my students became so excited that their buzzing was contagious. Mrs. Thompson, our principal, had to step in to get the children to calm down. "Now everyone," Mrs. Thompson says raising her arm, "I know that you are all very excited about this, but you need to quiet down so that you can hear what else Dr. Johnson has to say." Everyone in the gym begins shushing each other so that they can hear Dr. Johnson.

"Now," Dr. Johnson continued, "I am looking for creative, well-written science fair projects. I want to be able to clearly see your hard work, knowledge about the topic, and enthusiasm for science because I just love science." "Well," I think to myself, "I'm not sure how much enthusiasm for science he is going to see, but I bet they will fake enough if they have to in order to win that laptop." "Remember," Dr. Johnson went on to say, "Make sure that your project is neat, typed, and has graphics and any props or equipment needed to please the judges." Mrs. Thompson then tells our students that each teacher will talk more about the science fair contest in our classes.

When we get back to the class, my students' excitement was palpable. "Now," I begin, "You will all receive the science display board so you do not need to worry about purchasing those. I have several books in the class on different science fair projects that may interest you. For those of you with Internet access at home, you may search for science fair projects that interest you. Please make sure that you do not choose an experiment or project that involves animals or humans. We cannot have anyone or anything getting hurt." I look around my room and see the children whispering to themselves. "Any questions?" I ask before I pass out the information packets Dr. Johnson so kindly put together for each of the students.

"Ms. Simmons," Shawn begins, "Do you really think that we can win a laptop? I mean, why is he giving away a free laptop? Do you think he's crazy or something?" Now all of my students have quieted down and are looking at me intently. "I really think that any of you can win this contest, Shawn," I say and I mean it. "You are all very smart children, so I have no doubt that you can win. As for Dr. Johnson, I believe that since he's retired, he probably wants to make sure that your generation considers science and research as career options because that was his career and passion. I think he wants to encourage you all to work hard on your science fair projects, so he has offered to provide a laptop to the student who wins the contest."

"Well," Rachel begins, "I really don't care why he wants to give away a laptop. I just want to win it!" she says as she raises her hand in the air to get a high five from Melissa. "You are too crazy, Rachel," Melissa replies. "You know I'm going to win that laptop." After that, the floodgates open. "I'm gonna win!" "No you're not. I'm gonna win!" Before this goes much further and I have to make one or some of them change their cards, I start counting to get them back on task, "5, 4, 3, 2, 1, 0." When I get to zero, they all know they need to be quiet and have their eyes on me for further directions. "Thank you. Now, please get out your planners, make sure you write your homework assignments from the board on the appropriate day in your planner, clean up your area, and let's get ready to go home." With that, I hear chair legs scraping against our vinyl floors as my students look for their planners in their desks.

Three weeks later and the big day is here. I have bus duty in the morning, so I see all of the students getting off the bus, out of their parent's cars, and walking with their huge science display boards. As a few of my students exit the bus, they greet me as usual. "Hey, Ms. Simmons," Rachel says as Melissa waves with her one free hand. "Hello, Rachel and Melissa. Are one of those the winning science project?" I joke with them. "Yes," they both say in unison.

Next, Doug is dropped off by his dad who is carrying the display board while Doug carts a cardboard box. "Hi, Ms. Simmons," Doug and his father say in unison. "Ah," I say, "Looks like you have a lot of goodies in the box." Doug's father looks at me and says, "You know, Ms. Simmons. I'm really proud of him. He worked hard on this all by himself," he says as he rubs his son's hair. "I told him that even if he doesn't win the grand prize, he should be proud of himself." I smile and say, "Oh, Mr. Dodson, I couldn't agree with you more."

As Doug and his father walk off to put Doug's display together, the last bus pulls in. Several students greet me and I point them to the cafeteria where the science fair competition is being held. I almost think all of the students have gotten off the bus when Sylvia, the bus driver, informs me there is a problem in the back of the bus. As I board the bus, I see Caroline, one of my smartest, most inquisitive, and well-behaved students in the back crying. "Caroline, honey," I say, "What's the matter?" Caroline looks up at me and says, "I saw the other projects that people did. Mine is horrible. They have color graphs, typed their stuff out and had pretty paper, robots and everything. I had to write mine out because we don't have a computer. I couldn't even look stuff up because we don't have the Internet or encyclopedias."

As I look at Caroline's display board, I notice that she has handwritten her science fair project information on lined paper, tried to decorate her display board with a few stickers and artwork she created with crayons, and taped her sheets of lined paper to the strikingly white board. Caroline says, "I'm not going to enter this junk. I'm not going to win anyway. We are too poor to get all of the stuff to make mine look good."

Discussion Questions

1. What are some potential problems that come with major projects having to be done at home as opposed to school?
2. What are some possible solutions to help students who can't afford the supplies to adequately do major projects at home?
3. What is the school's responsibility when it comes to independent projects such as science fair projects, book reports, homework, research papers, etc.?
4. What are some ways that we as teachers can help parents and students who are having difficulty with science fair projects, book reports, homework, research papers, etc.?
5. What would you say to Caroline? Would you encourage her to enter the contest? State your rationale.

Advice from Veteran Teachers on . . . Poverty

- We would investigate why the cost of replacing the library book costs so much. If the parent is able to pay for the suggested retail price of the book, then it doesn't seem fair that the cost is so much higher. We would talk with our school librarian to get more information. If we still do not feel comfortable with the answers we receive from the school librarian, talk with your principal to find out why and what could be done to lower the cost of the replacement book for the parent.

- Suggest to the parent that she keep the library books, homework, school supplies, etc., away from their younger children. Encourage them to find a designated spot in their home to store these valuables.
- Let the children check out books from your class library. In order for us to have a well-stocked class library, all of us have purchased cheaper books from yard sales, used book stores, thrift stores, and libraries and have received free books from the book order clubs with bonus points, books from other parents in our classes, and from our PTA and PTO.
- With children who live in homeless shelters, who are homeless, or who move around a lot, you need to empathize with their situation instead of blaming them. Once again, we encourage you not to have preconceived notions about them based on their living conditions. Children whose parents are in the military move around quite a bit as well, yet no one would assume that they were behind or poor white trash because they moved around and attended several schools during their elementary school years.
- We let our students know that if they need anything with a school project, to please let us know. We can get the supplies needed to complete their projects. We firmly believe that you should not require them to purchase any supplies that they cannot afford. It's just not fair for those kids who cannot afford it.
- If students are required to use supplies that are not available through your schools (i.e., construction paper, markers, crayons, butcher paper, white paper, etc.), you may want to contact your local office supply store and ask them if they would donate those supplies. We've seen numerous letters on the walls at office supply stores where teachers and students thank them for donating supplies to their classes.
- We stay after school to help students with projects. Some may need time in the library or need to search the Internet to do their research, may need to type their reports or may need help assembling their reports/projects on the tri-fold board. That way, we can better even the playing field for our students.
- We do not make the at-home projects a huge part of their overall grade. That way, we can take into account the other work that they do both in and out of class.
- Since some parents help their children a bit too much with their at-home projects, we suggest that you make them do an oral presentation in order to double-check that they've actually done the research for their projects.
- In order to deal with parents who are doing a bit too much work on their child's at-home project, you should write a letter to your parents letting them know the specifics about their project and encourage them to allow their child to do the majority of the project as this is the best way that their child will learn the content.

Gang Activity

Birds of a Feather

"Miss Watson," I hear my principal, Dr. Elliott, say, "Are you available right now for a quick second?" I look up from my mail and say, "Would it be okay if I go to the restroom first?" Dr. Elliott laughs and says, "No problem. Just meet me in my office."

This is my usual routine after school. Check my mailbox, check if I have phone messages, and go to the restroom. After I finish washing my hands, I proceed to Dr. Elliott's office. I knock lightly on the door and when she lets me know that it's okay, I enter her office. "How may I help you ma'am?" I ask. Dr. Elliott says, "I just love that southern hospitality you always show me. My mom is from Mississippi, and she made sure that we said "ma'am" and "sir" to show respect." She then says, "Do you teach your third graders those same manners?" I think about it and then shake my head no. "You know what? I just don't think about it. Maybe I should," I say really meaning it. "You really should consider it," Dr. Elliott says, nodding her head.

"Anyway," Dr. Elliott continues, "I had a discussion this afternoon with several parents today about your treatment of some of your female students." I look at her in complete shock. "Oh my goodness. I don't even know what you are talking about or who could've complained about me." I am so cognizant about things like this. Especially since this is my first year teaching. "Dr. Elliott," I say with a now shaky voice, "Who complained?" Dr. Elliott looks at her notepad and says, "Mr. and Mrs. Hernandez." She then looks at me and says, "They believe that you are targeting their daughter and her friends as potential gang members because they are Latinas." Once again, I am just appalled and shocked by what I am hearing. "Dr. Elliott," I say, "You have to believe me when I say that I am not targeting her because she is a Latina. Chelsea, Monica, Lydia, and Darlena have been wearing clothing that looks like gang clothing. I asked them about it yesterday and they told me that they were not gang members."

Dr. Elliott looks as if she is pondering what I am saying. I must admit that I am a bit uncomfortable with this silence. Just when I think I can't take any more, she says, "What does gang clothing look like?" I think about this question before I answer. "Um, they were wearing red bandanas like belts. They were also all dressed alike in blue jeans, red button up shirts, white sneakers, red socks, and had their hair combed the same way." Dr. Elliott looks at me with what looks like amazement in her eyes. She then says, "You noticed all that?" I shake my head and say, "Yes. After that training session I went to on drug, alcohol, and gang prevention, I've been really paying closer attention to my students."

Once again, Dr. Elliott quietly ponders what I've just said. "What did Chelsea and the girls say when you asked them why they were dressed that way?" I think about that some and say, "They told me that they were going to go and take pictures after school and then go to the skating rink for Chelsea's birthday party." Following that, Dr. Elliott nods her head in agreement, "Yes, that's what her parents told me."

Once again, Dr. Elliott is quiet. With all of my nervous energy I say, "I'm not really familiar with gangs and stuff like that. I didn't grow up in that kind of neighborhood. So I thought that I was doing the right thing." Now I feel my throat tightening up and I feel like I'm about to cry. "Come on, Cheryl," I think to myself, "don't shed a tear." As hard as I was trying, I feel the warm tears streaming down my face. Dr. Elliott then hands me several tissues. I wipe my face and then wait to hear what Dr. Elliott has to say next.

"Okay, Cheryl," she says leaning over her desk to rub the top of my hand. "I thought that there was a reasonable explanation for what happened. I told her parents that you were a great teacher and that you really care about your students." I shake my head in agreement. "Oh Dr. Elliott, I would never purposely hurt my students' feelings like that." Dr. Elliott once again leans across her desk and rubs the top of my hand. "No problem, my dear. Now," she continues, "I have several questions for you." She then looks down at her notepad and asks me questions that she already had written on the notepad. "Now some of the questions are pretty personal, but I really want you to think about them in order to grow as a teacher." I look at her with wide eyes. She then continues, "Don't worry about memorizing the questions because I'm going to give you a copy of them. We can have another discussion tomorrow in order to give you time to think and reflect on the questions. "Okay, Dr. Elliott," was all I could say.

Dr. Elliott then begins, "Would you have accused the girls of being in a gang if they were white? What can you do so that this type of situation does not happen in the future? What will you say to your girls tomorrow when they come to class? What will you say to their parents in order to make sure they know that you are not accusing their girls of being in a gang because they are Latinas and that you really care about their girls?"

Discussion Questions

1. Would you have accused the girls of being in a gang if they were white? Why or why not?
2. What can you do so that this type of situation does not happen in the future?
3. What would you say to the girls tomorrow when they come to class?
4. What would you say to their parents regarding this situation?
5. How well do you think Dr. Elliott handled the situation?

Blood In—Blood Out

"Okay, folks," I say, "Let's get ready for the assembly. Please close your math books and put your math work in your math folders to take home for homework." I hear my fifth graders opening their desks and pushing their chairs back. During these transition times, there is a slight buzz in the classroom. I tell my students all the time that I don't care about the slight buzz, but if their noise gets above a level three in the class, I'm not going to be happy.

I scan the classroom to look for the rows that are neat, clean, and orderly. During this time, my students sit up a little straighter, lace their fingers together, and look at me with smiles on their faces. I walk over to the chalkboard and give each row ten points. I can see that they are proud as most of them mouth, "Yes," under their breaths. I move to the center of the room and say, "Great job, folks. Row three, please push your chairs in and line up." We all wait patiently until row three is in line. "Great job, row three. Now rows two and five, please push your chairs in and join row three in line." Finally I say, "Rows one and four, please join the rest of the class in the line." When all of my students are in line, I say, "Okay, folks. We are going to this assembly and you know what I expect. You may speak to your neighbor prior to the assembly with a level two voice. But remember, when the speaker begins to speak, you must be courteous and respectful and listen attentively." I look at my students and continue, "Are there any questions?" All of my students shake their heads and then I ask the line leader to begin walking down to the auditorium as I turn out the classroom lights.

Once we get to our spots in the bleachers, Jose looks to me and says, "Mr. Morgan, what's this assembly about today?" I think about it for a minute and reply, "Oh, it is on gang prevention. I think that several police officers will be here to talk about the problems with gangs and gang violence." Jose looks at me and shakes his head. He turns to his neighbor, Billy, and begins to chat before the assembly. Just then, our principal, Mr. Williams, taps on the microphone and says, "Testing, testing, one, two . . ." In order to remind my students of my expectations, I stand up and put my index finger over my lips. I scan my class to make sure that I get their attention and that they understand it is time for them to be quiet. I then sit down and we all look to the stage.

When he stops tapping the microphone, Mr. Williams says, "Hello, ladies and gentlemen. I know you will all be on your best behavior during this very important assembly." Mr. Williams continues, "Unfortunately, gang violence is on the rise. We are seeing more of our children, you—" he says pointing out at the audience, "—who are being hurt, incarcerated, and even killed." Mr. Williams turns to the guests on the stage and says, "This is Deputy Wilma Rodriguez, who is affiliated with the gang unit. Next to Deputy Rodriguez is Marcus Brown, who is a former gang member, and next to Mr. Brown is Delilah Eubanks, also a former gang member. Please put your hands together and welcome our first speaker, Marcus Brown." With that, Marcus stands up, gives Mr. Williams a hug, and takes the microphone.

"Hello everyone," Marcus begins. When only a few students reply, Marcus says, "Hello everyone," in a louder voice. "Hello," all of the students then reply. Marcus smiles and then says, "Now that's a hello."

Marcus was extremely nervous at first, but then I could easily tell how compassionate and knowledgeable he was about the topic at hand. "You see, I was initiated into my gang at age eleven. I had to cut my way into the gang, and when I decided that I didn't want to be in my gang anymore, I was cut on my way out of the gang." Marcus lifts up his shirt to show our students a huge scar across his chest. Most of our students and teachers gasp at the sight of his bulging scar. Marcus then continues, "You see, it all seems like a brotherhood when you first get in it, but then you realize it's not all that it's cracked up to be." Marcus puts the microphone down and I can see that he is choking up. Talking through tears with a cracked voice, he continues, "I've lost my father and one of my brothers to gangs; my other brother and sister are in jail forever cause of gang activity; and my best friend's little niece was gunned down playing in the streets."

Marcus is now obviously crying. "Please y'all, if you don't do nothing else. Please don't go down that same path. It ain't nothing but death and jail." Following Marcus's speech, Deputy Rodriguez and Delilah Eubanks told similar stories and made similar pleas.

As my students walk back to the classroom, I can tell that we are going to have to debrief prior to recess. Most of my students are in deep thought and quiet. I wonder how many of them are even scared. Once back in our room, I ask my students to please take out their journals and write down what they learned in the assembly. After twelve minutes, I ask, "Does anyone want to share what they learned today?" Kayla raises her hand and says, "I didn't know that there were white girl gang members like Delilah. I always thought that they were Mexican or Black." Rachel raises her hand and says, "Shoot, most of my girl cousins are in gangs and we're Vietnamese." I shake my head in agreement. "Yes, folks," I start, "gangs members are not only a Black and Latino issue even though that's how it's portrayed on TV and in the movies a lot of times." All of my students shake their heads in agreement. Ben, who I noticed was exceptionally quiet during the assembly and afterward, raises his hand and asks, "But what do you do if everybody in your family is in a gang like mine. I am scared of dying and going to jail like my brothers and cousins and stuff, but it's my family. I mean, how do I tell them no?"

Discussion Questions

1. What is your answer to Ben's question?
2. What support systems are available for children like Ben who have family members who are incarcerated, have been killed, or are in gangs?
3. What type of activities/lessons could you do in order to show your students how deadly gang affiliation can be?
4. For some students, a gang takes the place of their family. They may clothe them, feed them, protect them, encourage them, etc. What is your opinion regarding gang participation in this way?
5. What can you do to assist students prior to being initiated into a gang, if they are initiated in a gang, and if they want to then leave a gang they've been initiated into?

The Interviews

"Mrs. Doss," I ask Stephanie's grandmother, "Can you please tell my students how you were the first person to ever attend college in your family?" Mrs. Doss begins to shake her head and says, "That's right, boys and girls. I was the first person in my family to attend and graduate from college." I am really happy I decided to have parents and grandparents come into my class this year and share their life stories with my second graders. My students truly love to hear the stories, and it is doing great things with their interviewing, computer, writing, and even reading skills. It is amazing to me how much they get into preparing for the interviewee. I must say, I am very proud of them.

"I came from a family of farmers and my parents were very poor," Mrs. Doss continues. "I had thirteen brothers and sisters, and as the oldest, I felt responsible for taking care of them. My parents told me it was their job to take care of my siblings, but I still felt a sense of responsibility. But then my father sat me down one day and told me that I could do more to help my brothers and sisters by going to college and getting my degree. Not only would that improve our financial situation, but also, it would set a good example for my brothers and sisters to follow." Mrs. Doss then shifts in her seat and continues, "Now don't get me wrong, it was hard work. My parents had to work their fingers to the bone to help me with tuition, books, and expenses. But we made it." Mrs. Doss then beams with pride and says, "I am proud to say that nine of my brothers and sisters graduated from college and the others went to trade school and were able to financially take care of their families as well."

"Wow," my students exclaim in unison. Taj raises his hand and asks, "What did you do for a living, Mrs. Doss?" Mrs. Doss once again beams with pride. "Actually," she begins and looks over at me, "I was a teacher like Miss Henton." Looking at her, I ask, "How long did you teach?" Mrs. Doss says proudly, "For forty years." My students as well as I exclaim in unison, "Wow!" Taj then says, "Dang, that's a long time. How old are you, Mrs. Doss?" Mrs. Doss begins to laugh a hearty laugh as I jump up. "Excuse me, Taj," I say, "You are not supposed to ask a lady her age." Taj smiles and shrugs his shoulders. "Oh, Miss Henton," Mrs. Doss says, "I am not ashamed." She then squares her shoulders and says, "I am sixty-four years old." Once again, my students exclaim in unison, "Wow!" Mrs. Doss once again laughs with heartiness.

I move to the front of the class where Mrs. Doss is standing and put my arm around her shoulders. "Boys and girls," I say, "Please give Mrs. Doss a hand." My students begin to clap and some even whistle. Mrs. Doss continues to smile and laugh and takes a bow. "Thank you, boys and girls," she says, "for letting me share my story with you." Stephanie jumps up from her seat to give her grandmother a hug. Interrupting this special moment, I ask my students, "Do any of you have any other questions for Mrs. Doss?" My students look like they are really thinking about other questions to ask her, then they begin to shake their heads. I turn to Mrs. Doss and thank her once again. Following that, I look up at the clock and say, "Boys and girls, it's time for us to get cleaned up and ready to go home." As my students begin to get ready to go home, I look at Mrs. Doss and thank her again. "I enjoyed myself, dear," she says. "If you need me to volunteer for a fieldtrip or a party, just let me know because I sure miss being with students."

About five minutes later, I'm walking my students to the front of the school so that they can go home. This usually takes a few minutes because I find myself talking with parents, catching up with former students, and troubleshooting missing backpacks and homework planners. Just then, I hear my name being called. "Excuse me, Miss Henton," I hear. "I am Gerald Smith's father, Martin." Martin extends his hand to shake mine. "Why Mr. Smith," I say as I shake his hand, "It's so good to finally meet you."

I immediately notice Martin's tattoos on his forehead, neck, and arms. "Yes, I was incarcerated for the past twelve months and now I'm spending most of my time looking for a job," Martin says matter-of-factly. Admittedly, I am a bit put off by his disclosure and at a loss for words on what to say next. Thanks goodness he continues talking so I don't have to worry about it. "So," Martin continues, "How's my son doing in your class?" I shake my head and inform Martin, "Oh, Gerald is a top-notch student. He is well-behaved, works hard, and his peers respect him." Martin exhales and says, "Thank goodness. I really want him to do better than I did." I shake my head and say, "Well, it looks like he's right on his way to a bright future."

Just then, Gerald comes to both of us with his mother, Christina. "Hey Dad," Gerald says excitedly. "Did you ask Miss Henton if we can interview you in our class?"

Martin then chimes in, "Not yet, but you just did." Martin looks at me and says, "I would love an opportunity to come to your class and share my life story with your kids. I want them to go down a different path than I did. You know, staying out of gangs and getting in trouble and stuff. Shoot, the stories I could tell. I've seen people stabbed, shot, and robbed. I want them to know what it's like to always have to look over your shoulder cause folks are trying to kill you, to have to carry a gun everywhere you go, and to see your homies gunned down right in front of you." Pausing briefly, he continues, "They just need to stay in school and get a good job." He then looks at his family and says, "So, what do you think?" They all look at me expectantly.

Discussion Questions

1. What do you say to the Smith family regarding their request?
2. What questions would you and your students ask Martin Smith during his interview?
3. The teacher in the vignette made the assumption that Martin's last name was Smith because Gerald's last name was Smith. What would you say if you found out that Martin's last name was not Smith?
4. What would you say to parents who have some concerns and questions about Martin being interviewed by your students?
5. What are the pros and cons of Martin Smith being interviewed by and speaking with your students?

Advice from Veteran Teachers on . . . Gang Activity

- Shame on the teacher for assuming, if that is the case, that the student who is wearing the same type of clothing as her friends is a member of a gang. The manner in which the parents responded shows they are diligent and mindful of their child's friends and associates. Parents raising the racial issue is a legitimate concern. Would the teacher be as inquisitive if the students were white and all wearing stylish clothing from a Nordstrom's-type store?
- Former gang members can be a valuable resource in helping students to learn what not to do with their lives. The fact that he is the father of one of the students in the classroom should signal that he should not be treated any differently from the other parents. However, depending on the age of the students, if the teacher is going to allow other students to interview the former gang member with all the visible tattoos, it might be a good practice to conduct the interview in a controlled environment with the teacher present.
- If the parent is a convicted felon, the teacher should seek guidance from the school administrator before allowing the parent to volunteer in the classroom. In California, one cannot volunteer in a school setting if convicted of a serious or violent crime.
- The possibility of being forced to join an organized gang is a real possibility for some students. Depending on the neighborhood, gang affiliation provides some students with a real sense of belongingness and security. We also know that gang affiliation often leads to poor choices and bad consequences.
- The fact that the student wrote in his journal that he is afraid that he will be forced to join a gang is a sign that he is reaching out to a significant adult in his life seeking answers and reassurance. I would suggest the teacher find some private time to discuss this concern with the student. The teacher should not make judgmental comments about the student's family involvement with gang activity. The teacher's role will be to listen very carefully to the student's concerns and to assure the student that he/she has the right to make life choices that

are different from those made by other members of the family. It is important that the teacher provide other opportunities for the student to continue the dialogue whenever the student feels it necessary.

- It is very important that the teacher honor the student's privacy during these discussions. Talking to the student's parents or friends about the student's fear would be disloyal and a breach of trust. However, after gaining the student's trust, the teacher would want to ask the student if he/she would like to talk to the school psychologist or the school counselor about his fears.

Drug Abuse

Looking Good

"Girls," I say to April, Amanda, Brittany, and Chelsea in the back of the class, "if you don't put the brushes, lip gloss, and mirrors away, they will go into my desk and your parents will have to come up to school to get them." April looks up at me and says, "But Ms. Crane, it's almost time for lunch. I have to look good." The other girls giggle with April. I shake my head and say, "I understand, girls, but you need to wait until recess or lunch to groom yourselves." Carlton, who sits at the table next to the girls interrupts and says mockingly, "Groom yourselves." He then laughs and says, "I thought that only dogs groomed themselves." Several of the kids at his table give him fist bumps and then I hear Johnny say, "Then Ms. Crane is right. Only dogs do groom themselves." Now the whole back row is laughing. In order to get control and get it quickly, I say, "Just for that, Johnny, your table has just lost 100 points." I put my hand on my hip and maintain a stern look. I can look at their faces to tell that they are upset and disappointed. I then twist slightly and make the adjustment to our point chart on the dry-erase board. Now the whole class is quiet.

I look out at my class and say, "You all know that we do not comb our hair, apply makeup, or do any other things that disrupt our learning." I then scan the room to see if they are listening. "Second," I continue, "You know that we do not talk bad about one another. I will not tolerate anyone belittling anyone in this class. Do I make myself clear?" In unison, my fifth graders say, "Yes, Ms. Crane." I then look to the back and say, "And table 4," which is the table with April, Amanda, Brittany, and Chelsea, "You, too, lost 100 points for once again not following directions." As I look at their table, I can see that Amanda, Brittany, and Chelsea are disappointed. However, April shrugs her shoulders as if she doesn't care. Not to be deterred, I then tell my class, "All right everyone, let's get ready for lunch."

As my students get ready for lunch, I look over at April and wonder what I am going to do about this situation. She is a very popular student; a trendsetter, and if I allowed it, she would look at herself in her mirror during the entire class. But what I am concerned about is that her attitude as of late has been changing. She is so into the way she looks and now acts as if nothing bothers her. When I asked her mother about it she asked me, "Ms. Crane, do you have children?" Surprised by her question, I say, "Um, well, no." She nodded and with a smile on her face, said, "You see, Ms. Crane, I have three other daughters who have all gone through the same thing." As if thinking about what she wanted to say next, she closed her eyes and said, "Yes, it was about this time that each of my girls started their periods and then all hell broke loose." She then opened her eyes and said, "So you see, I anticipate that April will be starting her period soon, so her little hormones are gonna be raging for a while." After my conversation with April's mother, I felt sort of relieved. However, I am now wondering if there is something else going on. I mean, I can't ask April if she's started her period and if her hormones are raging. Shoot, she may not even know what a period is or what hormones are.

As I look around my classroom, I am pleasantly surprised by how fast my students have gotten the room cleaned up. I look up at the dry-erase board and say, "Now, we had a couple of tables who have lost points this morning. However, with good behavior they can earn the points back. I believe in all of you and know that you can all do your best and be on your best behavior." I look out at my students and see a few of them smile with pride. "Okay," I continue, "Table three, please line up." When all of my students are in line and ready for lunch, I remind Carlton to please turn the lights out as he is the last student in line.

As we begin to walk to the cafeteria, I hear a commotion coming from the middle of the line. I then see that April has accidentally dropped her purse and all the contents have spilled out onto the sidewalk. April then rolls her eyes up to the sky and says not really talking to anyone in particular, "Dang! Can you believe this?" As I bend down to help April pick up all her stuff, I notice several vials of what appear to be pills. I pick up one bottle and ask, "April, what are these?" April smiles at me and says, "Oh, they're not drugs, Ms. Crane. They're vitamins so that I can lose weight." Honestly, I am a bit taken aback by this and ask her, "Do your parents know about this?" She continues to smile and replies, "Oh they don't care. I got them at the store with them."

Discussion Questions

1. How do you handle this situation in the short term and the long term?
2. What over-the-counter vitamins, supplements, and medications are allowed and not allowed at your school?
3. What happens to students in your school who bring vitamins, supplements, and prescribed or over-the-counter medications to your school?
4. What is the official protocol in your district and school for children who need to take medication and/or vitamins during the school day?
5. What activities/lessons can you do with your students to teach them about possible dangers with over-the-counter vitamins or supplements and prescription medication?

On That Stuff Again

"Allan," I say looking on the rug for Allan Peterson. "Here, Miss Giroux," Allan replies with his trademark—missing two top and two bottom teeth—smile. I smile back at him and say, "Well hello there." He then covers his mouth with his chubby little hands and giggles. I continue taking roll. "Jobe," I say looking to the back of our rug to find Jobe. "Here, Miss Giroux. How are you doing?" I nod my head and say, "Why I'm fine, Jobe. How are you?" He tilts his head to the side like he's thinking about something and says, "Um, I guess I'm okay." As if thinking about it some more, he continues, "I am a little tired, mainly cause I ate a big breakfast." Sharell, who sits next to Jobe asks, "What did you eat for breakfast, Jobe?" Jobe then continues, "I had grits, bacon, eggs, biscuits and gravy, and some milk." I look at Jobe with an astonished look on my face. "My goodness, Jobe. That is a huge breakfast." He smiles at me as I continue, "I would be sleepy too with a breakfast like that." Jobe, still smiling says, "Yeah, but it was so good." He then rubs his belly, closes his eyes, and rocks on his bottom. The rest of my class then joins him in laughter.

Obviously, taking roll is taking a lot longer than I would like. But Jobe is one of the funniest little kids I've ever met. According to his grandmother, he has always been able to have conversations with just about anyone and has an unbelievable vocabulary. She went on to say, "That's why I had to put him in preschool because he was around grown-ups too much. Girl, he was all in our business and telling everyone at the church, store, and any and every where our business. So I thought that maybe if we put him in school he could talk to kids and have kids' stuff to talk about."

Getting back to roll, I then say, "Thank you, Jobe, for sharing with us. Okay," I then look to the third row and say, "Preston." When I don't see him in his usual spot, I say, "Preston McConnell." Gabriella speaks up. "Miss Giroux, he isn't here." When I finish scanning the rest of the rug, I nod and say, "Thank you, Gabriella. Now remember next time, please raise your hand." She then covers her mouth and gives a quiet giggle. She looks at me and raises her hand. After I call on her she says, "I'm sorry." I tilt my head to the side and say, "That's okay. Thanks for letting me know about Preston."

In the beginning of the school year, Preston was here every day and on time. He walked to school with his mother, Missy McConnell, was always well dressed, had his homework completed, and if I sent anything home to be signed, he always returned it the next day with his mother's signature. Unfortunately, he has been absent from school quite a bit lately, and when he does come to school, he is usually wearing the outfit he wore the day before, his hair is uncombed, he isn't returning or completing homework assignments, and he's always complaining that he's hungry. When I ask Preston about these things, his eyes get big and he will usually not reply.

Just then, the PA system interrupted my thoughts. "Miss Giroux," I hear Mr. Robinson, our principal say, "Is Preston McConnell in your class today?" I shake my head, and reply to the call button, "No, Mr. Robinson. He's absent today." There is no response over the PA system. "Mr. Robinson," I say hitting the call button again, "Are you still there?" Finally, Mr. Robinson comes back on and says, "Yes. I'll call back later." Just as quickly as his voice streamed into our classroom, he was gone.

I then take my seat at the front of rug and go back to taking roll. Before I can get started, Mr. Robinson comes over the schoolwide PA system and says, "Will Preston McConnell please come to the office? Preston McConnell, please come to the office right now." I look over at my students a bit confused and concerned. However, I want to make sure that they don't get too scared, so I continue with taking roll.

When I get to Patrick Zavala's name, I close my attendance folder and get up to move us to Language Arts. Just then, the door to my classroom opens and I see Preston's grandmother standing there with tear-stained cheeks. "Mrs. McConnell, is everything okay?" I say with concern. She shakes her head and says, "Preston left for school with Missy and then I receive a call from Grant Guillory telling me that he saw him in the park. He's supposed to be here." She then puts her face down as she continues, "I know that I shouldn't have let her take him today. You know she's back on that stuff again. She came home and didn't even know he was missing and now she's at home scream-ing and paranoid cause she's high and stuff." Just then, I feel Jobe tug on the sleeve of my blouse as he asks, "What stuff is she on, Miss Giroux?" Shocked back to reality, I hear Gabriella shout, "Oh, Miss Giroux," and then she quickly covers her mouth and raises her hand. Shaking my head in frustration I ask, "Yes, Gabriella." Gabriella then points to the window and says, "There's Preston on the playground."

Discussion Questions

1. What is your immediate reaction to this situation?
2. What is your legal responsibility with a situation such as this?
3. What social support services are available in your school and community for children like Preston whose parents are on drugs?
4. What social support services are available in your school and community for individuals like Missy McConnell?
5. What safety measures are in place at your school so that family members or even strangers cannot come directly to your class like Mrs. McConnell did?

Dots on His Feet

Today is our end of the year trip to Logan Park at 10:00 for the fourth grade. I grab my duffle bag from the trunk, lock my car door, and plan out my strategy. I will go into the office, say hi to everyone (I learned that during student teaching), grab my attendance folder, check my mail, and pick up my students just in the nick of time. But, just like with teaching, things rarely go *exactly* as I plan. "Ms. Donaldson," Joyce, our secretary says, "a parent called today and wants to meet with you about her kid's grades. I put a note in your mailbox." I can tell that Joyce is about to go into great detail about her conversation with this parent, my shoes, etc. But I am on a mission. To get my kids in the nick of time. I quickly say, "Thanks, Joyce," trying to get my attendance folder. "I really appreciate that." Joyce smiles and I leave the front office. "Whew, that was close," I say to myself as I go into the teachers' lounge.

"Hello, Ms. Marsha," our custodian Mr. Kennedy says to me, "Are you talk-ing to yourself again? Now, I told you about that." I just love Mr. Kennedy. "I know, Mr. Kennedy," I say. "You know I'm not a morning person, so I have to talk to myself to keep me going." Mr. Kennedy laughs and continues to clean out the sink. "Oh, by the way," I say, "Thanks for the extra paper towels. My kids go through paper towels like there's no tomorrow." He looks up and says, "Then that's good." As he continues to clean the sink, "That means they are washing their hands." I smile and say, "You know, I never thought of it that way." Mr. Kennedy looks up from the sink and says, "Every-thing is all in the way you look at things. My grandfather taught me that." As I move to the door to exit the teachers' lounge, I say. "Have a great day, Mr. Kennedy." He nods and says, "You do the same."

I look up at the clock and realize that it's almost time for us to leave for Logan Park. Just as I am about to hit the bell to signal the end of Language Arts, Mr. Walters, Mrs. Willoughby, and Ms. Williams come in with visitors' passes on their chests. They have volunteered to walk with us to the park. I see their children waving at them as I gently hit the bell on my desk, which tells my students that I want their undivided attention. "Good job, everyone. I see everyone's eyes. Fantastic. I will put five marbles in our jar." My students get excited because they know that a root beer float party is coming when they fill up the jar. "Now," I continue, "it's almost time for us to leave for the park. I want you to please put your reading books away, make sure that you have the Language Arts assignment written in your planners, and clean up. You have a three-minute warning, so please begin." I set the timer and watch them work. About one minute into their cleanup time, my cell phone rings. It's Mrs. Martinez telling me that she and several parents are already at the park barbecuing hot dogs and hamburgers and that everything else is all ready for us.

As I look around the room, I can feel a buzz in the air. The kids are so excited about our trip. We are really lucky that the park is behind the school so we can walk there. Admittedly, I was initially concerned about the safety of our students and a swimming pool. But, the fourth-grade team has been doing this end of the year celebration for years. Plus Michael, our team leader who has been teaching for fifteen years and is a trained lifeguard, has asked the park services to provide two lifeguards. So with all of those precautions, I feel better.

Just then the timer goes off. I look around the room and notice that my students are all sitting up with their backs straight, shoulders squared, with smiles on their faces. The three parents in the room begin laughing. Ms. Williams then says, "Are they always this well behaved?" I look at my class. "Actually, Ms. Williams," I begin, "They are a great bunch of kids. That's why they get five more marbles in the jar." I hear several of my students say, "Yeah!" I then say, "Okay, ladies and gentlemen. Let's get ready to go to the park."

Our walk to the park takes just about fifteen minutes. In all, there are three fourth-grade classes so it seems like there are kids everywhere. Some of the kids are already in the pool, while others are sitting on the lounge chairs talking. Michael and the two lifeguards are perched in their lifeguard stations looking at all the students. As I continue to scan the children, I notice that Kevin is sitting in a lounge chair by himself. He has on his swimming trunks and I know that he can swim because his grandmother indicated that he could on his permission slip. However, what is surprising is that he has socks on. He stands up and walks to the edge of the pool when I blow my whistle. As students look up, I shout, "Kevin Henderson, please come here." I begin walking in his direction and when I get to him I ask, "Why are you wearing your socks? You can't wear socks in the pool." Kevin turns his face down and says, "But I have to wear socks, Ms. Donaldson." As if expecting him to continue, I look at him and ask, "Why do you *have* to wear your socks?" Kevin looks down and away from me. He looks up with a look of embarrassment and finally says, "My mom and dad used to shoot heroin in my feet so I wouldn't cry when I was a baby. I still have dots all over my feet." He looks at me and asks, "Now can I swim with my socks on?"

Discussion Questions

1. What are the pros and cons of Kevin wearing socks in the pool?
2. What are the long-term problems for children exposed to heroin as infants?
3. What would you say to Kevin's grandmother if you got a chance to have a conversation with her?
4. Which school officials could you discuss this issue with? What would you tell them?
5. What's your legal responsibility with a situation such as this?

Advice from Veteran Teachers on . . . Drug Abuse

- The teacher should confiscate the pills from the student and report the incident to the school nurse or the principal. Hopefully, the school will follow up with a call to the parent. If the pills are vitamins, the parents should be informed of the proper protocol for taking medication at school.
- A fifth-grade student who is that conscientious about the way she looks often suffers from poor self-esteem issues. Taking pills to lose weight at this age could lead to other types of addictive behaviors in the future. It should be suggested to her parents to seek the advice from a family doctor to help the student modify her diet and to exercise more. The family doctor may refer the student to a child psychologist to deal with the self-esteem issues.
- As a mandated reporter, the teacher is obligated to report the parent who injected the baby with heroin. Although the student is now in the fourth grade, heroin could still be used in the home, constituting a dangerous environment for the student or any other siblings.
- The student is obviously self-conscious about the needle marks in his feet. However, the wearing socks in the pool will draw even more attention to him. We would suggest the teacher help the student to enter and leave the water in an area were his feet would be the least noticed. Once the student is in the water the needle marks will go unnoticed.
- The teacher should speak with the student to let him know that he is not responsible for the inappropriate actions of adults. The focus should be on the positive aspects of the boy's life and what he can do to prepare to become a responsible adult and parent.
- Once the grandparent reports to the teacher that a student is living in an environment where illegal drugs are being abused, the teacher is mandated to report this information to the proper authorities. If the teacher knows, or should have known, that a child lives in an abuse situation, the teacher could be held liable if the student were harmed as a result of the mother's addictive behavior.
- It is the teacher's professional responsibility to deflect questions such as "Why is she crying?" or "What stuff is she on?" in order not to discuss the personal matters of others in the classroom.
- Teachers need to also be aware that students can get high from inhaling glue, rubber cement, permanent markers, aerosol computer dusters, and bathroom and kitchen cleaning supplies, to name a few. If you suspect that a student is using these products inappropriately, let your administrator know as soon as possible.
- Children can bring alcohol in thermoses and clear alcohol in water bottles. Keep your eyes, ears, and especially your nose open for these as well.
- Marijuana is the drug of choice for many. Unfortunately, marijuana is a gateway drug for harder drug use. Some students have parents who smoke marijuana and consider it a natural herb—not a drug. Thus, their children may not consider it a drug. Regardless, it is an illegal drug, and if you smell it on one of your students, it should be reported immediately to your administrator.

Alcoholism

I Learned From Them

"Back to School Night is such a stressful time for me," says Yvonne in the teachers' lounge. Yvonne has been teaching first grade for fifteen years. Geraldine, in her first year of teaching, looks surprised. "I thought that it would get easier," she says in a naïve voice. Yvonne shakes her head no. "But you've been teaching for so long. Surely you have mastered how to keep the stress level down," Geraldine continues to probe. Yvonne thinks about it for a minute and finally replies, "Nope. Every year is different. It's always stressful for me." After a few seconds of silence, Yvonne continues. "But every year, it's stressful for different reasons. No two years have been the same." The other veteran teachers in the lounge shake their heads in agreement with Yvonne.

Geraldine looks over at me. "Bob, what do you have planned for Back to School Night? Do you have a speech ready? Your outfit planned?" "Wow," I think. "Geraldine really is stressed!" Back to School Night is seven days away! "You know, Geraldine," I begin, "I don't worry about my outfit as much as others." The other teachers in the lounge begin laughing and nodding their heads in agreement again. "I take this time to really get to know my parents and to have them hopefully get to know me. I try to keep things as low-key as possible."

Holly, another fifth-grade teacher who has been teaching for three years just like me, says, "Bob, what are you posting on that back wall? That big old sheet of yellow construction paper is blinding." Our principal, Mrs. Janice Peterson, comes into the lounge just then. "Tell him, Holly. I've been trying for over a month to get him to put students' work up on that wall." They are right—I have had that construction paper up for over a month. And yes, Janice has been on me every other day to get something up on that wall. "What will parents think when they come in here and there's barely any student work up? That whole wall is blank. Cover it!" I try to explain to her that we are working on writing autobiographies, and as with most things, it has taken a lot longer than I previously thought. I am so surprised that my students are having this much trouble with their writing skill development. If they can learn to write a coherent paragraph and include relevant information, I will be more than happy. "I am posting their autobiographies up on that "blinding" back wall. I think that folks will be impressed," I say with confidence and pride.

Just then, the bell rings signaling the end of lunch. Yvonne quickly looks over at me as she cleans up her lunch. "Just make sure that you read those autobiographies before you hang them up. I had to learn the hard way about ten years ago that sometimes, kids like to add things at the last minute."

I look at her in puzzlement . I totally trust my students. "Oh, Yvonne," I begin, "I don't think I have anything to worry about." Yvonne shrugs her shoulders, and says, "Okay," and walks out of the teachers' lounge, closely followed by Geraldine who is asking Yvonne, "What do you mean you had to learn the hard way?"

"Hey kid," Ronald, who has been teaching third grade for ten years, says, "You should listen to Yvonne," he says as he takes a bite of his sandwich. When he swallows, he continues. "She had to go to court and everything regarding that issue. It really got ugly. Just cover yourself." I think about it for a minute. Although I still trust my fifth graders whole-heartedly, I say, "Well, it can't hurt to reread their autobiographies," as I leave to pick up my students.

After school, I decide to take the other teachers' advice and peruse my students' autobiographies. Most write about their parents, siblings, pets, hobbies, and extracurricular activities. "See," I think to myself, "I knew that I had nothing to worry about." After counting to make sure that I have twenty-seven autobiographies, I realize that I have only twenty-six. I count them again and come to twenty-six again. I decide to put them in alphabetical order, and when I do, I realize that I am missing Steve's autobiography.

Steve is one of the most creative students in the class. His writing skills are extremely well developed. He has a sense of audience, humor, and timing that you rarely see in children as young as him. He loves to write poems, raps, and short stories, and he tells me that he's working on a chapter book. Because his writing skills are so good, I submitted several of his poems into a competition hosted by the local community college. Just last week, we found out that he won the grand prize for his poem titled, "My Legacy." I am so proud of Steve.

The next day, I ask Steve where his autobiography is and he tells me that he needed more time to work on it because he wants to make it the best paper he's ever written. Since he is usually punctual with his assignments, I do not question his motives. On the morning of Back to School Night, Steve finally hands me his autobiography. "My whole family is coming tonight to see you give me my award for the poetry contest," Steve informs me. "Good," I say. "You and your family should be very proud of your accomplishment."

During lunch I decide to read over Steve's autobiography. To my horror, the last part reads, "My grandparents were alcoholics—so are my parents. That's why it shouldn't be a shock to them that I, too, drink. One of my earliest memories is drinking the "leftovers" after they had blacked out or went to bed. I also remember making them drinks when I was younger. I can still make a mean martini." Steven then goes on, "I just love the warmth of the alcohol as it goes down my throat. Just then, I get a calm that I can't get any other way. After that, I can write fabulous pieces. It helps me be so creative."

Discussion Questions

1. What do you say to your administrator regarding this situation?
2. What are the pros and cons of censoring Steve's autobiography?
3. Do you post Steve's autobiography the way it is currently written? Give a rationale for either choice.

4. Steve has admitted to continuing to drink. Who are you obligated to report this information to?

5. What help is available at your school and in your community for children who are drinking?

The Carpool

This year I decide to focus more on storytelling with my fifth graders. My great-grandparent and grandparents used to tell me wonderful stories about the "Old Country" all the time. I loved hearing stories about when they were young and how they finally made their way to America, fell in love, had children, and made a life for themselves. Also, this is a great lead-in for our unit on biographies. So I begin by telling my students what I learned about an interesting woman by the name of Mrs. Tooley.

"I met Mrs. Belle Tooley when I went to Jamaica on spring break to visit my grandmother." I continue. "Mrs. Tooley told me that she was ninety-two years old." I hear my students gasp. "Really?" "Oh my gosh!" and "No way!" are just a few of the comments that I hear them utter. I raise my hand to get them back on task. "Mrs. Tooley told me that her grandparents and parents all lived to be real old. She told me that her great-grandmother lived to be 107 years old!" "Wow!" was the overwhelming response from my students.

I then tell them that Mrs. Tooley is a mother of ten children who are all alive. "According to Mrs. Tooley," I say, "most of her children live in Kingston, but she does have two kids who live in California and one who lives in New York." "Also," I continue, "Mrs. Tooley's husband passed away twenty-five years ago. She told me that she didn't want to remarry because she liked her freedom." I chuckle at this comment. "Mrs. Tooley laughed when she said that." Several students chuckle, too, while others shrug their shoulders in confusion.

"I also found out that Mrs. Tooley was a doll maker for most of her life. She told me that she used to sell her dolls to the tourists who came in on the cruise ships." I then look at the doll on my desk and say, "I brought in one of my dolls from Jamaica. My grandmother bought it for me when we went there for our family reunion." As I continue to gaze at my doll I say, "Mrs. Tooley said that she used to make a whole bunch of dolls all the time, but now she has problems with her hands and fingers, so she can't make as many dolls as she used to."

The boys and girls in my class look at the doll with amazement. She is beautiful. She has dark brown skin, hair made of yarn, eyes made of seashells, a vibrant dress, little patent leather shoes, and bright red lips. I then tell my students, "Mrs. Tooley makes all the material that she uses to make the dolls. She even dyes the material herself." I continue, "Mrs. Tooley told me that she learned how to dye material because when she was a little girl, she worked on an indigo plantation, and she had to dye material all of the time. As a matter of fact," I continue, "her hands were blue." I hold up the palms of my hands to show the students what parts of Mrs. Tooley's hands were blue.

"Mrs. Carter," Jack asks, "is that true?" I nod my head. "Oh, yes, that is true," I respond. "There are countless stories of slaves who worked on indigo plantations who suffered the same fate as Mrs. Tooley. As a matter of fact, in some of the history literature I've read, once slavery was abolished, many people were so embarrassed by their marked hands that they wore gloves every time they went in public." Jack looks at me with a baffled look on his face. Then Chelsea, his neighbor, chimes in. "Why were they embarrassed? I thought that we learned that they didn't have a choice." I nod my head again. "You're right," I tell Chelsea, "slaves didn't have a choice. However, can you imagine walking around the rest of your life with blue hands? To many, it reminded them that they had been slaves at one time."

As Chelsea shakes her head, I continue. "Unfortunately, Mrs. Tooley is sick. So I am lucky because I got one of the last dolls she'll probably ever make." With that sobering comment, I ask, "Does anyone have any questions?" After five questions, which take twenty minutes, we are through with this activity. I then say, "You see, this is the type of information that hopefully you will get when you interview your family member, family friend, or person in your community." I then smile and look around the class again. "Since there are no more questions, you may get ready to go home for the day."

The bell rings and my boys and girls rush to get ready to leave. Jack stands up and says, "Whew! No homework cause it's Friday!" Several other kids get excited too. Truth be told, I'm happy they don't have homework as well. I miss teaching kindergarten where their homework packets were much easier to grade. Now with research papers, essays, longer math assignments, etc., the grading is overwhelming at times.

As I walk my students up to the front of the school, Jack, Lisa, Duncan, and Samantha stay close together. These are the students who told me on the first day of school that they were trying to help with global warming and had encouraged their parents to carpool. I was and still am pleasantly surprised that their parents actually do carpool at their children's encouragement. I see that Jacqueline Brando, Jack's mother, is outside of the front office door holding her nine-month-old-daughter, Megan. "Hey, Mom," Jack yells out to his mother. Mrs. Brando turns and quickly scans all of the kids with Jack. "Well, it looks like you have the troop with you," she says. "Hello, Jacqueline," I say, "how's the little one treating you?" Jacqueline looks at Megan and leans closer to me, places her hand on my shoulder, and slurs, "Oh, she keeps me on my toes. But overall, I can't complain."

'Whew!' I think to myself. The smell of alcohol was apparent.

"Well," Jacqueline continues, "we better get going, troops." Jacqueline then turns around and stumbles. She drops her purse and almost drops Megan. "Whoa," she says. We both look on the ground at the contents of her purse. Jacqueline quickly begins to pick up the contents with Megan on her hip crying. The last thing she picks up is a small empty bottle, the kind you get on an airplane, of what appears to be alcohol. We look at each another and she begins to giggle. "I am such a klutz sometimes." She then looks over at the kids and says, "Come on, troop. Let me get you all home."

Discussion Questions

1. What's your immediate reaction?
2. Which faculty members or administrators do you notify regarding this situation?
3. What do you say to Jacqueline Brando to stop her from driving with the kids?
4. What is your legal responsibility in regards to this situation?
5. What activity/lesson can you do with your students to encourage them not to get in cars with adults whom they suspect have been drinking?

Maybe It's Just Mouthwash

I put my lunch that I probably won't want or like when 11:30 comes around in the fridge; quickly grab the book order forms and flyers for professional development opportunities out of my mailbox, and turn around to see Mrs. Brown going through her mail. She wants me to call her Sylvia but I have such a hard time with that because she has been teaching for thirty-two years, thirty of which have been in kindergarten. Shoot, she could've been one of my elementary school teachers. When I asked her if she ever wanted to teach another grade, she told me that she loved the little ones the best. "I just love how innocent they are," she always says to anyone who asks her. She describes herself as the quintessential kindergarten teacher—she is the happiest person on the face of the earth, has cute names for all of her students, wears the clothes and earrings that let you know which holiday and season is coming up, and always maintains eye contact when she talks to me. Plus, she just loves children, books, crafts, cooking, singing, and everything else that comes along with being a kindergarten teacher.

"Hi, Sylvia," I say, "are we doing book buddies today?" She swallows and says, "Definitely," rubbing my back like she does to her students, "my kindergarteners just love when your third graders come to read books with them." I nod my head in agreement and say, "Oh, so do my students."

"But, let me tell you a little secret," she says as she leans in closer. "One of my parents, Mr. Hartman, is from Louisiana. His son is Roger—I'm not sure if you remember him." I shake my head no. "Well, he is coming in today to tell the kids stories about working in the swamp lands in Louisiana—although I'm not sure what type of work he actually did there," she says as she seems to be thinking about it. "Anyway, he's a delightful man, and he'll talk about how he saw alligators, ate coons, opossums, and squirrels, swatted mosquitoes the size of his hand, and he'll even read them a book. I thought that would be a fun thing for our book buddies to do today."

"Wow! That sounds great. Thank you," was all I could say.

"We'll see you at 1:30 then," Sylvia says as she exits the lounge.

As she walks out of the lounge, I begin to question what just happened. "Was that alcohol I smelled on her breath?" I ask myself. "No, it couldn't be." But I know the smell of alcohol, and that sure smelled like it. I continue to tell myself, "No one else seems bothered, and I know that she talked with others before she got to me today. What should I do next?" I ask myself. "Maybe it was just mouthwash," I say. Then the first bell rings, which tells our students to line up. "Yeah, it was probably just mouthwash," I say to myself, but aloud this time. Then I go pick up my students.

I set the timer for two minutes, then look around the room at my students. Jamilah is helping Stephen, whose arm is in a cast, put his math worksheet in his folder. "Jamilah," I say as we finish up our math worksheets and get ready for lunch, "thank you for helping Stephen out with his folder. I really appreciate it." I continue to look for other kids whom I can praise for doing a good job. "Marcus, thank you for putting my books back on my desk." "Cynthia, you have a warning." Cynthia looks up with that "I-can't-believe-you-saw-me" look on her face. I raise my eyebrows at her, letting her know to get to work. She smiles that famous smile and begins cleaning up.

When the bell rings, I shuffle the numbers in the bowl on my desk. "Okay," I say, "Table 1 gets a check today." Table 1 is a little excited and a little nervous. Last time, Johnny didn't have his assignment written down, so they didn't get the prize. They all take out their planners and math folders, as I walk around and quickly check to make sure that their math books are back in their desks, the worksheets are in their folders, and their area is clean. After I've checked everyone's planner, desk, and folder, I raised my right thumb up to let the class know that they all had completed their tasks. "Good job, Table 1. You may come up to the front and pick out one piece of candy." When they are finished and back at their desks, I excuse each table one at a time to line up for lunch.

When I get to the refrigerator in the teachers' lounge, I realize that I was right. I do not want my lunch. But I guess I'll have to eat it. Payday is a couple of days away. When lunchtime is over, I see Sylvia in the parking lot. "Marsha," Sylvia says in her ever-so-cheery voice. "I just want to make sure that we are still on for book buddies. You know that I have a storyteller coming in today."

"Yes," I say in surprise. "You told me about him earlier this morning."

Tilting her head to the side, Sylvia then says, "Oh, so I did," then walks off. "See you at 1:30."

I can't pretend that I don't smell the alcohol this time. It's even stronger than before. "That's not mouthwash, Marsha, and you know it," I say to myself. Plus, Sylvia's face was all red and her brow was sweaty. In deep thought, I walk silently to get my students.

Discussion Questions

1. Who do you talk to first regarding this situation?
2. What do you say to them?
3. Do you bring your principal into the conversation? When?
4. What will you do if the parent, Mr. Hartman, and your students smell the alleged alcohol on Sylvia's breath?
5. Do you think that it's appropriate for you to talk with Sylvia regarding her alleged drinking? Why or why not?

Advice from Veteran Teachers on . . . Alcoholism

- First things first—read your students' papers before the Open House and before you even consider hanging any of their work on your bulletin board. That way, if there is something in there that is puzzling or concerning you, you can have a conference with the child. You learn a lot from talking with the child. It could be an editing conference. Following that conference, you can then decide if it's appropriate or inappropriate to display the paper as is or ask the child to revise it.
- Would we post the paper in its current state? Yes. In all of our years of teaching we have found that other parents don't usually read other kids' papers. They usually compare handwriting as opposed to what other children have written—the content. Letter formation, handwriting, and the neatness of the other children's work are what parents look at.
- Talk to the parents first in a diplomatic way. Maybe read the letter to the parents during a parent-teacher conference or an afterschool meeting. Listen to what they have to say. If they think that it's a joke, then take it further. If the parents are surprised, then I would take them seriously. I would have to see their reaction. Possibly report to the principal: that there could be neglect or child endangerment.
- If you've developed a friendly rapport with the parent(s), you may suggest that they consult their child's pediatrician and/or go to family counseling for further assistance.

- The carpool—we would stall and ask her to follow us to the office. Then get an administrator involved. If there is no administrator available, ask the secretary to get on the walkie-talkie to request immediate assistance.
- The parent could become violent, indignant, or begin to cry uncontrollably. Either way, get an administrator involved.
- If you are required to walk your students out to the front of the school with your class, get another teacher involved. Get eye contact and whisper that you need help.
- Talk to the other parents in the carpool to let them know about the situation. They may be in a better position to talk to the parent who has been drinking.
- If a colleague is drinking, immediately talk with your principal or your team.
- The teacher could be on medication and having a reaction—either way, it's not your job to investigate this situation. So contact your principal immediately so that he or she can investigate.
- Remember your legal obligation to your students. You have to protect the children. So, you need to report problematic or dangerous behavior to an administrator.
- If a parent or another child smelled the teacher's breath, let them know that you talked to the principal and it's being handled. Or if you feel comfortable with the parent, encourage them to speak to the principal to voice their concerns.

18

Divorce

Kids Are So Resilient

"I can't believe that Beverly heated up that fish in the microwave," Jessica says to me. "I hate the smell of fish." I look over at Jessica and say, "Well, at least her lunch is healthy." We both laugh as we look down at Jessica's lunch—a huge submarine sandwich, chips, cookies, and a soda. I don't know how she can eat those heavy lunches and still stay awake in the afternoon. Just then, Bill, another teacher, comes in from the front office and sprays air freshener all over the teachers' lounge. "Good thing Beverly is in the restroom," I say to Jessica, "She may be hurt that everyone thinks her lunch stinks."

After another few minutes of eating our lunches in silence, Jessica interrupts my thoughts by asking, "So, what are you all doing this afternoon, Melissa?" I swallow a bite of my salad and say, "Science and writing our letters to the manager of Hometown to thank her for donating the supplies for our jog-a-thon." Hometown, a local grocery store, has donated orange juice, snacks, and fruit for each of our second-grade students who participated in the jog-a-thon for juvenile diabetes awareness. Our students raised $1,276.50 for the Juvenile Diabetes Foundation and were so proud about how much they learned about juvenile diabetes and how they were able to make a difference in the lives of others.

Once again, Jessica interrupts my thoughts, "Now where did you get the idea to do a jog-a-thon for juvenile diabetes?" I say, "Davin was diagnosed with Type I diabetes in the beginning of the year. We were so scared because we didn't know what was happening and because he was gone so long." As I think about it more, I continue, "Then Ebony was at Hometown with her mother and saw a sign-up sheet for a walk-a-thon for diabetes, but only adults were allowed to participate. So I asked Maria and she said that we could do one here." Our principal Maria is all for the students being involved in service learning activities. I sip my water and say, "I mean, it was a lot of hard work, but it was worth it. The kids really got into it and they did a great job." Just then, as I was finishing my lunch and cleaning up my spot, Beverly comes back into the lounge and says, "Ummm, my lunch sure smells good." I get up and throw away my trash, looking at Jessica and then back at Beverly to say, "I sure hope you enjoy it." Jessica begins to giggle as I walk out the door.

When I get back to my class to get ready for science, I hear a knock on the locked door. I see Natasha, Jordan, and Sydney standing there smiling. "Yes ladies," I say, "How may I help you?" Natasha looks up at me and says, "We just wanted to know if you needed any help?" These little ones are always so helpful. On most days they know exactly when I come back in the class and ask me if I need any help. On most days, I don't.

"You know what?" I say as I look back at the back table by the sink. "I really could use your help today. Come on in." As they walk in, I tell them, "Today we are going to do a lesson on repelling and attracting with balloons." I look at their little confused faces as I continue, "It will make more sense when I do the lesson." They all smile and look at each other and then at me. "But for right now," I continue, "I need for you to blow up balloons for me as I cut the yarn." The girls then look at me with excitement. I hand them the balloons and tell them, "We are going to need thirty balloons because each team needs two." I look at each of them and ask, "Any questions, girls?" They shake their heads and dive into the balloons.

I go to get the yarn on the front table. The girls giggle as they try to blow up the balloons and it makes me smile. At the beginning of the year, Natasha's mother was so concerned about her daughter because her divorce was finalized over the summer. I pull out Natasha's folder from the small crate I keep on the floor next to the front table and find the note her mother had written to me. She wanted me to make sure that her daughter wasn't exhibiting signs of depression or anxiety. She wanted me to let her know if her daughter was sleeping in class, crying in class, moping in class, not turning in homework, complaining about being sick, begging to go to the nurse's office, not eating, eating too much, being mean to classmates, being too nice to classmates, or vomiting. According to her mother, Natasha is extremely close to her father, and due to the judgment by the court, she is able to see him only every other weekend, one week over major holidays, and for one month during the summer. So, she was sure that Natasha would be having a difficult time with the divorce.

Surprisingly, however, she seems like a well-adjusted second grader. She is happy most of the time, does all of her class work and homework, and plays and works well with her classmates. When the bell rings signaling the end of lunch, Natasha and her friends stop blowing up balloons and say, "Should we go outside and line up, Mrs. Larkin?" I answer, "Yes, girls, and thank you for your help." As the other girls walk out of the room, I say, "Natasha, come here for a second, sweetheart." I ask her, "So, how are things going with you? I've been thinking about you." Natasha looks up at me, tilts her head and says, "Oh, do you mean the divorce thing?" Admittedly, I am caught a bit off guard by her question. "Um, yes." I finally say. "Well," Natasha continues, "Actually I am so happy that my parents divorced. They were arguing all the time and screaming at each other. I like it the way it is now. Just me and my mom and then just me and my dad. Hopefully, it'll stay that way forever."

Discussion Questions

1. Are you concerned about Natasha? Give your rationale for why you are or are not concerned.
2. When you have an opportunity to talk with Natasha's parents, what will you say to them?
3. If Natasha's parents' situation should change (e.g., either begins to date or even get married), what problems/concerns would you anticipate?
4. What support services would you seek for Natasha?
5. What service learning opportunities can you create for your students?

The New Baby

"Cecelia," I say to the other third-grade teacher as we walk to the playground to pick up our students, "Are we still on for book buddies with Karen and Nichole today?" Our third-grade classes meet as book buddies with Karen and Nichole's PM kindergarten classes. Our students read books, talk about books, write, laugh, and just enjoy one another. I am so impressed with the way my third graders have taken to their younger peers. In class, they want to make sure that they pick interesting and funny books for their book buddies, plan meaningful "lessons," and just show their buddies that they care about them. Some of my parents have said that they wish their children cared as much about their own siblings as they do about their book buddies. Although I don't have children of my own, I remember my two younger brothers being such brats, so I know that this is a lost cause until the siblings are older.

Cecelia looks at me and then swallows a sip of coffee and says, "Yes. I saw them in the lounge and they said that we are on." "Well thank goodness," I say, "Not only would my students be upset, but shoot, I didn't plan for anything else." Cecelia starts laughing. She has been teaching for about fifteen years and has been a great mentor to me. "I heard that," she says. "Plus," she continues, "It's Friday, too. We'd have to do something together if those two cancelled on us." We laugh together because we both know that's the truth.

Just then, Stephanie, one of my students, approaches me. "Miss Washington," she says with her quiet voice, "I don't feel good again." I look at Stephanie and place my hand on her forehead. "You don't feel warm, honey," I say. "What's hurting you?" "I think it's my tummy, Miss Washington," she says while diverting her eyes from my direct gaze. I look at Stephanie and think. In the past few months, Stephanie has "suffered" from more tummy aches, headaches, sore throats, and aching muscles than any other kid in history. Just about every day she lets me know that something is ailing her and then she begs to go to see Mrs. Franklin in the nurse's office. Although I think that sometimes she may actually be hurting, most of the time I think that she's not telling me the whole truth. According to her dad and stepmother, who is expecting their first baby in four months, these bouts of illness started a few months ago at home as well. "I mean," her father told me at a parent-teacher conference, "As soon as we let her know that we were expecting the baby, she started getting sick." None of us believe that this is coincidental. However, I don't think any of us really know what to do about the situation.

I look over at Cecelia; who is watching me to see how the new teacher handles this situation, and then say, "It's still early, Stephanie. Why don't you get in line and join us in class. Then if you still don't feel better by lunch, I'll call Mrs. Franklin." Stephanie looks as if she is considering what I'm saying and then says, "Okay, Miss Washington. I'll try." She then walks slowly to the playground holding her tummy.

Cecelia smiles at me as we both get to the playground where our students are lined up and waiting to begin their school day. Kayla comes up to the front of the line and excitedly tells me, "Miss Washington, my Mom had the baby yesterday. She named her Rebecca after my great-grandmother." Smiling, I say, "Congratulations, Kayla. Are your mommy and Rebecca still in the hospital?" Kayla put her hands on her hip and said, "My mom says that they don't let you stay in the hospital no more. Last night, she kept saying that you got to be almost dying after you have your babies before they will let you stay in the hospital." I just love Kayla's gift for gab. Cecelia, who just recently came back from giving birth to twin boys, overhears our conversation and chimes in saying, "That is so true. If I hadn't had twins and a slight fever, I would've been home that night." Kayla nods her head just like I've seen her mother do while saying, "See, Miss Washington." I giggle and then tell Cecilia I'll see her at lunch and to have a great morning. I then blow my whistle, and say to my students, "Let's walk safely to our class."

When we get to class, I take roll and lunch count. We then do the Pledge of Allegiance and I let the kids know of the two announcements we have concerning the walk-a-thon and the recycling drive that the sixth graders are doing so they can go on their end-of -the-year school trip. Following that, Kayla raises her hand and asks, "Can I give an announcement, Miss Washington?" I look up at the clock and do the "come here" gesture with my index finger. Kayla then gives her usual smile and walks up to the front of the class proudly. She clears her throat and says, "My mom had a baby girl yesterday. She weighed over eight pounds and according to my mom, she's just as long as I was." She then looks up with a perplexed expression on her face. "Although I don't know how long that is." She then shrugs her shoulders like that information is not too important to her overall speech and continues. "My mom is home but my dad had to stay because he was feeling all queasy and stuff and thought he was gonna faint." Celine raises her hand in the back and I call on her. "What did your mom name the baby and why did your dad almost faint?" Kayla begins to laugh and says, "Oh I forgot. Her name is Rebecca. My mom said that my dad almost fainted cause he was in the room with her when she had Rebecca." I begin to laugh as some of my students say, "UGH!" I thank Kayla and ask her to please keep us posted on the baby, and her mother and her father's progress. I then announce, "Let's get ready for math. Please get out your homework so that we can grade it. You have 1½ minutes," I set the timer as my students get ready.

While I'm looking for my teacher's edition math book, Stephanie interrupts me, holding her stomach, and says, "I am really not feeling good now, Miss Washington. I think I need to see Mrs. Franklin now."

Discussion Questions
1. What do you say to Stephanie?
2. Do you allow Stephanie to go to the nurse's office? Explain your rationale.
3. If you have a chance to talk with Stephanie's parents and Stephanie at the same time, what would you say to all of them?
4. What support services are available for children in your school who are possibly anxious and/or depressed?
5. What activities can you implement in your class to help children express themselves? To help them deal with their feelings?

We're Poor Because of Mommy

As I pull into the parking lot, I am already feeling overwhelmed. I can't believe that there was an accident in the center lane of the freeway. Traffic was stopped for miles. Finally, the accident was cleared and we were able to continue our commute to work.

Thank goodness I didn't have morning recess duty. I would then have had to call the office on my cell phone and let them know that I would be late. As soon as I put my car in park, I jump out, grab my wheelie with all of my stuff in it, grab my lunch, and head to the front office to get my attendance folder and check my mailbox.

When I get to my mailbox, I finally catch my breath and calm down enough to act like I'm not late for work. Then, I see Jonathan, another fourth-grade teacher, and say, "I can't believe that Christmas break is over already." "I know," he says, "They seemed like the two quickest weeks in the world." Our school secretary, Mrs. Velma Johnston, begins to laugh at us. "I can tell you two aren't parents. I know for a fact that it's not as quick for parents. Look at all of those happy, smiling faces outside." We all look out the big picture window in the front of the office and agree. Jonathan says, "I mean, they look like they've won the lotto or something." I nod my head in agreement, "Okay. They are laughing and everything like it's a party or parade outside" Velma chimes in, "It is a party because y'all are taking care of their kids from 7:30–2:50. Now if that's not a party then I don't know what is." We start laughing and then bid her a good day.

We then go to the teachers' lounge and get all of the stuff out of our bulging mailboxes. I can't believe how fast these things fill up. "Pam," Jonathan says to me, "What do you have planned this morning?" I think about it while looking at my mail and say, "I am going to give them an opportunity to write about what they did over break. Then, we are going to take a spelling test and then do Literature Circles." I look up at him and ask, "What are you doing this morning?" He laughs and says in a quiet, whisper-like voice, "What you plan on doing sounds good. I think that I'm going to have my kids do the same thing." Our principal, Ms. Neal, has been on Jonathan about not planning his lessons, but he doesn't seem to feel it's important. The bell rings, signaling the beginning of another school day.

After we get to the classroom, my students immediately begin talking about what they got for Christmas and where they went for Christmas. Since I have to get several things in order before we truly begin our school day, I say, "I am going to give you ten minutes to catch up with your friends. You may talk quietly to your neighbors." I hear some of the kids cheer and clap. I then raise my hand and say, "Now if the noise level gets too high, we will have to stop and put our heads down. So please be courteous to your neighbors."

As I begin to tidy up my desk, I overhear Megan say, "My family went to Telluride and we went skiing and stayed in a huge log cabin. It was so nice. Just like on that TV show." She continues telling several kids, "My dad surprised me and got me a new laptop, a new saddle for my horse, a new cell phone, and an iPod Touch". Several of the kids at her table look obviously impressed with everything she received. Megan then looks up at Jennifer and ask, "What did you get for Christmas?" Jennifer leans over and says, "I got another laptop like you. A pink one." She stops and thinks before continuing. "Oh, I also got new skis, and a whole bunch of clothes and shoes." She stops again before continuing. She finally says, "I got a whole bunch of stuff, but I can't remember right now."

Megan then looks at another member of their table group and says, "Marcus, what did you get for Christmas?" Of all of my students this year, Marcus has had a really hard time. His mother was the one who was working and financially supporting the family and she just left one day. Since she left and is not contributing to the family's welfare, according to Marcus's father, they are struggling financially. They've had to move from their 5,000-square-foot home in the hills to a one-bedroom apartment where they are barely making the rent payments. On numerous occasions, Marcus has expressed that he is concerned about his father and two older sisters because they cry all the time. As a matter of fact, Marcus has said, "Some days my dad doesn't even get out of bed. He just stays there and cries all day." Marcus's father has told me that he is so happy that his son seems to be doing well even though his mother has left the family. However, there are many days that Marcus does not seem to be doing well with this, and this seems to be one of those days.

"Marcus," Megan says, tapping on the table to get Marcus's attention, "What did you get for Christmas?" Marcus looks like he's thinking about what to do or say next. As soon as we make eye contact, Marcus's eyes well up with tears and he begins crying. He stands up and say, "Nothing, okay, Megan!" Marcus then looks at me again and says, "You all know my mom left and now we're poor. I hate my mom! I hate her!" He then runs out of the classroom and heads to the front of the school.

Discussion Questions

1. What's your immediate reaction with this situation?
2. What types of support services are available for families like Marcus's, who are experiencing difficulties financially supporting themselves?
3. What types of support services are available for children like Marcus who are dealing with emotional difficulties?
4. How do you feel about teachers like Jonathan, who refuse to plan their lessons?
5. In your school, what happens to teachers (both tenured and untenured) who do not follow the stated protocol such as planning their lessons every day?

Advice from Veteran Teachers on . . . Divorce

- The situations leading up to divorce vary greatly. In some cases, the divorce may come after violence or infidelity, or be a total surprise. We cannot be sure what the child/ren has/have been living through before, during, and after the divorce.
- Some children have a very difficult time dealing with their parents' divorce. Be on the lookout for behaviors such as cruelty to other students, siblings, or animals, fire starting, lying, disrespectful behavior, etc. You will need to immediately discuss your observations with your administrator in order to get the referral process going so that extra support can be provided to this troubled student.
- Some students may be emotionally sensitive during this time. They may cry at the drop of a hat, whine a lot, daydream, sleep in class, be very clingy, require more of your attention, or have outbursts when they do not get their way. You may want to have one-on-one conversations with the child in order to let them know that you are supporting them. You should take those times to discuss their behaviors and to offer suggestions on how they can work through their problems.
- We have had cases where the divorce is seen as a good thing. The child may very well be happy that their parents are no longer together. However, just keep your eyes and ears open and monitor their behavior. Although they may have initially been happy, their feelings can change. Plus the closer they get to you and the longer they know you, they may trust you more and may open up to you.

- You may want to allow the children to keep a journal where they can discuss their feelings during this difficult situation.
- Seek professional help from the school counselor or encourage the parents to seek outside counseling. This information may be useful for the child as well as the parents.
- Dual household—when the child is living with both parents but in different homes. You may need to conduct two parent-teacher conferences, make copies of the report cards and progress reports, and make sure that both parents get the copies. If there are long-term homework assignments or projects, you should make sure that both parents have the instructions as the child could be at both parent's homes during the time of the long-term assignment.
- If both parents get along, you may want to have a conversation with them in order to head off some of the problems that can occur with the child/ren living in two households. All of us have had the situation where the child completed their homework, but left it at the other parent's house. You may want to establish how they are going to make sure that homework is completed and kept in one backpack that the child takes to both homes.
- If the parents do not get along, you may want to have the above conversation with them separately. Be prepared to let each parent vent their frustration, but remember to keep an open mind and be as objective as possible. More than anything, we all encourage you not to get personally involved in their tumultuous situation.

Different Family Structures

My Foster "Families"

"Casey," I say as I check my mailbox before school. "Did you bring a lunch today?" Casey starts laughing and says, "I did, but I'm not sure if I'm gonna want it when lunch time comes around." I look over my other shoulder and say, "How about you, Margie?" Margie doesn't check her mailbox as often as she should and her arms are full of things like book order forms, mailers for conferences, new books in the field with great ideas for all teachers, and outdated coupons for the teachers' store. She, says, "You two know that I am planning on getting married next August. How am I ever going to fit into my dress if I keep eating out with you?" I look back over my other shoulder and tell Casey, "Okay Casey, I guess we don't want to be bad influences on Margie. So, Margie," I say looking over my other shoulder again, "You're not invited to lunch with us." Casey begins to laugh and then so does Margie. "Now," Margie continues, "I didn't say all that. I just said that you're bad influences on me." Then Casey chimes in while giggling and trying to act serious, "Oh, we don't want to be bad influences, Margie. We under-stand." After giving it some more thought, Margie says, "Okay, how about Mr. Pete's for turkey and swiss sandwiches?" We all laugh. That is our favorite place for lunch.

From the teachers' lounge, I go straight to the playground to pick up my students, who are waiting in line for me. When we get to our class, the kids pick up their back-packs that are lined up along the outside wall of our classroom. When I see that they are once again in straight lines, we enter the classroom. By this point in the school year, my third graders know the routine by heart. The first thing they do is put their homework in the homework bin; the attendance person waits until I take roll and picks a partner to walk it up to the office. The lunch person waits until I take the lunch count, then picks a partner and they walk that number up to the cafeteria while the rest of my students are quietly reading. These are just some of the benefits I have found teaching third grade—they're able to take on more responsibility.

Just as I am about to hit the bell to let the kids know we are moving to Language Arts, a flyer on my desk catches my attention. "Win a Trip to Magic Kingdom for Your Whole Family" is written on the top of the bright yellow sheet. The contest is being sponsored by a local organization and interested students will need to include a picture of their family and write a three-page paper about what makes their family special in order to enter the contest. I begin to think—this is probably a great opportunity for my students to work on their writing skills. I then hit the bell and wait patiently as my students put their books, magazines, and newspapers in their desks.

When I am satisfied that all of my students are paying attention, I hold up the flyer and say, "I think that this may be a worthwhile contest for all of you to enter. The grand prize is a trip to the amusement park Magic Kingdom for your whole family." I then hear "Ooohs" and "Ahhhs" from my students. "You will need to include a picture of your family and also write a three-page paper letting the judges know what makes your family special." I look up at my students' happy, smiling faces and say, "Anyone interested in entering the contest?" All my students raise their hands enthusiastically. A few chime, "Me, me, me."

"Miss Washington," TJ says, "When is everything due?" I look back at the flyer and read, "April 16." I think about it and say, "So that gives us about one month to get everything in on time." My students are all chatting about what they want to say in their essays. Looking in the back of the classroom, I see Joshua. His facial expression shows me that he is perplexed at best.

Joshua is a tiny, young boy who has lived a life that most of my students, and even most teachers, know nothing about. I found out that Joshua's biological parents were killed in a car accident when he was just a baby. Unfortunately, he did not have any other family members, so he was placed in foster care. At last count, Joshua told me that he has lived in ten foster homes. According to Joshua's journal, "Just when I get used to things, they move me to another place." So, as I look in the back of the room and see the sadness in his eyes, I think that I may know what he's thinking about.

"Joshua," I say, "Can you please come up to my desk?" Joshua walks slowly up to my desk and says, "Yes, Miss Washington?" I look into his face and say, "You look a little upset. Is everything okay?" Joshua takes a few seconds before responding. Finally, he says, "I don't have a picture of my family, so I guess I can't enter the contest." He puts his head down and continues, "As a matter of fact, I don't even have a family."

Discussion Questions

1. What would you say to Joshua in order to help him deal with his current sadness?
2. What can you do as a teacher in order to get Joshua an opportunity to enter the contest?
3. Which holidays and classroom activities alienate children who are in foster care or who do not currently live with their parents?
4. What are some activities you can do in order to help children who may be having a difficult time dealing with not living with their parents or other family members?
5. What support services are available in your school and community for students like Joshua?

Granny and Paw Paw

I just love it when the weather is like this, slightly cool and crisp. Springtime is a fun time to be teaching. But I have found I have to do more with my management skills because after a long winter cooped up in the classroom, my second graders are a bit more rambunctious and excited about getting the opportunity to go outside and play. There is also another downside to this time of year—allergies. We go through several boxes of tissue every day due to the trees and flowers now blooming. Although they are beautiful, the blooms wreak havoc on our noses, throats, and eyes.

As I look up at the clock, I realize it is almost time for me to get my students. Trying to mentally prepare myself for another day, I think about the fact that it is Friday and we get to have our Homework Party Celebration. I learned about this party idea from a good friend of mine who does this every month with her students. All the students who have completed all their homework during that month get to eat popcorn, drink juice boxes, and play balloon volleyball in the classroom for the last twenty minutes of school on the last Friday of the month. It is amazing how much my students love to do this. I am also glad I asked my classroom parents to help me with the cost of popcorn, juice boxes, and balloons.

Now, I'm not an unfair teacher. If I have a student who didn't do their homework for a day, I give them an opportunity during recess or their lunch time to make it up. I also encourage and remind them on a daily basis about how much fun the party is. Additionally, in cases of emergencies, I tell my parents they can simply write a letter explaining why their child could not complete their homework. I do not penalize them for emergencies. But, they have to make sure they return the letter or they do not get a reprieve.

As I glance over at the homework chart, I see that about 90 percent of my students will get to participate in today's party. Those students not participating, must stay in the class. I take that time to conference with each of them to see how I can best help them complete and return their homework.

Brrriiiinnng! The bell goes off and brings me back to my morning reality. I open the door and stand in the doorway; several of my students are coming down the hallway. "Hello, Mrs. Mourning," Jake, Katie, and Aaron say in unison. "Why hello, kids," I say back to them. "You may go into the class and get yourself ready for today." Jake looks up at me and smiles that sly smile and says, "Sure thing, Mrs. Mourning." He then giggles and goes into the classroom. As the rest of my students come filing into the class, I greet them with a "hello" or "how are you doing?" and let them know that they can go into the class and get ready for learning. Just when the tardy bell is about to ring, I see Helene running down the hallway. I put my hand up to let her know that she needs to slow down and walk. She comes right up to me totally winded. "Am I late, Mrs. Mourning?" Helene says with big sad eyes. "I ran all the way here." I look into her doll-like face and say, "No, actually, you are right on time." I give her a thumb's up signaling that I am proud of her. She gives me her bright smile, minus the four teeth she lost in the beginning of the year, and saunters into the classroom. As I close the door behind me, I tell Helene, "Honey, why don't you get some water to cool down." She looks up at me and says, "Thanks, Mrs. Mourning," as she moves to the water fountain.

Helene is the one student who I am most concerned about. She has not been turning in homework consistently all year. I know she is living with her grandparents, because she always talks about her Granny and Paw Paw. Once she told me her mother was on drugs and left them in the house alone and that her father was in jail and that's why she and her sibling are living with Granny and Paw Paw now. As a matter of fact, I believe there are also some cousins who are living with the grandparents, too.

During lunch, I go through the homework folders in the crate to see who will be able to go to our Homework Party Celebration. Once again, I notice that Helene's folder is empty. This means once again she will not be able to participate in today's party. I look up at the clock and realize I have twelve minutes before lunch is over. I take out my cell phone and look through my list of students' phone numbers until I get to the number of Gertrude and Melvin Luke, Helene's grandparents.

Mrs. Luke answers the phone and I can hear a baby crying in the background. "Hello, Mrs. Luke," I say, "How are you doing today? This is Helene's teacher, Pat

Mourning." Mrs. Luke says in her familiar southern drawl, "Well hello honey, how are things going? Is that girl in trouble?" I quickly answer, "Oh no. Not really. I'm just calling to see about her homework again. Once again," I continue, "she won't be able to participate in our homework celebration because she doesn't have all of her homework with her." I wait for a second, "So, Mrs. Luke, what can *we* do to make sure that Helene participates next week?" After a few seconds, Mrs. Luke says, "Honey, look. We are barely making it over here. Financially, emotionally, everything. Shoot, we barely can get to church most weeks. You see, I have all of my grandkids living with me. They each have so much homework to do, and some of that stuff me and my husband can't do. I don't know nothing about denominators and stuff like that. So you tell me. What *can* we do to make sure that she participates next week?"

Discussion Questions

1. What is your response to Mrs. Luke's question: What can we do to make sure she participates next week?
2. What after-school programs are available in your community for children who have difficulty completing their homework?
3. What family situations are privileged with the whole concept of homework?
4. What family situations are disadvantaged with the whole concept of homework?
5. Is a Homework Party Celebration fair for all students? If so, how? If not, how can you make it fair?

The Fieldtrip

"Mr. McDonald," Jenny says during literacy center time. She has a worried look on her face and looks on the brink of crying. "My dad isn't here yet for the fieldtrip." She looks out the window hoping he'll appear. "Oh my goodness, Jenny," I say gently hitting the side of my head and blushing, "I forgot to tell you that your dad called before school and told me that he would be coming right at 9:00 because he wanted to get everyone a surprise for the fieldtrip. He also told me to make sure and tell you so that you don't worry."

"Oh, okay, Mr. McDonald," Jenny says looking totally relieved now. She starts to go back to the writing center when she quickly turns around and asks, "What surprise?" I smile at Jenny and say, "Now would it be a surprise if he told me and then I told you?" Jenny started laughing and I could see that her bottom teeth were just beginning to grow in. Giggling, she says, "No, but you can tell me anyway. I promise I won't tell." I pretend like I'm really giving this request some consideration and say with a smile on my face, "I think it's best if you wait for the surprise just like everyone else." Jenny says, "Oh dang," and then smiles and saunters back to the writing center.

My first graders are buzzing with excitement and it sure is contagious. They are finally going to see the exotic animals they have been learning about for the past month. The thought of seeing snakes, a komono dragon, polar bears, lions, tigers, koalas, and lizards makes me giddy too. Just then, my classroom phone rings.

"Mr. McDonald," Gladys, the school secretary, says, "Your bus just pulled up. Make sure you remember your first aid kit, plastic bags for those who don't know that they get car sickness, and your lunches." "Thanks, Ms. Gladys," I say before hanging up.

Ms. Gladys has been the secretary for Highpoint Elementary School for over thirty years and has worked with seven principals and thousands of children and their families. I appreciate the way she is always looking out for me and I just love all of the little tidbits of wisdom she passes on. Like the plastic bags for the kids who may barf. I wouldn't ever have thought of that on my own.

"Okay, boys and girls," I announce to my class. I pause and wait for all of them to stop what they are doing and look me in the eyes. "It is time for us to clean up our literacy centers and get ready for our fieldtrip to the zoo." I can immediately see all of the little smiles on their faces. "Let's show the parents who are here how well, fast, and safely we can clean our classroom." I then set the timer for two minutes and tell them, "You may begin."

As the kids begin to clean up the class, I go over my list one more time. I check off everything I'll need or think I'll need to ensure this fieldtrip is a success. Every few seconds I look up to make sure my students are still cleaning up. I must say though, there really is nothing like a fieldtrip to make the kids clean the classroom just a little faster than usual. As I peruse the classroom, I hit my bell again and say, "Boys and girls, I am so proud of the way you are working hard and working together. Keep up the great work." Most of my students look up at me beaming. "You may get back to cleaning."

Just then, I hear Jenny say, "My dads are here," as she excitedly runs up to the front door. The classroom door then opens and in comes Jenny's father, Michael, with a tray full of cellophane goodies. Behind him is another man holding a similar tray full of goodies. Jenny then grabs hold of Michael and says, "Daddy, what's the surprise?" Michael says, "Hold o, sweetheart," as he almost drops the cookies. "I'm going to drop all of our hard work." Jenny then removes herself from Michael and hugs the other man just as tightly as she hugged Michael.

Michael then looks up at me and says, "I am so sorry, Mr. McDonald, that we are late. It took some time for the cookies to cool." He then sets the tray on the kidney table and reaches behind himself to grab the other man's tray. He says, "Please forgive my rudeness. This is my husband and Jenny's father, Barry. Barry, please meet Mr. McDonald." I look at Barry and then say, "Please call me Kyle. It's a pleasure to meet you." I look down at my table and say, "And thanks for the treats. What are they?" Barry answers, "They are cookies shaped like animals that the kids will hopefully get to see today." Jenny then jumps up and down and runs to tell her friends about the surprises her fathers brought for them.

The timer goes off to let me know the kids have had their full two minutes to clean the room. I look around the room, and as expected, see all of my students sitting in their chairs behind their desks in a tidy classroom. "Okay, boys and girls," I begin, "We now have all of our parent volunteers here. I would like to intro . . ." but just as I was about to introduce Michael and Barry to my students, Millie Van Patton comes up to me and whispers, "Can I please see you outside for a minute?" I say, "Boys and girls, please give me a minute while I talk with Mrs. Van Patton. You know that I expect you all to be on your best behavior." My students nod their heads and I follow Millie.

When we get just outside the door, Millie clears her throat and says, "Now, are those two going on the fieldtrip?" I look at her quizzically and say, "Why yes. Those are Jenny's fathers." Millie looks back at me and says, "But aren't they gay?" I look back and her and say, "Well, I guess so." Millie looks at me again, puts her hand on her hip, and says, "And you're going to allow those types of people around our children?" Before I can reply to Millie's statement, Ms. Gladys comes down the hallway and says, "Mr. McDonald, the bus driver said you need to hurry up and get your students down to the pickup station so you aren't late for the tour at the zoo."

Discussion Questions

1. What is your immediate reaction to this situation?
2. How do you handle Millie's questions and concerns?
3. If you then see Millie discussing her concerns with other parents, how do you handle that situation?
4. What activities/lessons can you do to introduce different types of families to your students?
5. What are the pros and cons of doing activities and lessons in question 4 in your district and school environment?

Advice from Veteran Teachers on . . . Different Family Structures

- We would encourage the child who has foster parents to enter the contest, drawing pictures of his foster family and how he thinks he might have looked like as a baby. We would also look through magazines to help him find pictures of toddlers who he thinks he might have looked like.
- We would also talk to the foster parents to get more information from them. We would like to know how he is doing at home, how he is doing emotionally. Do they think that he will be with them for a while or do they feel he will be moving soon? We would also let them know that he is considering entering this contest and ask for their assistance with this project.
- We would talk to the organizers of the contest to let them know that we have a special case where a child does not have pictures of himself or his birth parents, yet would like to enter the contest. We would let them know that we encouraged him to draw his pictures and to write his essay about his foster family.
- If the grandparents, great-grandparents or even parents/guardians are unable to help with homework, we would offer to tutor the child after school. This is especially true if the child is behind. Otherwise, if the child is not behind, we would give them time to do their homework after school. If they are independent, we would work separately in the room and be available to answer any questions the child may have.
- In some cases, we had an after-school homework program on campus. This service was free for students. In those cases, we tried to make sure that the child/ren was/were enrolled in that program.
- Most of us have had children who have either two mommies or two daddies. We would welcome those parents into our rooms and on our fieldtrips. If there are parents who have trouble with this, we would suggest that they speak with the principal. Hopefully, the principal will be supportive of what we've told the complaining parent.

Self-Inflicted Injuries

I Need to Go to the Restroom

"Mrs. Anderson," Juliet comes into the room smiling after eating her lunch. "Did you read my journal last night?" I look up at Juliet and say, "I sure did. Congratulations on getting a solo at the dance recital." Juliet beams with pride. She has been telling everyone who will listen about how much she loves dancing. She is taking tap, jazz, ballet, and hip-hop. She is a rather tall, thin girl and looks like the quintessential ballerina. Sometimes, when she has practice or a performance right after school, she even wears her hair in a tight bun. On the first day of school, when we were introducing ourselves and telling everyone our dreams for the future, Juliet told us that she wanted to go to Julliard in New York City and be a ballerina with the Alvin Ailey Dance Company and a Rockette for Radio City Music Hall. She then told us that when she is "old . . . like in my twenties," she'll pursue a dancing career on Broadway. "So," she told us, "although it's a lot of work now, I know it'll pay off later." I must admit, she is a driven, talented, and confident young lady. These traits will probably take her very far.

Juliet then says, "I can't believe that I got that solo. I worked so hard for it." She then closes her eyes and continues, "I was practicing for hours every evening." Jennifer, who was already in the room, says, "Is it a ballet?" Juliet nods her head. "Um hum." Then Juliet gets on her tippy-toes and spins around. Armando says, "How do you stand on your toes for so long?" Juliet looks over at him, but before she can answer, Jennifer chimes in, "And to think, they do it with a piece of wood in their shoes." Armando's eyes get big and then he says, "Are you for real?" Juliet answers, "Um hum, our ballet shoes do have a block at the toe." Armando, still not understanding asks, "But why? That's got to hurt." I quickly interrupt, "That's *got* to hurt?" Armando thinks about it for a few seconds and then says, "Oh, that *haaas* to hurt." He then smiles at me.

Juliet looks at Armando and continues, "It does kind of hurt in the beginning of our training. But I've been taking ballet since I was three years old. So now it doesn't hurt nearly as bad." Jennifer jumps in and asks, "What do your toes look like? Do you have hammertoes?" Armando and Jennifer begin to laugh. Actually, so do I. Juliet sticks out her lips and says, "No, I don't!" She then says, "But my instructor, Mrs. Ballentine. Whoa! Her feet look horrible!" Jennifer then asks, "Aren't you scared your toes are going to look like hers later on?" Juliet sighs and says, "No. My mom says that Mrs. Ballentine's feet probably looked like that way before she ever started dancing." Just then the bell rings. As we all laugh together, we walk to the playground to get the rest of the class.

When we get to the line, Juliet looks over at me and asks, "May I go to the restroom, Mrs. Anderson?" I look over at Juliet like I can't believe that she is asking me this question. "Juliet," I begin, "You know that you should've gone during lunch." Juliet then looks at me with pleading eyes and says, "But Mrs. Anderson, I came to the classroom and we got to talking and everything. I just lost track of time." I look back at Juliet and say, "Even with that, you will lose two tickets when we get back in the room." Putting the choice back on her, I continue, "So it's up to you. Two tickets from the raffle or go to the restroom?" Juliet looks at me and says, "I think I'll go to the restroom." I nod my head and tell her to come right to the class when she's finished.

After lunch, my students take out their independent reading books for twenty-five minutes. Most of my students like this time of the day. I still have those who take all twenty-five minutes to search the library for a book that they want to read. When they finally select a book, it is usually time to move on to social studies or science.

About three minutes into our independent reading time, Juliet returns to class. She flashes me a smile and puts two of her raffle tickets on my desk. She quickly goes back to her desk, sits down, and begins to read. After several more minutes, I look up to check on my students. I see Juliet lean into Armando to ask him a question. Then I observe him contort his face and say, "Dang, did you throw up?" Juliet's eyes get wide as she looks around the room at all of the kids now staring at her. She then replies, "Shut up, Armando! You don't know anything."

Discussion Questions

1. How do you handle this situation?
2. What do you say to Juliet to find out if this is an isolated case of vomiting or if she is in fact bingeing and purging (bulimia) on a regular basis?
3. What school personnel should you immediately contact regarding this situation?
4. What do you say to Juliet's parents regarding this situation?
5. What are the short-term and long-term physical, social, and psychological/mental effects of bingeing and purging?

It Hurts So Much!

"I think that I'm going to have to cut P.E. short today," I say to Chris, another fourth-grade teacher as I wave my hand in front of my face trying to get some air flow. I continue to rant by saying, "The heat is unbearable." I swat at a gnat and continue, "Plus, my allergies are acting up." I continue to swat at the same gnat and say, "I think I'm gonna faint out here if we don't get some shade soon." Chris starts laughing. "Look at you," he says. "See, that's what happens when you grow up in the freezing northeast instead of the balmy south." I smile back at him, "I don't know how you all do it. I am about to melt out here." Chris continues to laugh. "It's really not that hot today, Millicent. Plus, that's why we are having them walk instead of run today." I look out at my students, most of whom have red faces and sweat pouring down their faces. But I must admit, they are still walking around the track, talking, sipping water from their water bottles, and appearing to enjoy themselves. Well, some of them.

After looking at the track again, Chris shakes his head and says, "What's with Sabrina? It's hot as hell out here and she has on jeans, a T-shirt, boots, and a hoodie." Chris continues to shake his head and adds, "Now she's going to faint out here with all of those clothes on." I look over at Sabrina. I have been wondering about her all year long. She is usually by herself. In class, she sits with a group of other girls, but rarely interacts with them. When I get the chance to see her on the playground, she is usually hanging close to a building by herself or walking around the periphery of the playground by herself. But what really concerns me is that she is always dressed in heavy clothes such as the ones she has on today. When I ask her about this, she always says that she's cold. But there are days like today that I actually see that her face is red and she appears to be perspiring.

I look up at Chris and ask, "What do you think? Do you think that's odd that she's wearing all of those clothes?" Chris looks down at me and says, "You know what? I don't know." Chris continues, "I was raised with five sisters, so I just chalked it up to girl stuff." He smiles and continues, "I remember when we were little. They could be happy, sad, mad, and then happy again in the blink of an eye." He then looks at me seriously and asks, "Do you think she's . . . um . . . got . . . um . . . her period or something like that?" I look at him and reply, "You know, I don't know. How do you ask a young girl if she's started her period?" Chris leans back and laughs. "You expect me to have the answer to that question? You should know better than me." We both laugh and then look back at our students.

Just then, several boys come up to Chris and me walking fast and ask, "What's our time?" I look down at my watch and realize that I forgot to pay closer attention to the time. Luckily, Chris chimes in, "Remember, today we weren't timing ourselves. We were walking for exercise only." All of the boys exclaim, "Ugh!" as we both laugh. Chris then lets them know that they can go over to the grass and rest while we wait for the other students to finish their two laps.

"Ms. Rosewood," I hear. I look down and see Sabrina standing right beside me. "Can I go to the bathroom?" Chris, ever the jokester, chimes in smiling, "*Can* you?" Sabrina gives him a half smile and then says, "May I?" I nod my head and then she heads off to the restroom. Several minutes later, all of our students are sitting on the grass cooling down. "Okay, folks in my class," I announce, "please line up . . ." Just then, I feel a hard tap on my shoulder. I turn around and find Selita Moore, one of our noon duty supervisors, standing with Sabrina at her side. I look into Sabrina's eyes and realize that she is crying. Selita then looks at me and then Sabrina and says, "She says that she is a student of yours." I nod my head and ask, "Yes, what happened?" With that, Selita lifts up Sabrina's right sleeve, which is covered in bloody scratches and old scars. "I found her in the restroom cutting herself with this paperclip." With that, she hands me the bloody paperclip.

Discussion Questions

1. What is your immediate reaction to this situation?
2. Since your other students saw this interaction take place, what are the pros and cons of discussing this situation with them?
3. What does Sabrina's self-mutilation indicate to you?
4. In case of emergency, what should you take to the playground when you are conducting physical education?
5. What should Selita Moore have done regarding taking precautions against the transmission of blood-borne pathogens?

We're Only Holding Our Breath

"So that's what I want to be when I grow up." Sebastian takes a bow and walks back to his seat. I look back at my class and say, "Thank you, Sebastian for your presentation. I learned a lot about dog grooming." Sebastian looks back and gives me a thumb's up. I say to the class, "Please give Sebastian a hand." With that, my fifth graders begin to clap. I look at my clipboard and realize that it's Roger's turn to present his future career choice. "Roger," I say, "Are you ready?" Several of his friends cheer for him as he jumps up and says as he salutes me, "Ready, Mr. Fitzgerald!" I shake my head. Roger is a cutup.

We have been able to get through about four presentations a day, so we should be finished with these by the end of the week. The presentations have really been interesting. Most of my students have expressed wanting to be models, actors, and professional athletes. I was rather surprised and a bit concerned when Raquel did her presentation on the career of being "Rich and Famous for Absolutely No Reason At All." She went on to support her career choice by saying that there are so many reality stars out there now who do nothing more than go to parties and be where the paparazzi are at the right time. Raquel stated in her presentation, "They get to buy the latest purses, shoes, clothes, fly all over the world, date famous people in movies and sports, and go to parties all the time. Why would I want to waste my time and energy going to college when I can just be rich and famous?" When told that most of these young people come from families of pretty impressive wealth, she replied, "My mom is a doctor and my dad is a lawyer. That should be enough."

Following her presentation, I contacted her parents who came after school one afternoon to talk with me about her career choice. Apparently, Raquel had since, changed her mind about her career choice. According to her mother, "We showed her how many of these famous starlets have been incarcerated, on drugs, have trouble with their body image, and have embarrassed themselves and their families with tapes of them in compromising positions." After a few minutes, Dr. Malone continued with a smile, "We also told her that we'll cut her off right now if she keeps this up." I guess that Raquel thought about it and agreed.

Coming back to my own reality, I scan my room and say, "Great job, everyone. I will be putting five marbles in our jar. You have all had wonderful questions, have been attentive, and have been great listeners. I really appreciate that." I then turn my back and place five marbles in our jar. When it's full, the kids have voted for twenty minutes of free time in the classroom. I thought about it and concluded, "It's free and they'll earn it. No problem."

I say to the class, "Please welcome Roger Sedaris to the stage." After giving them a second to clap, I look at my clipboard and say, "Roger has expressed interest in pursuing a career as a stunt double." I then look at Roger and say, "You may begin."

A wonderful orator, Roger says, "Thank you, Mr. Fitzgerald. That is correct. I would like to be a stunt double when I enter the work force. Now, in all honesty, my parents are not too excited about my career choice. My mother has expressed concern about the danger of the job. I told her that the danger is one of the reasons that this career choice entices me. I believe that I am an adrenaline junkie like my uncle Rich." Roger continues, "My uncle Rich skydives, scuba dives, rock climbs, base jumps, and bungee jumps." For the next fifteen minutes he spellbinds all of us with thrilling details of his uncle's job.

"He probably does other things, but these are the things that he is willing to share with me." Roger looks up to the ceiling and continues, "I would love to be able to join him, but my mother is havin' none of that right now." Roger then smiles and concludes his presentation by saying, "But I was thinking. I would love to do exciting things like that, so why not get paid to do them?" With that, Roger takes a bow as the class roars with clapping. Several hands go up from kids who have questions for Roger, but since his presentation went on longer than the others, and the bell rings signaling morning recess, I say, "Please save your questions for Roger until after recess. Please line up." With that, my students line up and I excuse them for recess.

About eight minutes into recess, my door is opened swiftly, and Dori, Maria, and Gwendolyn come running into class. "Mr. Fitzgerald," Dori says, "The boys are playing that hold your breath game again. I look down at the three of them and say, "Hold your breath game? What are you talking about?" Dori looks at me and says, "You know, when they're trying to faint." The look on my face must've indicated that I still didn't understand, so Dori elaborates, "They hold their breath while they're kneeling. Then they jump up fast, and when they get up, they faint." Maria looks at me and says, "And this time, Roger was out for a long time, Mr. Fitzgerald." And with that, I follow the girls out to the playground to find Roger, Bruce, and Clint coming from behind the kindergarten classrooms laughing and stumbling over one another.

Discussion Questions

1. What do you say to Roger, Bruce, and Clint as soon as you get to them?
2. What needs to take place following your discussion with the boys?
3. What are the short-term and long-term dangers of playing a game such as this?
4. What other dangerous games such as this are children playing today?
5. What would you say to your other students in order to dissuade them from playing dangerous games like this?

Advice from Veteran Teachers on . . . Self-Inflicted Injuries

- These are serious situations that can go from 0 to 100 in seconds. A child could "accidentally" cut a major vein or artery, or not be able to be awakened. Thus, serious injury and even death can occur.
- We would talk with our administrator about these types of situations so that those on recess duty can be on alert for children who hide behind buildings during recess or stay in the restroom stalls too long.
- Once again, these cases bring up the fact that teachers always need to have their eyes, ears, and noses open. If children begin to dress differently, wear inappropriate attire given the weather (i.e., big bulky sweatsuits on hot days), have thinning hair, look gaunt, complain about severe throat pain or burning, or smell like bile, then you need to begin questioning that child in private to get more information. That way, early intervention can hopefully prevent a more serious end.
- We would also talk with these children's parents about taking their children to primary care physicians/pediatricians to deal with the physical aspect of their self-inflicted injuries. We would also suggest that they talk with this medical professional about possibly referring

them to a psychologist, who can help children deal with possible emotional issues causing them to inflict injury to themselves.

- Hopefully, in particular with those who are holding their breaths and passing out, your administrator, either during an assembly or morning announcements, can discuss school-wide the seriousness of playing the hold your breath game. Additionally, your administrator can also take this time to discuss the dangerous consequences for those children both participating and watching such behavior, and make it clear that this is not a game and that death can and has occurred in some cases.

Death

Dear Mrs. Johnson

"Okay, everyone," my principal, Mrs. Plummer, says, "Let's get the meeting started." With that, the faculty quiets down. Lori, the other fourth-grade teacher, looks over at me and mouths, "Thank goodness" while she points to her watch. I smile and mouth back to her, "I know." We both want to leave soon to make it to the half-yearly sale at the mall.

What I quickly notice is that it is super quiet in the library. You really could hear a pin drop. Then, I almost panic when I see Mrs. Plummer looks up. She is the strongest and most well-composed woman I know. I am shocked to see that she has puffy, red eyes, a red nose, and tear stains on her face. I see that most of the front office staff, custodial staff, and cafeteria staff are in this meeting, which is extremely unusual because generally only teachers attend our faculty meetings. Lori and I look at one another and shake our heads. "Oh my goodness," I think. "What can this be about?"

Mrs. Plummer, who called this emergency faculty meeting at 2:00, lowers her head and moves her lips silently as if she is praying. She takes several deep breaths, and then finally, she clears her throat and begins to speak. "Well, as you all know, Melita has been battling breast cancer since early October." With that, she clears her throat again and blinks her eyelids several times. I am now feeling uneasy because her usually strong and confident voice is scratchy and weak. After what seems like an hour, she looks up, sucks her lips in, and lowers her head. I look over at Lori and she is pale as a ghost. Finally, Verina Lopez, who has been teaching first grade for twenty-five years at Westland Elementary School, stands up and hugs Mrs. Plummer, saying, "It's all right, Felicia. It's all right." Wide-eyed, I look around the library and see others who are crying too. Now my throat hurts.

When I took over Melita Johnson's fourth-grade class in October, I was not told why she was not returning to school for the entire academic year. I quickly found out that not only was she well loved and respected by the faculty, staff, and parents at Westland, but the kids, too, loved her deeply. "Whew!" I remember thinking. "What have I gotten myself into?"

Following this difficult time, Mrs. Johnson did so many amazing things. She came in and told her students personally what she was going through. I will never forget how strong she was. She maintained her composure and held several students who were crying. Then, when she was going through chemotherapy and radiation, she wrote letters to each student. In her letters, she was more concerned about their well-being than her own. I was amazed at how much she knew about her students. She knew that Kyle was moving up in his belt class in karate, how Laila was working so hard to land her figure eight in ice skating, and that Brian was improving his reading at the local library. When she got weaker, she dictated letters to her husband and he wrote them out and sent them to the class. On many occasions, the kids asked me if they could visit her, but I told them it wasn't possible. I made sure that we wrote her letters, cards, and even videotaped our fieldtrip. According to Mr. Johnson, Melita loved seeing "her babies" laughing and having a good time at the tide pools. I'm getting misty-eyed just thinking about all she's done.

After about a minute and several tissues, Mrs. Plummer begins to speak. "I spoke with Melita's husband today and he told me Melita had been having a hard time breathing for the last few days. So he took her to the hospital this morning." Several teachers begin crying. Mrs. Plummer nods her head slowly. "I know. I know." She takes another deep breath and continues, "The doctors originally thought they had removed all of the cancer, but apparently it had metastasized to her lungs." Now, the majority of the faculty and staff are crying and rocking back and forth. The others simply look shocked. Continuing, Mrs. Plummer says, "I hate to tell you all this, but Melita passed away this afternoon." Next I hear a collective gasp, and folks begin to wrap their arms around each other and cry out loud.

Mrs. Plummer says, "I just can't believe it." She shakes her head and says, "Please go home and hug those you love the most." She then wraps her arms around herself and begins rocking back and forth. "As soon as I hear about the funeral arrangements, I will let you all know." Still sobbing, she grabs a tissue and walks quickly out of the door.

Discussion Questions

1. In your district, how are children told about the death of a teacher, student, or anyone in general?
2. What emotions can you expect children to display after hearing that their teacher has died that day, the next week, and even after a month?
3. What services are available to students in your district who have lost their teacher due to sudden death?
4. What are ways that parents can be notified about Melita Johnson's death?
5. What are some activities that you can do in your classroom to help your students process Mrs. Johnson's death?

Scared to Death

Gary Bullock, our principal, comes into the teachers' lounge after school. He is a no-nonsense kind of guy. I remember when I interviewed, he told me he believed in shooting straight from the hip, so if I was shy or sensitive, I would need to get over that quickly, because he was "all about the kids." I remember looking down at his well-worn cowboy boots, cowboy hat, and bolo tie and thinking that he looked like John Wayne. I soon found out that he runs our school like I would imagine John Wayne running a school—not touchy-feely, just business.

"Oh good, you three are all here." Gary says looking at Robin, Monica, and me. It is the end of the school day and we just came back from our fieldtrip. We finally got the last of our fourth graders on their way home. Whew! Although I love going on fieldtrips, they are so tiring.

Interrupting my thoughts, Gary says, "I just heard that there was a car accident this morning." We all look at one another silently and then back at Gary. "One of our students, Marvin Viera, and his mother were on their way to school and the car blew a tire and spun out of control," Gary continues. Gary looks surprised when Monica screams, "No!!" I scoot over closer to Monica and place my hand on her shoulder. Marvin is in her class and she always talks about what a great kid he is.

Not knowing what to do, Gary looks down at his vibrating cell phone on his hip. He actually looks like he's going to answer his phone, when Robin says, "Well, what happened? Is he okay?" Looking back up, Gary continues, "Sorry about that. Um . . ." He then looks up and looks like he remembers what he was going to say. "Marvin's mother is fine, but Marvin is not doing so well. Apparently, he was not in his seatbelt and went through the front windshield." We all gasp. "Marvin is in the ICU and as soon as I hear anything, I will update you." As he exits the lounge, Monica lays her head on the lunch table and continues to cry.

I am just shocked. I don't think I can even walk right now. We all sit and stare at one another. Robin rubs Monica's back. We are really lucky to have Robin on our team. She has been teaching for thirty-two years and still loves it. I so appreciate that she gives us suggestions, constructive feedback, support, and words of encouragement on tough days. "Are you two okay?" Robin says in her soothing, compassionate voice. Monica still looks shocked. After dabbing her eyes with a tissue, she says, "No." Thinking some more she says, "I just don't know what I'm going to tell my students if . . . if . . . if . . ." she then shakes her head and begins rocking back and forth. Robin places her hand on Monica's, and looks up at me. "And how are you, Gabby?" I look at her and say, "I just don't know how to feel." I look over at Monica and say, "What am I going to tell my kids?" Shaking my head, I look back at Robin and say, "They are going to be devastated." Monica is now crying harder and shaking her head in agreement.

Placing her hand over her mouth, Robin looks away from me for a second. She says, "Unfortunately, this is not the first time I've had to deal with sick kids or children dying." Her voice cracks and she dabs her eyes with a napkin. When she gains her composure, she continues, "Tomorrow, we will all meet with our students in my class and I'll let them know what information we have right now. I will also talk with Gary about getting a letter typed up and sent home to the parents as soon as possible." She quickly writes herself notes on another napkin and continues, "Our students need to write to Marvin and his family. It will be good for them and for our students." I nod at this idea. I really appreciate it when she gives me pointers on what to do. "We also need to set aside a little over an hour to give the kids time to ask questions and just vent." Thinking, she continues, "I can tell you that they are going to be scared about their own mortality." Now Monica is crying harder. "I didn't go into teaching to bury kids," Monica says. Robin looks at her and rubs her back, "None of us did. But, sometimes this happens and we have to deal with it as best we can to help our students deal the best they can." I have to admire Robin's resolve.

Robin looks around the lounge and says, "Gabby, sit with Monica until she calms down." I nod my head. Getting up she continues, "I'm going to take care of the letter." With that, she exits the lounge. After about a half-hour, in a daze, Monica and I somehow get home for the evening.

The next day, I get to school late because there was an accident on the freeway. I am upset because I have yard duty too. So I just rush to the playground and begin to monitor our students' behavior. On my BlackBerry, I get a text from Robin informing me that she has taken care of everything and reserved the library so that all our students can sit comfortably while we discuss Marvin's situation. I take a deep breath and continue looking out at the playground. This sure is going to be a difficult day.

A group of my students come to me on the playground and ask, "Did you hear that Marvin Viera was in an accident yesterday?" Not sure how to respond, I simply nod my head and say, "Yes, I did." Natalia asks, "Is he okay?" I look at her and say, "You know what, Natalia, I'm not really sure. As soon as I hear something, I'll let you know." After about fifteen more minutes, the bell rings and all the kids on the playground line up. I blow my whistle and shout, "All right everyone, let's walk safely to our classes."

When we get to the classroom, Gary, Robin, and Monica are at my door with several strangers. When I look into their faces, I can tell that something is seriously wrong. Robin takes me to the side and says, "I have been trying to find you all morning. I hate to tell you like this, but Marvin passed away early this morning. Gary got the call a little while ago." Joining us, Gary adds, "These are counselors from the district office who are going to help the students with processing their feelings." I look over at the "guests," then at our fourth graders who are silent and look like they've been hit by two-by-fours. Monica looks like she's in a state of shock. Instantly, I feel the tears burning my eyes.

Discussion Questions

1. What activities would you do with your students after the principal and the counselors leave?
2. What children's books dealing with death are available?
3. What services are available for teachers in your district who have had a student die?
4. What are ways that parents can be notified about a student's unexpected death?
5. What should parents be told to look out for in relation to their children processing the death of a peer?

Robbie the Hamster

"If you can hear the sound of my voice, clap once." With that, some of my second graders clap. Saying it a little louder, I say, "If you can hear the sound of my voice, clap twice." This time, the majority of my students clap. "If you can hear the sound of my voice, clap three times." After that, all of my students clap and look up at me for further instructions. I look at each table, then say, "This was much better. It took only three times to get everyone's attention." Thinking about it some more, I say, "And that's not too bad considering we were doing art projects." Nodding my head, I once again peruse my class and continue; "Now next time, I want to get it to two claps." Diamond, one of the funniest kids I know, gives me a thumb's up and says, "You got it, Mr. Michaels" she says, flashing her million-dollar smile. "Okay, class, "I say. I'm going to hold you to Diamond's promise." I quickly look at the clock and say, "Now, it's time for recess." The kids get excited and begin to push their chairs back on the tile. "Wait, wait," I say as I raise my hands to get their attention. "We aren't going anywhere until this room is sparkling clean." I look at my watch again and say, "Let's get this room clean in two minutes. If you do, I will add three blocks to our jar." I look around the room and say, "You may begin."

I walk around the room as the kids clean up. Felix, who sits in the front of the room, is staring squarely into the cage of our class hamster, Robbie. I walk over to his desk ready to ask him why he isn't cleaning the room like his friends. But when I get closer, I see why he is staring into Robbie's cage. Robbie is lying on his side and breathing erratically. Realizing that I am standing right behind him, Felix says, "Mr. Michaels, Robbie doesn't look good. Is he okay?" I look back at Robbie and tell Felix, "I'm not sure." Now I am kneeling down on one knee looking into the cage. I gently tap the cage and wait for Robbie to respond. He doesn't. I look over at Felix whose face looks panicked and say, "Now don't worry. After school, I will take Robbie over to my brother's house. He's a vet. I'm pretty sure that Robbie is just tired." Not sure if this is helping Felix or not, I say, "Um, now why don't you go over to the library and help Rebecca's group straighten out the books." Looking at me, Felix nods his head in agreement, and then scurries off to the library.

I am still looking at Robbie's cage when Diamond comes up to me and says, "Mr. Michaels, the room is clean." She then looks into Robbie's cage and shouts, "Oh my God! Robbie's dead." I jump up quickly and turn to look into the shocked faces of my second graders. Trying to quickly contain what could possibly be a disaster, I say, "No, he's not. He's still breathing." I look at Diamond whose eyes are as big as golf balls. "See, Diamond," I say, "his chest is moving up and down." She slowly moves her eyes from me and back to Robbie's cage. Now the majority of the class is clustered around the tiny space that houses Robbie's cage. "Oh," Maria says, "I see his chest moving." Other students chime in, "Me too, me too." Feeling like this is just too much to deal with, I quickly get my students lined up and out to the playground for recess.

After school, I call my brother, Louis, and ask him if I can bring Robbie over to his clinic. I let my principal, Mrs. Uribe, know that I am taking Robbie to a vet, and check out early. As I gently place Robbie on the floor of my passenger seat, I think to myself, "Please don't let this hamster be sick or die. I don't know what I am going to do if he dies." Needless to say, the ride to my brother's clinic was long and thought provoking.

After I've waited for about twenty minutes, Gayle, the assistant in Louis's office, flags me to the back. In an attempt to make small talk, she says, "Now who do we have here, James?" I smile at her and look back at Robbie's cage. "This is my class hamster, Robbie. I don't know exactly when he went on his side and began breathing like this, but by about 1:30 this afternoon, several of my students noticed it." Needing any kind of comforting words, I ask, "Do you think he'll be okay?" Gayle, who has yet to take her eyes off Robbie, says, "You know, I'm not sure. Louis is the doctor, so we'll let him do a thorough check to see what's going on." She then looks up at me and says, "Why don't you have a seat and Louis will be with you as soon as he's finished with his other patient."

As I get comfortable in room 2, I look back at Robbie's cage. He is still on his side and his breathing is now labored and infrequent. Just when I am about to panic, I hear a knock on the door and Louis enters the room. "Hey kid brother," he says. "What's going on?" Feeling a bit relieved, I say, "I'm doing okay, but I'm not so sure about Robbie." Louis tilts his head to the side and peers into Robbie's cage. With a look of concern on his face, he says, "Honestly, this little guy doesn't look good." He tilts his head to the other side, picks up Robbie's cage, and continues, "Let me run some tests on him. Just have a seat and I'll be right back." With that, he rushes out of the room, leaving me to myself.

After what seems like a lifetime, Louis comes back into the room and says, "James, I don't think that there's a need to run tests on Robbie. I felt several lumps on him, and now he's vomiting and convulsing." Not wanting to hear what he's saying, I ask, "Are you saying that he's dying?" Nodding, Louis says gently, "That's exactly what I'm saying. My best guess is that he has some type of cancer. I've seen this before." Looking up at the lights, he continues, "I think that the most humane thing for us to do is to put him down." I nod my head, giving my brother permission to put Robbie to sleep.

Discussion Questions

1. How would you tell your students that Robbie has died?
2. What are the pros and cons of having class pets?
3. What are the pros and cons of getting another class pet following Robbie's death?
4. What is your school and school district's policy regarding class pets?
5. What are the pros and cons of telling your students that an animal has been "put to sleep" instead of saying that it is dead?

Advice from Veteran Teachers on . . . Death

- Most times the child is very shocked that the death occurred. The parents/family members may not have been able or willing to let the child know that the person is so sick that they may potentially die.
- Academically, you have to make some concessions. Sometimes you have to put the academics on hold in order for the child to fully heal. We don't believe that children will learn anything while grieving the death of a loved one if they're being "forced" to complete assignments. They may not be able to concentrate long enough to do work. Let them do what they love to do academically. If they love to read, write, or draw, allow them to do that.
- Request the counselor through the school district. Not all schools or districts have onsite school psychologists. If counseling is not available, let the parents know that there are available psychologists who charge their fees on a sliding scale.
- Pay attention to changes in social behaviors, eating habits, sleeping habits, etc. Students may display tempers, show aggression, cry, be passive, daydream, and be unable to focus. Children grieve differently from adults in many cases.
- If children bring religion into the conversation, we suggest that you answer the best that you can. After a child asked, "Did he go to heaven?" several of us have answered, "Some people believe that he is in heaven." Then suggest that the child talk with their parents about where people go when they die.
- Check in with the parents on a regular basis to see how things are going at home.
- If a teacher passes away, hopefully there is a system in place so that faculty will be notified in a timely fashion. If your school does not have a phone tree, then you might want to suggest one; it can spread the information quickly to other teachers.
- If you are the one who is responsible for telling your students about the death of a teacher or a student, let them know what happened. Let them know that accidents and terminal illnesses don't happen all of the time. The kids need to know that the child was sick or if it was an accidental death. We've had cases where children have died at our schools, and when the other children were not told how the child died, they made up stories on how they

thought the child had died. Also be upfront when telling students about the death or illness of a class pet.

- Allow them to have a conversation about any deaths they've experienced or how they are feeling with this current death. You have to let them talk about their feelings and fears. This may be tough for you, but it's important that they have a safe place to express their feelings. You have to be vulnerable and let them know if you've been through the experience of losing someone or something as well. Following that conversation, you might want to give the kids some down time. They may want to read, write, draw, or even play games. Some might want to write or draw about their feelings or write letters or cards to the deceased or the deceased person's family.
- If your district allows you to have class pets, have the same type of discussion as suggested above. We don't suggest that you have a ceremony for the class pet. Maybe in a week or so, you may want to get another class pet. Have the class decide on the kind of pet or the name of the new class pet.

Internet Usage

Inappropriate.com

"Whew!" I say to Manuela, another fifth-grade teacher. "I am so happy that this field-trip is almost over." The fifth-grade team, four classes in all, has taken our classes to the museum as a complement to our Social Studies program, which is U.S. History. The museum has wonderful exhibits on Native American history, the Civil War, the Civil Rights Movement, the Women's Suffrage Movement, and the Japanese internment camps. In my opinion, it was a great experience for our students to see all of the photographs and artifacts, and to hear the docents, dressed in attire worn by those they represented, tell stories of the past. But in all honesty, this bus ride is driving me crazy. It's warm outside and these windows aren't letting in enough wind to deal with the heat and our fifth graders and their questionable body odor.

"I know," Manuela says, interrupting my thoughts, "Although it was a great experience, it sure was long." I nod my head in agreement. "I was thinking the same thing. I wonder if we could do this fieldtrip over two days." Manuela looks at me as if she is considering my suggestion. "I mean," I continue, "It's just so much to try and squeeze into one day." Manuela says, "We should ask Charles and Monica. They've been doing this for years." Charles has been teaching fifth grade for fourteen years, and Monica has been teaching it for eight years. Charles and Monica's classes are on the other bus. I wonder if their bus is hot too.

Manuela then leans closer to me and says, "Plus, it's hot too and some of these kids are stinking. I mean," she continues, "did they bathe in the cologne or perfume?" I nod my head, "Bathe in it? Did they skip the shower and swim in it?" Manuela and I both laugh. "Just think about it though," Manuela continues, "If we push for this field-trip to be over two days, that's two days of being on a bus!" "Girl," I say to Manuela, "Forget I ever made that suggestion." I look around at the faces of all sixty-four fifth graders, who look just as hot as we do. We both lean back and brace ourselves for the thirty-minute bus ride back to school.

When we get back, it's really too late to do a significant lesson. That bus driver must have picked up speed because none of us planned on having any school time after the fieldtrip. I thought we would have the kids get their stuff, say goodbye, and be on their way. But just as luck would have it, it didn't work out that way. Next fieldtrip, I will plan on having an activity ready just in case things happen like they did today.

Once settled back in our classroom, I have to think of an "educational" activity the kids can do for the little over thirty minutes before the end of the day. I put the kids into groups and say, "We are going to do Internet searches on several of the topics we learned about during our fieldtrip. This is just the start to a larger project." Surprisingly, my students are listening intently. "So," I say, "I will need one group to look up several key figures in history on the Civil Rights Movement, the Trail of Tears, the Women's Suffrage Movement, and the Japanese internment camps." Hands begin to go into the air quickly. I select a group and ask them which topic they would like to search.

As usual, one of the computers in the classroom is not working. We have only four computers. I guess I should be glad that three of them are working. Usually, it's a real good day when two are working properly. Just then, Juana asks, "Ms. Smith, would it be okay if I use my I-Phone? I can download images off the website and everything." I look up and ask, "Do you have to pay extra for that service?" Juana laughs. "No. I used to, but when my mom got my first phone bill with all of the downloads and texting, she got me unlimited." Thinking that this will not be a problem, I agree to let Juana and her group sit close together and do their Internet search on the Women's Suffrage Movement.

As I walk around the room to monitor my students, I see Juana's group is sitting awfully close to one another. Initially, I brush it off because they are looking at a screen the size of a small calculator. But as I turn my back to check on the group in front working on the Trail of Tears, I hear Juana's group giggling and Juana saying, "Shush!" In order to catch them off guard, I go around the class and pretend I am looking for something on the back wall. When I get back to Juana's group, I peek down and see pictures of Juana on the screen dressed in a bikini. I see other pictures of her with several friends who also wear bikinis. Just then Caitlin looks up and says, "Oh my God! It's Ms. Smith." I look at the girls and back at the phone. "What are you doing?" is all I can ask. Juana clears her throat and says, "I was, um, looking, um, at my MySpace page."

Discussion Questions

1. How could this situation have been avoided?
2. What types of protective software are available on your classroom computers?
3. What words or keyword searches can get through the protective software? (e.g., *Little Women*)
4. What would you say to your whole class about Internet responsibility?
5. What is your school's policy regarding cell phones and Internet usage?

It's Easy Money

"Okay, folks," I say to my fifth graders, "Today we are going to work with adjectives." I continue, "When I'm reading some of your pieces, if I close my eyes, I can't get a rich picture of whatever it is you're talking about because you haven't given your reader the descriptors or adjectives necessary to create a clear mental picture of the image you're thinking about." I turn to the dry-erase board and write "cat" on the board next to a picture of a cat I had cut out from an expired calendar. I turn back to my students and ask, "Now let's look at the image on the board. What are some words I can use to describe this cat to people who do not have a picture of this cat to look at?"

My students look at me as if I have gone crazy. Cornelius, a boisterous and outgoing young man with a sly smile, says, "Um, gray." He turns to Marcellus, Keisha, and Sarah and gives them high fives. Not moved by this display, I write "gray" on the board and ask Cornelius, "Does the cat have only gray fur?" After looking at the picture of the cat, he responds, "Oh no, Mr. Brown. It's gray with white paws and white fur on the tips of its ears." I smile and say, "Exactly." I then ask my students, "Please close your eyes and visualize what this cat looks like in your mind." I look at the picture and say out loud, "It's a gray kitten, with whiskers that seem too long for its small face. It has white paws, and the tips of its ears are white as well. The kitten also has a small, triangular-shaped black nose. It also has a small red bow on its left ear and a fuchsia collar around its neck. There's even a little dirt on the kitten's front paws."

I walk around the room and ask my students to open their eyes. "Look at the picture of the kitten on the board. How did your mental image of the kitten compare to the actual image?" I see my students nodding their heads. "Now," I continue, "Look at what this level of description gives your readers. It allows them to see the pictures you have in your head of the objects or concepts you are writing about." I go to my desk and pick up a sheaf of calendar pages. I have twenty-seven pages with animals, little kids, and national landmarks on them. I spread them out on the front table, then turn to my students and say, "You are each going to select a calendar page. Then take out a blank sheet of paper and give us a rich description of the object in the picture. After that, we will read our descriptions in small groups while the other group members have their eyes closed. They will give you feedback on the quality of your description when they open their eyes." Some kids are looking directly at the front table as if they are trying to figure out which calendar page they want to select. Before I transition them to the next stage of this project, I say, "You may talk with your neighbors during this activity. Pointing to our Voice Level chart in the front of the room, I say, "You may talk at a level two." I begin calling rows up to select their calendar page.

While my students are working, I walk around and monitor their progress. Some students raise their hands and ask for help with vocabulary. Dominique asks, "I mean, I know what it is, but what is the name of the thing that is made of clay and has a face and is on castles? I remember it from that movie, but now I can't think of what it is." I make a mental note, "Need to work more on vocabulary." I am finding they can describe what object they're talking about, but do not have the official label or word for it. I look down and say, "Gargoyle, Dominique." Before she asks me to spell it for her, I say, "Sound it out, look it up, or get on the computer." She smiles and continues working.

When I get to Cornelius's row, I stand back. I notice he is trying to whisper, but because he sits in front of those he is talking to, I can hear him as he twists around to address them. Then I hear him say, "Yo, it's so easy. I got more money now than I know what to do. And all they want is for me to take off my shirt. It can't get no easier than that." He then continues, "When y'all come over tonight, all you have to do is take your shirts off. I got the webcam all set and everything." Several of the boys around Cornelius begin to get giddy. "Just think," Charlie says, "We got a four-day weekend. It's about to be on and poppin'."

Discussion Questions

1. What's your first reaction regarding this situation?
2. What school personnel need to be notified immediately regarding this situation?
3. Imagine that you have to call the parents involved in this situation. What would you say to them in a group meeting to explain to them what you've overhead?
4. What are the pros and cons of webcams for personal use and in classrooms with elementary age children?

5. How would an elementary age child set up an Internet site so that he or she could receive remuneration from strangers for acts such as these?

Looking for Love

"Jamilah . . . Jamilah. . . Jamilah," I say to the girl staring out the window with her head tilted. Finally, Maria touches her on her shoulder and points to me and says, "Mrs. Whitfield wants you." Jamilah's eyes get big and she looks up at me with concern on her face. She saunters to the front of the classroom where I am seated. I am grading my third graders' spelling tests, but I always make sure to look up and check on my students. That's when I noticed Jamilah staring out of the same window again.

When she finally gets to the table where I'm sitting, she asks, "Yes, Mrs. Whitfield," in her usual whisper-like voice. I look at her and whisper, "Honey, are you okay today?" I motion for her to have a seat next to me. As she takes her seat, I look up at the rest of my students, who are supposed to be finishing up their math assignments. "Boys and girls," I announce, "You have more than enough time to get your math work done. Most, if not all of you, should be able to finish before lunch. Then you won't have to take the rest home for homework. So I encourage you to get to work." I look back at Jamilah and quickly back to the class. "Oh, before I forget," I say, "You all know that you may read when you are done or sign up to help others in the class who may have questions." I scan the room to make sure they are paying attention. "Since you all know what to do, I expect you to work hard. Any questions?" The kids shake their heads. "Okay," I announce, "You may get back to work."

I turn my attention back to Jamilah. "Yes, honey," I say quietly. "Sorry about that." I reach over, touch her hand, and lean toward her before saying, "I have noticed that you've been sort of out of it all day." Jamilah turns her head down. She usually does this when she believes that adults are lecturing her or punishing her in some way. I continue, "Is everything okay?" Jamilah doesn't say anything and her facial expression is frozen. I then say, "You're not in any trouble, Jamilah. I just want to make sure that everything is okay. But I can't help you if you don't tell me what's going on." Jamilah is now moving her eyes back and forth. I can tell that she is thinking whether she should trust me or not. She sucks in her lips and lets out a great sigh. But, she still doesn't say anything or look up from the table. Once again, I try to get her to open up to me. "Jamilah, would you feel more comfortable talking with another teacher or our principal?" With that, she looks up quickly and shakes her head vigorously. I say, "It's okay, sweetie." I lean in closer to her and ask, "Would you feel more comfortable if we go outside and talk?" Slowly, Jamilah nods her head.

I get up and count to three. This is the universal signal in room 31 to stop what you're doing, remain quiet, and look up to me and wait for further instructions. "Boys and girls," I say, "I am going just outside the door to talk with Jamilah." I look at our Chore Chart and see that Megan is the class captain this week. I look over at her and say, "Megan, if anything should happen, come and notify me, okay?" Megan nods her head. I look over my class again and say, "Keep up the good work." With that, I motion for Jamilah to join me outside of our classroom door.

Once we are outside of the classroom, I ask, "So Jamilah, what's going on?" With her head turned down she says, "I'm . . . um . . . um . . . scared." She then sniffs, covers her eyes with her hands, and begins crying. I lean in closer to her and embrace her. With that, she begins to cry even harder. "Jamilah, honey, why are you scared?" I ask. When she is finally calm, she says, "I heard my sister on the phone with one of her friends." Interrupting her, I ask, "Which sister?" Jamilah says, "Indira, the one in seventh grade." I ask, "What did she say on the phone, Jamilah?" She then says, "She told her that she was going to get on a plane to fly to meet her boyfriend in Germany. The one she met on the Internet." She looks up and continues, "I heard her say he bought her a ticket, sent her a fake passport, and when she gets to him, he is going to shower her with presents and love." I then ask, "Jamilah, do your parents know about this?" She shakes her head and says, "When she saw me, she told me we would both get in trouble if they found out. So please don't tell, Mrs. Whitfield. Please don't tell."

Discussion Questions

1. What do you say to Jamilah about the fact that you are a mandated reporter when any child is in danger or in need?
2. What are your next steps regarding this situation?
3. How well do you think Mrs. Whitfield handled her conversation with Jamilah?
4. What are some lessons/activities that you can teach to promote Internet safety with your students?
5. Mrs. Whitfield uses many terms of endearment and touches Jamilah. Are these appropriate with all cultural groups? How about across gender groups?

Advice from Veteran Teachers on . . . Internet Usage

-   In most districts, Internet usage is highly restricted. Make sure that this is the case in your district. We've had colleagues who had their students reading Louisa Mae Alcott's classic *Little Women* when pornographic images and websites came up. So, in order to protect yourself, double-check to make sure that your district has provided safe computing environments for your students.
-   Although it seems great that a student has Internet access on her phone, you have no way to require parental locks or even closely monitor the websites and links that she is checking. We suggest that you tell her thank you, but no thank you. Then, find the students something else to do.
-   As far as students having cell phones at school, this is becoming more popular; it is problematic for elementary school teachers. Most districts have strict policies on when children can use their cell phones. As some of these phones have Internet access that you cannot monitor, adhering to your district's policy regarding cell phones is crucial.
-   We have all had students who have *MySpace* or *Facebook* pages. We encourage you to have discussions with your students on how to responsibly use these services. Most of our students who do have web pages on these sites have been far too trusting and simply assume that their friends are the only ones who can access their webpage. Thus, they post their private thoughts, phone numbers and home address, pictures of themselves in bathing suits, in front of their houses, in their bedrooms, at their school, etc. Then, once again, a pedophile who is manipulative and cunning can pretend to be a young child who empathizes with this child in order to begin communicating with this child. Additionally, this pedophile now knows what the child and possibly their friends look like and where they live and attend school. As you can see, this can potentially lead to tragic consequences.

• With the other cases, you need to notify your administrator immediately. Trafficking children for sex is sadly a booming international problem. Thus, although it may seem like they are just taking their shirts off or just communicating with a friend, pedophiles are manipulative, cunning, and extremely dangerous. These situations can turn bad quickly with kidnapping, prostitution, drug abuse, rape, and death being real possibilities. Once again, notify your administrator immediately.

Incarceration

Possible Careers

* Physician	* Teacher	* Electrician	* Artist
* Lawyer	* Principal	* Mechanic	* Hair Stylist
* Teacher	* Secretary	* Pharmacist	* Sales Person
* Veterinarian	* Bouncer	* Astronaut	* NBA Player
* Singer	* Model	* Dancer	* MLB Player
* Actor/Actress	* Store Owner	* Dog Walker	* NFL Player
* Military	* Police Officer	* Correctional Officer	* Writer

Career Day

After studying the list we just created on the chalkboard, I turn back to face my fourth graders. "This is a good list to start our discussion on possible career choices for your futures. We are going to investigate what type of education you will need to pursue for these careers and other careers we discover through our research. Some may require you to go to college to get a bachelor's degree or even a master's degree. Some may require you to keep going to college and earn a doctorate." I look back at the list and point to several of the career choices listed. "And some may require you to go to a trade school or do an apprenticeship, and some don't require you to go to school at at all, such as an NBA or major league player." I then hear some of my students in the back cheer. I look back there and say, "Now, you may think going to school is a drag . . ." I say and I notice some of them nodding their heads in agreement, "but we will find that there are few spots in those careers, thus decreasing the likelihood that one of us would be able or even qualified to get one of those coveted positions."

Reggie raises his hand and says, "I know that's right. I used to tell my grandma that I wanted to play professional basketball. Grandma used to laugh at me and say 'You're too short to ever play in the NBA.'" Reggie and a few students giggle. Then Monique chimes in, "Plus you ain't got game, Reg." Now all of my students begin to laugh. I chuckle too. Reggie says, "That's cold, Monique." He looks up and says, "I really don't have game, Ms. Fields. My grandma says I better keep my butt in school for as long as I can."

Still laughing, I say, "See, that's a great example. We may want to do one of these career choices, but we may not be tall enough or may not be good in that area. When I was growing up, I wanted to be a doctor. Then I took Biology and we had to dissect a frog. I thought I was going to be sick. I kept thinking, "There's no way that I can get to medical school where you have to dissect a human body if I can't even dissect a frog."

Most of my students say, "Ugh!" Monique raises her hand and with her nose scrunched up asks, "You have to dissect a human in medical school?" I reply, "You sure do." Once again, I hear students say in unison, "Eeeyooo!"

Excited by this discussion, but realizing that the bell is about to ring in about five minutes, I say, "We're going to go through each of these careers and talk about the specific training you will need for them." I pick up the flyers I created for our parents about our career day and ask, "Do any of you have questions?" Several kids raise their hands. I call on Miriam, who looks down at a list she's been making. "What's an apprenticeship, a doctorate, and a trade school?" Several of the kids who had their hands raised lower them. I look at Miriam and at the clock and say, "Don't worry about those right now. We're going to discuss all of these terms during the next few weeks." Miriam and a few kids nod their heads so I continue. Passing out the flyers and response sheets, I say, "Please let your parents know we need them to come to our class and talk with us about their careers in order to make this a great Career Day." Then the bell rings signaling the end of our school day.

The next day, Matthew comes into the class early and drops his backpack on the floor. "Ms. Fields," Matthew begins, "My dad wanted me to make sure that you get this. He told me that I had to bring it to you before I go to the playground." I smile because I have been working with Matthew on being more responsible. "Thank you, Matthew. I am so proud of you for taking care of business." Matthew smiles and hands me a crumpled response sheet. Then, just as quickly as he entered the room, he headed for the playground.

I look at the response sheet and read the note written by Matthew's father.

"Dear Ms, Fields. I want to be a part of your Career Day. I made bad decisions regarding my future and career and sold drugs. As a matter of fact, I was convicted of running a meth lab. That got me a ten-year stretch in prison. While incarcerated, I lost touch with my kids, saw so many friends get killed and stabbed in jail, and there were no programs in prison to better myself. Plus, try getting a job on the outside with felonies and having to check in with a P.O. all time! Prison ain't no place to be and I think the kids need to know that. I am in no way proud of this and am working hard to make sure my kids don't follow in my path. I would love to come and let your kids know that selling drugs is a career choice, but one that will lead to death or jail. I look forward to hearing from you soon. Please call me at 555-1234. Sincerely, John Rogers.

Discussion Questions

1. What are the pros and cons of Matthew's father being a part of career day?
2. What is your opinion regarding Mr. Rogers saying that selling drugs is a career choice?
3. How will you respond to Mr. Rogers?
4. If you choose to have Mr. Rogers as a part of career day, how would you introduce him and his career?
5. Would there be repercussions in your district and school setting if you allow Mr. Rogers to speak to your students? If so, what do you think they would be?

It Was Illegal, but Was It Wrong?

Anna, a third-grade teacher, says as we walk from the parking lot early in the morning, "Did you see the protest on the news last night?" Both morning people, we usually get to work well before most of our colleagues. This is a benefit because that means we can prep before the mad rush closer to the beginning of the school day. We have open access to the copier, the die cutters, the butcher paper, and the book-binding machine. I also have time to organize my thoughts and get ready for my fifth graders with few interruptions from others. Today, however, Anna has other plans for me.

"No," I say honestly. "I went home last night, worked out, showered, ate dinner, graded a few papers, and then went to bed." Anna says, "About fifty members of my church protested that abortion clinic over there on Third Avenue." She takes a sip of her steaming cup of coffee and continues, "I just wish they would get rid of that abortion clinic. They claim to talk about responsible parenting, birth control and stuff like that. But who do they think they are fooling? We all know those types of clinics are nothing but places where confused young girls go and have their babies sucked out of their bodies."

Remembering to lock the front door behind us, we continue to the back of the office. When I turn the corner to the teachers' lounge, I see Marvin, one of our custodians, bending over picking paperclips up off the carpet. "Hello, Marvin," we say in unison. Marvin looks up and smiles. "Hello there, you two." Seeing what he is doing, I say, "I just hate when paperclips get on carpet. They are so hard to pick up." Marvin says, "And try picking them up with hands as big as mine." He displays his hands and we nod our heads in agreement. "Do you need any help?" I ask Marvin as Anna puts her lunch in one of the refrigerators. "Oh no, you two get ready for your kids. I'm done here. I'm going to Mr. Hollis's room to change some lights." With that, Marvin puts the full box of paperclips back on the table with the telephone and exits through the side door.

As if she simply put her thoughts on pause, Anna continues with her earlier discussion. "Like I was saying, I am so proud of my church. I couldn't go because I can't get arrested with me being a teacher and all. But I am still proud of them." As if waiting for me to respond, Anna looks at me intently. Not really knowing what to say, I finally say, "Um, I didn't get to watch the news. I was so tired." I put my lunch in the same refrigerator and try to change the subject. "So, are you all ready for your fieldtrip to the zoo tomorrow?" Anna nods and says, "I am so happy that Blossom is on my team. She is such an organized and happy-go-lucky person. She took care of the lunches, first aid kits, the buses, copying the permission slips and everything. The two things I had to take care of were getting three parent volunteers and making sure my students returned their signed permission slips." Anna says, "Are you going to work in here or do you want to go to your classroom?" Not sure which way to go, I say, "I'm going to work in here. I have some copying to do. What about you?" Anna answers, "I'm going to stay in here, but I'm going to work at the table so I can finish grading their math tests." I smile and say, "Okay, Anna. If you need anything, I'll be in the Xeroxing area."

I was able to get everything done and ready for school to begin. Just then the first bell rings signaling our students to stop playing, walk faster, finish their breakfast, or quickly go to the restroom and head to the classrooms. As Anna and I walk toward our classes, I see my students are lined up outside the door. I also notice a commotion and get closer to investigate with Anna right by my side. Marisol turns around and says, "Oh, Ms. Rothchild, Kimberly is crying!" I move to the front of the line to see Kimberly weeping uncontrollably. "Kimberly," I say, "What's going on?" Kimberly continues to cry. Elaine, who is Kimberly's best friend, jumps in and says, "Her mother was locked up for protesting at that abortion clinic last night." She then continues, "She said her mother wanted to keep it opened and stuff." With that, Kimberly begins to cry even harder. When I look over at Anna, I notice her bristle.

Discussion Questions

1. How do you immediately handle this situation?
2. How would you handle a situation if your students want to further discuss the protest and the clinic?
3. If Anna wants to continue this discussion during lunch, how would you handle that situation?
4. As a teacher, can your certification/credential be revoked for a misdemeanor? Can it be revoked for a felony?
5. What school officials or community agencies are available for children who have parents who are incarcerated or have been incarcerated?

Monkeying Around

". . . and the little monkey and his mother and three brothers and two sisters went home and lived happily ever after. The end." I say as I close the book. The ten boys and nine girls in my kindergarten class begin clapping. They've been doing that since the beginning of the school year. I'm still not sure if they are clapping because they like the way I read stories or because they think it is almost recess time. I look up at the clock and realize we still have eight minutes before recess. I decide to ask questions. "Did you enjoy the story?" While most of the kids nod their heads, Leah and a few others shake their heads no. "Leah, would you like to share why you didn't like the story?" I ask, curious to hear what she has to say. Leah says, "I didn't like the book because the book was ugly." I think to myself, '*Ugly?* Oh my goodness. What do I say to a response like that?' I keep thinking and then remember, "Scaffold! That's what I was taught to do, right?" "Leah," I finally say, "What do you mean, ugly?" Leah looks up at me and says, "It's just ugly, Mr. Lange." Once again, I am perplexed. "OK," I think to myself. "That didn't help and we still have seven minutes left." Then I have that ah-ha moment all new teachers look for. "Leah, what about the book was ugly?" I ask.

Leah gives me that look that lets me know we are finally on the same page. "The pictures was ugly. They didn't have no colors on them," she says. "So," I reframe her responses so that I don't embarrass her, "You didn't like the pictures because you thought they *were* ugly and because they didn't have *any* color on them?" I ask. "Did anyone else not like the pictures?" Now all of the hands go up. "So," I ask, "What could the illustrator have done to make the illustrations or pictures more appealing to you?" Several students raise their hands. I scan the rug and call on Mimi, who says, "I think that maybe he could've used some crayons or something like that." I nod my head. "Does anyone else have a suggestion?" My students look like they are really thinking about this question. Rodney raises his hand and says, "Mimi took my answer." Not deterred, I say, "What about paint? Maybe the illustrator could have used watercolors like we did in class. Or maybe even photographs." I twist my body and point to our bookshelf. We have a lot of books in our Book Nook that have photographs in them. Just then, Rodney, who is one smart kindergartener, says, "But Mr. Lange, you always say that only nonfiction books have photographs." He continues, "You just said that during science when you read that book about snakes."

Once again, they didn't teach me this in student teaching. He is right. I did say that this morning. "You know what, Rodney? You're right." I say nodding in agreement. "I did say that and that's not right. There are fiction or narrative books that have photographs. As a matter of fact, I have one right here." I reach over to the books close to my rocking chair and hold up a book. Rodney looks really confused now. "So did you lie to us, Mr. Lange?" Surprised, I say, "Oh no, Rodney. I just made a mistake." Rodney thinks hard and nods his head. "Okay, Mr. Lange." I scan the rug and apologize to my students. My mother, who is a teacher too, has always told me that when I became a teacher that I would make mistakes and that I need to be honest with my students, accept it, and then apologize. I think that they are learning valuable lessons with this as well. That I don't have all of the answers.

I look back up at the clock and find that we have three minutes left. Thinking quickly, I say, "Now let's look at their family. Their family may look a little different than some of our families, right?" All of the children are looking at the last page intently. Just then, Rodney raises his hand and says, "Oh yeah. Where's their daddy?" I look at the book and reply, "They don't mention the daddy in the story?" I scan the rug again and ask, "Where do you think their daddy is?" Several hands go up. Rodney is now waving his hand in the air, but he has shared several times already. I decide to call on Grace. "I bet he's at work," she says. I nod. "He may be at work. Does anyone else have a guess?" Luther's hand is up and I call on him next. "Maybe he's asleep in the bed." Once again, I nod. "Good guess." I scan the rug and decide to call on Lillian. "Maybe he's in jail." I then hear a loud gasp on the rug and most of the children cover their mouths with their hands. I, too, am surprised and find it hard to hide it. Then I hear Rodney say, "He ain't in jail." Lillian then chimes in, "You don't know that. He could be in jail just like my dad and my aunt." She looks at me and says, "Huh, Mr. Lange?"

Discussion Questions

1. What is your response to Lillian?
2. Are you concerned about Lillian? Give your rationale as to why or why not.
3. What are the benefits of planning read alouds prior to actually reading books to your students?
4. What are the pros and cons of reading books that may deal with sensitive issues both directly and indirectly?
5. How do you handle a child who is monopolizing the conversation in your class, like Rodney?

Advice from Veteran Teachers on . . . Incarceration

- Regardless of race, ethnicity and class, anyone can be arrested and charged with a crime. There are individuals who are imprisoned for protesting something they believe in, those who are falsely imprisoned, and some who are wealthy, yet commit crimes. So we encourage you to not be biased but to be open-minded in your opinions regarding incarceration.

- You need to let the child know that they are not a bad person and neither is their incarcerated parent. They may have done a bad thing, but that does not mean that they are necessarily bad. Please remember, it's not the child's fault that their parents are incarcerated.
- You might want to find out if the child is allowed to visit their incarcerated parent. Then they may want to write them letters or make holiday cards or gifts for them.
- Understand that most prisons are far away from where the child currently lives. If the family travels to the prison to visit their loved one, the child may be tired on Monday. They may also be disappointed, scared, confused, or even angry. We've had the case where a family went to visit their loved one and forgot the child's birth certificate. He was consequently unable to visit his father. When he came back to school, he was visibly upset the whole day.
- We would probably talk to the principal about the parent who wanted to talk with your students about being incarcerated. We would also suggest that the parent come on a different day to speak with your students. We think that what he has to say is valuable, but that it may be better received at a time different from career day.
- If you are reading a book with your students, once again, be honest. You do not have to get into a lengthy discussion with them about this situation. If a student suggests that a parent may be in jail or they may be at work, accept their response and move on.
- Initiate counseling at school. Also encourage the family to seek outside counseling if more counseling services are needed.

War/Terrorism

I'm Not a Terrorist—I'm an American

I pull down the map of the United States. "Now," I tell my fourth graders, "you may also turn to page 219 in your social studies books for a map of the United States to help you with the states." I look back and continue, "I am now going to tell you a bit about my background and will allow you time to guess where I'm from." This is the lead in to our social studies state projects. Each student will have to write a three-to-four-page report on their state, complete a visual display of interesting facts and landmarks in that state on a tri-fold board, and give an oral presentation.

I look out at my students and say, "I was born in a state with red clay-like dirt. My ancestors were the original people of the United States. They were great warriors, spiritual leaders, and hunters." I look around at my students and see some of them are buzzing about where they think I am from. "Unfortunately, many of my ancestors were killed by disease and war." I stand up straighter and say, "The state where I was born is in the Midwest. It is known as the "Sooner State" and has a great tradition of college football." I smile as I see that some of the students are pointing to Oklahoma in their textbooks. I continue, "There are many oil reserves in my birth state." Thinking about another hint that I can give them I say, "During the summer it's rather hot and humid there, and during the winter it snows. But what I remember most when I was growing up were the ice storms." I look out and finally say, "So, can anyone tell me where they think I was born?"

Several students raise their hands. I call on Charlotte, who looks down at her social studies book and then up at me. "I thought I knew the answer until you said that it snowed out there. I don't think that it snows in this state." I say to Charlotte, "Well, go ahead and tell us your guess anyway." Charlotte says, "Oklahoma?" Her guess sounds more like a question than an answer. I look at the rest of the class and say, "How many of you think that I was talking about Oklahoma?" Most of my students raise their hands. I look over at Charlotte and say, "You're correct. I was born in Oklahoma. Okmulgee, Oklahoma, to be correct."

My students begin talking amongst themselves about their guesses. Then Elijah raises his hand and asks, "I didn't know that it snows in Oklahoma, Mrs. Elliott." I nod my head and say, "Yes, it sure does." I look around the room and say, "It doesn't snow as much as it does up here. But it does snow." Niecy raises her hand and I call on her. "I almost thought about New Mexico because when my family and I drove through there this summer, we could see the red dirt on the sides of the mountains." I nod my head and say, "Yes, I know exactly what you're talking about. But there are parts of Oklahoma that have this red dirt that really looks like clay." I think about it for a second and continue, "As a matter of fact, where I went to college in Oklahoma, the red dirt would mess your clothes up if you got it on them. It would dye the color of your clothes so you had to be careful." Some of the girls shake their heads and then Niecy says, "Okay, I can't go to school there." Several girls say, "Okay," in agreement with her.

I look up at the clock and realize that it is almost lunch time. I announce, "Great job, everyone. We are going to talk a little more about your state projects after lunch." I look around and say, "So please clean up your areas and get ready for lunch." With that, my students push their chairs back, place their social studies books in their desks, and start to line up. After dropping off my students at the cafeteria, I head to the teachers' lounge. I know I am not in the mood for the microwavable lunch I brought today, but it's four days until payday so it'll have to do. After going to the restroom, checking my mailbox, messages, and getting my lunch from the microwave, I finally settle down to each my spaghetti marinara. Sheila, our attendance clerk, comes up to me and says, "You have an upset student in the front. I can't seem to calm him down."

I immediately get up and find Abdul sitting in a chair in the front office. I can see that he is crying so hard he is having trouble getting air. His shoulders are heaving up and down and I hear him gulping air. I sit next to him and ask, "Abdul, what's wrong?" Startled, he looks up at me and says, "Mark, Joshua, and Derek keep messing with me." He takes in another breath of air and continues, "They took my lunch and threw it in the trash." I look at him and ask, "Did you tell anyone?" He shakes his head and says, "They said that they would beat me up if I did." Surprised by what I'm hearing, I ask, "How long has this been going on, Abdul?" He looks up and says, "All year." He then cries even harder and continues, "I told them that I was born in Michigan, but they said that I am still a terrorist." He goes on to say, "They said that they are going to beat me up because they don't want my kind in America." He then shows me fresh scratch marks on his upper arm.

Discussion Questions

1. What is your first reaction to this situation?
2. What would you do if any or all of Mark, Joshua, and Derek's parents agree with their boys' statements and actions?
3. What can you put in place in your class so that students feel comfortable talking with you sooner when they are being threatened or teased incessantly by other students?
4. What activities/lessons can you teach in your class to promote understanding and appreciation of difference?
5. Are there greater legal ramifications for Mark, Joshua, and Derek's actions? If so, what are they?

Is She Gonna Die?

"Um," Julian continues, "I got this football from my father. I visited him last weekend, and he gave me this football." Julian looks at the football, twists it to the side, and continues, "My father and I threw the football in his backyard all weekend, and he promised that when my mom signs me up for peewee football, he will go to all of my games." Julian looks up at me and says, "Well, he said he will try because with his work he has to fly all over the place," I smile at Julian. "Did your father play football when he was a little boy, Julian?" I ask. He thinks about it for a second and says, "Yes, he did." He gets a big smile on his face and says, "So did my mom." Most of my students gasp. Admittedly, I was shocked too. I chuckle and say, "Are you serious?" Julian says, "Yes, Mrs. Rogers. She was the quarterback."

After a few seconds, Derek, one of my most precocious first graders, raises his hand and I call on him. "Yes, Derek." Derek looks at Julian and says, "Girls can't play football." Several of the girls shoot him evil eyes. But before I can say anything, Diamond jumps in and says, "Um, excuse me. I play football." She rolls her eyes and says, "And I bet I could beat you." Derek turns around to reply, but I jump in just in time. "Okay, kids," I say and then give Diamond and Derek "that look" to let them know I mean business. I say looking at Derek, "Now, it is true that not many girls play football." I then look at Diamond and continue, "But there are girls who do play football and who are very good." I nod my head and say, "We now know of two girls who play or have played—Diamond and Julian's mother." I point to the wall behind my desk and show him the picture of Diamond in her football uniform and say, "Okay, Derek." Derek looks at me like he still isn't totally convinced, but finally says, "Okay, Mrs. Rogers." I look up at the clock and realize that Julian's show-and-tell time has gone over the usual three minutes. I say, "Let's thank Julian for sharing his football with us." With that, my students begin to clap. Julian takes a bow and walks to his cubby to place the football in it. Thinking quickly, I say, "Julian, we have to remember you are only allowed to play with that football during lunch and recess, okay." Julian nods his head and joins his peers on the rug.

I look at the board and realize that our last presenter for today is Marsha. "Marsha," I say, "You may come up and tell us what you brought to share with us today." Marsha comes to the front of the rug and stands near me. "Today," she begins, "I brought in some pictures that my mom took in Iraq." I turn my head when I hear several of the students on the rug say, "Wow!" Marsha fumbles with the pictures and I ask, "Would you like for me to hold up each picture while you explain what's going on?" Marsha nods her head. I take the pictures from her small hand and hold up the first one. She looks closely at the picture and explains, "This is my mother in front of her tank. Beside her are several of the guys in her unit." When I flip to the next picture, she looks at it intently and explains, "This is a picture of my mom in the mess hall. My mom says that the food isn't too bad out there. But she does miss Big Macs." Marsha looks at the last pictures and explains, "This is my mom when she is driving the jeep. She said she was leading a convoy and taking supplies from her base to another base." I look out at my students and see several confused faces. I then ask, "Does anyone know what a convoy is?" All of my students shake their heads. I continue, "A convoy is when a group of cars, trucks, or jeeps go from one place to another. It allows them to carry a lot of sup-plies and protect one another in case of trouble." Following that I ask, "Are you done, Marsha?" She nods her head and turns her attention to her classmates.

I ask if anyone has a question for Marsha. Inga raises her hand and says, "Does your mom carry a gun?" Marsha looks at Inga and says without elaboration, "Yes." Derek raises his hand and I call on him. "Has she killed anyone?" With that question, Marsha looks at me and shrugs her shoulders. She then says, "I don't know." Derek puts his hand in the air again, but admittedly I concerned about what his next question might be. So I call on Sarah. "Marsha," Sarah asks, "Aren't you scared your mom is gonna get shot and killed like all those people on the news?" And with that, Marsha looks up at me and her doe-like eyes fill up with tears.

Discussion Questions

1. What is your reply to Sarah?
2. How do you console Marsha?
3. What would you say to Marsha's father or caregiver to let them know that this discussion took place today?
4. What activities/lessons can you do for young children dealing with parents or other family members in the military who are stationed overseas?
5. What activities/lesson can you do so that your students can help soldiers who are overseas?

My Stomach Hurts

It is early in the morning and I look out at my fourth graders, who are working on their Father's Day cards. I thought I would give them some time this morning to have some fun with arts and crafts. Usually, I do these types of activities in the afternoon, but I thought I would mix things up today. It actually seems to be working. Most of my students seem to be getting energized by talking with their peers and doing something they enjoy. The test will be when we have to transition to Language Arts. Will they still be able to use their newly found energy productively? I guess I'll have to see.

As I scan the room, I see that John is looking listless and lethargic again. Lately, John has been complaining about headaches, stomachaches, and constant fatigue. I talked with his mom about the situation and she said she has noticed that he is having trouble going to sleep at night. "I have gone into his room around midnight and have found him in his bed with the light on looking up at the ceiling. Then when I ask him about it, he tells me that he's praying for the world." His mother continues, "But the problem is when it comes time for him to wake up for school, it's like pulling teeth. And now he's complaining about being sick all the time." She then continues, "On several occasions, we've awaken to find that he's made a pallet on the floor at the foot of our bed." Following that conversation, I haven't heard anything else from John's mother about his insomnia.

I look over at John again and say, "John, will you please come here." John looks shocked I called on him. He slowly saunters up to my desk and says, "Yes, Miss Dowling." I can tell he is tired. His eyes are red and puffy. Plus, his hair is mussed up. I look at him again and say, "Are you okay? Do you feel all right?" John looks at me intently. He finally says, "I really don't feel good. My stomach hurts." I look at his stomach and back up at his face. I lean closer to him and whisper, "Do you feel like vomiting?" I think I actually see his eyes light up. He rubs his stomach and says, "Actually, I do. Can I go to the nurse's office?" I look at him and ask, "What about your card? You don't want to finish making your Father's Day card?" While continuing to rub his stomach, he looks back at his desk with the blank piece of construction paper and says in a weaker voice, "Maybe I can finish it when I feel better. Maybe after lunch."

I look at John and try to think of the best way to handle this situation. Several times I have sent him to the nurse's office and he ends up sleeping and snoring so loud that he bothers others in the office. Our nurse, Mrs. Holtorf, is not going to be happy with me sending him to the office again. She always tells me, "You are just letting those kids run you. That boy is not sick. He's sleepy. You need to call his mom and dad and make sure they get him in the bed at a decent hour." When I contacted his parents, they, too, didn't really know what was wrong or what to do. Yet, according to Mrs. Holtorf, who has been a school nurse for almost thirty years, "Kids will continue to try to get out of work no matter what. This one has you wrapped around his finger. You better toughen up if you're gonna keep teaching." Thinking of what Mrs. Holtorf would say, I say to John, "Now, Mrs. Holtorf is probably not going to let you just sleep in her office. If you are really sick, she is going to call your mom and see if she can come get you to take you home." I look him and continue, "Now, are you sick enough to go home?" With that, John looks and finally says, "I don't know."

As I am just about to suggest that we go outside, the fire alarm goes off! I quickly look at John who begins to panic and breathe erratically. Just then, over the PA system we hear, "We apologize, everyone. It was a false alarm. Please go back to your regular class schedule." Still panicked, John begins to dry heave and breathe erratically. In shock, I say, "John, what's going on?" Finally, with pressured speech he says, "We're all gonna die soon when the nuclear war happens. I saw on the news that North Korea shot one in the air and Iran is getting bombs." He looks up and around the class and with a petrified look on his face says, "We are all gonna die and our skin is gonna burn and melt away." Following that, he continues to dry heave and gasp for air.

Discussion Questions

1. What signs and symptoms did John exhibit that indicate that he may have been depressed or anxious about something?
2. How do you handle students who fall asleep in your class?
3. What services are available at your school for children such as John who may be dealing with the fear of dying?
4. What do you have in place to deal with students who try to get out of work by feigning an illness?
5. What types of activities/lessons can you do with your students to encourage peace locally, nationally and internationally?

Advice from Veteran Teachers on . . . War/Terrorism

- The concerns expressed in the vignettes are real concerns. Honestly, these are not only concerns for children, but for most adults too.
- In some communities, in particular those closest to military bases, a lot of families have at least one family member who is stationed overseas. Having other students who are going through the same situation, such as missing their loved one and being concerned about their safety and well-being, may be a comfort to some. If possible, your school counselor/psychologist may conduct group therapy sessions with these children in order to give them an outlet and strategies for how to deal with their anxiety and sadness.
- If you have a group of children or just one child who has a family member overseas, or children who are anxious about the war in general, you will want to let all of your students know that they can come to you any time if they become fearful, anxious, sad, or confused. Then, make sure that you listen to them and provide them with the necessary support.

- Some children may be especially anxious or depressed and require more support than you can give. Some children become so anxious that they vomit, complain incessantly about tummy aches, and begin not to sleep at night. This may be especially true if a loved one or someone else's loved one is killed in the line of duty. In those cases, talking with your school counselor/psychologist or the child's parents immediately will be crucial to them getting the help that they need.
- If you have children who have parents or other family members in the military who are stationed overseas, you may want to ask the parent, guardian, or family member who is the physical custodian of that child if there are available services such as group or art therapy on base or through the armed forces.
- You may help your students become proactive. Some suggestions are that they write cards and letters to soldiers to thank them for their service to our country and let them know that they care. They can also collect goods and send the soldiers care packages during the holidays.
- Your students can write letters to members of Congress and the House of Representatives, as well as the President and Vice-President of the United States, to express their concerns about war. One of your students may have a suggestion that hasn't been tried yet that may be plausible. Maybe you can even videotape your class reading the letters and send the video as well.
- Older students may be able to do an in-depth study on the conflicts going on around the world. They could examine the roots of the problem(s) and the attempts to resolve the conflict and investigate new suggestions/solutions to help with the strife. Additionally, they could examine the war from an economic, historical, social, or religious point of view.
- Once again, teasing or bullying of any kind is unacceptable and should be dealt with immediately and consistently. In particular with the case presented, you may want to talk more about the Islamic religion and Middle Eastern and Persian cultures with your students as these are the ones that are overwhelmingly portrayed negatively today.

Epilogue

Teaching is one of the most difficult professions one can enter. We have to deal with constant federal and state curricular changes, difficult parents, difficult students, and even difficult colleagues. Most of us perform our jobs without being adequately financially compensated for all we do. Some of us tutor before and after school, attend our students' extracurricular activities, spend hours planning lessons, prepping, and grading papers, and just thinking about how to best help our students on our way to school, at home, and even in the grocery store. But what I do know is, although teaching is difficult, it is the most rewarding profession one can have.

After my first year of teaching I wrote this poem after a parent asked me how hard could teaching be when I was "only playing with five year olds all day long."

To Be a Teacher . . .

I was given the snazzy title of _**Teacher**_, OK
but now I know, it's misleading.
For my role was much more than
the one who only taught them how to . . .
read,
write,
color,
count,
think critically,
make friends,
keep friends,
stand in lines,
check out library books,
take turns,
tie their shoes,
swing without needing a push,
and
say thank you and you're welcome.

For you see, in addition to the "Teacher" activities above,
I was a . . .
Psychologist,
social worker,

police officer,
nurse,
lawyer,
judge,
politician,
historian,
mathematician,
scientist,
computer scientist,
librarian,
crossing guard,
painter,
sculptor,
crafter,
dancer,
musician,
food service worker,
custodian,
surrogate parent,
cell and I-Pod confiscator,
frugal shopper,
mediator,
softball/soccer/basketball/volleyball/tetherball player,
score keeper,
and even
an organizer,
a comforter,
an empathizer,
a sympathizer,
and
a hairstylist for picture day.

I don't want to be a mediocre teacher,
I want to be a fantastic teacher.
Thus . . .
I need to be able to
Listen attentively . . .
Genuinely and sincerely understand and care about my students and their families . . .
Think before I act . . .
Set a great example . . .
Be a role model . . .
Be creative . . .
Be encouraging . . .
Be knowledgeable . . .
Be committed . . .
Be determined . . .

Be willing to have fun and let my hair down;
while at the same time,
Be willing to praise and discipline consistently when working with my students.
SO . . .
Is teaching hard?
YES
Does it make you go home in a daze sometimes?
YES
Will you be able to pay your student loans off in five years with the salary of a
beginning teacher?
NOOOOOO!

But I can guarantee that being a teacher and educating children is one of the most
rewarding professions out there.
So, although the rewards may not be monetary,
They may be . . .
A little smile from one of your students . . .
A thank you from a parent . . .
An improved score on a spelling test . . .
A student doing much better on a running record . . .
The custodian complimenting you on how neat your classroom is . . .
A compliment from a colleague about how straight and quiet your students are in
line . . .
One student who usually is in trouble not getting in trouble for a full day . . .
The little red apple sitting on your desk that a student left for you after lunch . . .
Your principal telling you that one of your parents has said nice things about you . . .
A younger sibling of one of your students asking to be in your class when he or she is
older . . .
and . . .
Those times when you get to just look at all of your students
Actively engaged in
Thought-provoking work
Working collaboratively
Sharing supplies
Smiling
Laughing
And just having a great time being in your class.

Index